MRS BEETON HOW TO COOK

For my grandmothers Nora Baker and Elsie Hinch,
who spanned the gap between Isabella and me.

Gerard Baker

MRS BEETON HOW TO COOK

220 CLASSIC RECIPES FOR THE MODERN KITCHEN

ISABELLA BEETON & GERARD BAKER

First published in Great Britain in 2011 by Weidenfeld & Nicolson

1 3 5 7 9 10 8 6 4 2

Text copyright © Weidenfeld & Nicolson 2011
Design and layout copyright © Weidenfeld & Nicolson 2011

Design & Art Direction by Julyan Bayes
Photography by Andrew Hayes-Watkins
Illustration by David Wardle. Additional illustration by Carol Kearns
Food Styling by Sammy-Jo Squire
Prop Styling by Julyan Bayes and Giuliana Casarotti
Edited by Debbie Woska and Constance Novis
Proofread by Diona Murray-Evans
Index by Cherry Ekins

A CIP catalogue record for this book is available from the British Library.
ISBN-978 0 297 86597 1

The Orion Publishing Group's policy is to use papers that are natural, renewable and recyclable products and made from wood grown in sustainable forests. The logging and manufacturing processes are expected to conform to the environmental regulations of the country of origin.

Printed in Germany

CONTENTS

INTRODUCTION

W hen Isabella Beeton first published *Beeton's Book of Household Management* in 1861, Britain was still a rural society in which large numbers of people were involved in farming and many grew their own fruit and vegetables at home. As a result, most households ate very simply, in tune with the seasons. The repertoire of home cooks was small and economy was vital, so the emphasis was on getting the most out of each and every ingredient.

But change was already underway. Just as the Industrial Revolution moved people from the country to the cities, the development of modern transport networks, refrigeration and kitchen appliances brought a world of food to our fingertips. Yet, sadly, those same developments led to a steady decline in the numbers of people cooking at home, and a loss of the basic skills and techniques that were taken for granted 150 years ago.

With today's renewed interest in seasonality, traceability and sustainability, the resurgence of forgotten or underused ingredients and the increased numbers of people cooking at home for economic reasons, Mrs Beeton's expertise is more relevant than ever. The recipes celebrated in this collection are both timeless and delicious, and offer the perfect opportunity for both new and experienced cooks to rediscover good, old-fashioned home cooking.

The author

Today, most of us have a mental image of Mrs Beeton as a matronly figure – brisk, efficient and experienced in the kitchen. In fact, Isabella Beeton was young and recently married, juggling working outside the home with running her household and coping with the demands of a husband and young family. Having worked on it through her early twenties, she saw her book published at the age of 25 and died just three years later.

Isabella was born in London, grew up in Epsom and began her married life in Hatch End (which was then on the outskirts of London). Although she wrote of housekeepers, butlers and valets, her world was far from the big country houses of the preceding century, and although it is likely that she had some help in the kitchen, she almost certainly managed her home and most of the cooking herself. Her book was inspired by an awareness of the challenges faced by women like herself, and a wish to use the knowledge and experience she had gained to help other young women in her position:

> *What moved me, in the first instance, to attempt a work like this, was the discomfort and suffering which I had seen brought upon men and women by household mismanagement. I have always thought that there is no more fruitful source of family discontent than a housewife's badly cooked dinners and untidy ways. Men are now so*

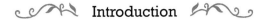

well served out of doors, at their clubs, well-ordered taverns, and dining-houses, that in order to compete with the attractions of these places, a mistress must be thoroughly acquainted with the theory and practice of cookery, as well as be perfectly conversant with all the other arts of making and keeping a comfortable home.

There is no question of Isabella Beeton having written all the material herself. As a young woman with limited experience of running a home, she would not have been able to compile so authoritative a text without help. What she did have was an understanding of the kind of information that women like herself wanted to have at their fingertips – and with that in mind, she used her position as editor of *The Englishwoman's Domestic Magazine* to pull together the best recipes and advice from a wide range of sources.

For the matter of the recipes, I am indebted, in some measure, to many correspondents of the 'Englishwoman's Domestic Magazine', who have obligingly placed at my disposal their formulas for many original preparations. A large private circle has also rendered me considerable service. A diligent study of the works of the best modern writers on cookery was also necessary to the faithful fulfilment of my task. Friends in England, Scotland, Ireland, France, and Germany, have also very materially aided me.

Having gathered together her source material, Mrs Beeton then set about sorting it into as accessible and comprehensive a form as possible. She was among the first revolutionary food writers to style recipes in the format that we are familiar with today, setting out clear lists of ingredients and details of seasonality, time taken, average cost and portions produced (this last being entirely her invention). She also offered notes on how to source the best food for her recipes – placing particular emphasis on such old-fashioned (or, in our eyes, surprisingly modern) ideas as the use of seasonal, local produce and the importance of animal welfare.

In essence, her success was in identifying that her own needs were shared with her readers'. And her book clearly found an audience: it sold in huge numbers from the outset and has been in demand, in its various incarnations, ever since. It is easy to see why. Mrs Beeton's core themes – buy well, cook well and eat well – are as relevant today as they were 150 years ago.

The ingredients

Up to the building of the first railways, food distribution in Britain was essentially local. When Mrs Beeton was writing, the suburbs of our major cities still contained market gardens – London was once ringed with them – and the surrounding countryside provided supplies for the cities' ever-increasing populations, with historic drove roads and market routes funnelling animals to population centres.

However, this was a time of massive social, technological and agricultural change. Four-crop rotation techniques had been adopted from Europe under the influence of Charles 'Turnip' Townshend 100 years earlier, increasing agricultural yields and allowing greater animal productivity. At Ballindallach castle, within sight of the fishermen in the Junction pool, the breed we now know as the Aberdeen Angus was being developed by Sir George Macpherson-Grant, and other advances in animal and plant breeding were gathering pace.

The power of the British Empire meant that in many instances food could be imported more cheaply than it could be produced. Processed foods were also beginning to appear on the market – and being seized upon with enthusiasm by a new generation of women who, unlike their forebears, could not afford staff and had to manage the kitchen, as well as the rest of the household, themselves.

The change in the nature of our food supply was underway. Developments in pesticides, fertilisers and machinery changed the face of farming by the middle of the twentieth century, with a constant stream of workers being forced off the land and into the cities, where they would gradually lose touch with their food and the way in which it was produced.

In the background, voices have always challenged the direction in which our national food production has developed. When Eve Balfour championed low-input mixed farming techniques and campaigned to set up the Soil Association in 1946, she was considered a radical pioneer. Today, the organic and slow food movements work to protect traditional farming methods all over the world. There is hope, too, for many of our traditional animal breeds, which are being revived by the Rare Breeds Survival Trust.

And consumers are increasingly concerned about the provenance of their food, too. More and more of us are now rejecting exotic and well-travelled foods in favour of the fresher, tastier, more nutritious ones that we can find (or grow) in our own backyards. We are choosing to shop at farmers' markets and farm shops and patronise our local butchers, fishmongers and greengrocers rather than just buying everything at the supermarket. Seasonal vegetables and locally produced organic meats, smoked fish, cheeses – the sorts of things that we are increasingly seeking out – would all have been very familiar to Isabella Beeton. In a sense we have come full circle.

The recipes

The original book was written with an awareness of household economy that we can take lessons from today. Because we have access to so much so easily, we often forget to consider how to get the most out of each ingredient – yet maximising flavour and nutrient value and minimising waste is as relevant in the twenty-first century as it was in 1861.

However, the recipes themselves have needed careful adaptation. Many of the ingredients that may seem at first glance quite universal – flour, butter, yeast and apples, to give just a few examples – are so different today from those varieties Mrs Beeton would have been familiar with that using them in the original way can give quite different results to those intended. For those reasons, quantities needed to be not only converted but checked and altered. And all those cases where Mrs Beeton advised adding salt or sugar or honey or spices 'to taste' needed to be pinned down in real quantities, always keeping in mind both flavour and authenticity.

In many instances, recipes have been altered only as much as is necessary to give a truly authentic result. the portable soup on page 33, for example, is a faithful and very Victorian recipe, and certainly merits trying today.

In the case of many of the meat and fish dishes in particular, the modern recipes are amalgamations of more than one Beeton recipe or suggestion. Where a Victorian cook would have happily chosen a plain meat from one chapter and a sauce from another, we tend to prefer the convenience of having everything in one place. The grilled mackerel with gooseberry sauce on page 65, for example, can be found in the original book only as a gooseberry sauce which is suggested as an accompaniment for mackerel. Mrs Beeton did not put the two together as a complete dish.

In a few other cases, a recipe has been inspired by a flavour combination mentioned in passing by Isabella in her original book, although she did not herself offer a recipe for it. This is the case with the lamb chops braised with spring vegetables on page 138, which arose from a simple note that peas and asparagus work well with lamb chops. In these cases, thought has been given to how Mrs Beeton might have combined the ingredients, in order to produce a dish that she would, hopefully, have been happy to include in her own edition.

Cooking methods, too, were in some cases not replicable and in others simply no longer the best way of achieving the desired results. A significant factor in this is that the domestic oven was in its infancy in 1861, and Mrs Beeton was not able to make full use of it in her book. Most kitchens would instead have been equipped with old-fashioned ranges, and there is much mention of setting things before the fire, turning and basting. Roasting meat, which we now consider a simple process, required constant attention 150 years ago, and even toasting bread was a laborious process deemed worthy of several paragraphs.

Oven temperatures, therefore, have all had to be deduced from a mixture of reading between the lines, comparing modern recipes, and testing, testing, testing.

In the process of updating the book it became clear that some of Mrs Beeton's recipes were forerunners of dishes that we are now familiar with under a different name. In these cases, the name of the dish has also been modernised. For that reason you will find here among other things eggs Florentine (see page 193), a plum crumble (see page 243) and a Victoria sandwich cake (see page 302), in spite of the fact that those dishes were in fact probably all invented – or at least named – after Isabella Beeton's death. The essence, nonetheless, comes from her.

The legacy

After Isabella Beeton died early in 1865, her book took on a life of its own. It was endlessly enlarged and added to, and eventually lost almost all trace of the woman whose name it bore. In any one of the many twentieth-century editions of *Mrs Beeton's Cookery and Household Management*, most of the recipes are entirely modern: they are neither rooted in, nor do they take their inspiration from, Mrs Beeton's original work.

What has been sadly lost in the many, many, editions of the book that have been published in the past 150 years is the spirit of the original. The picture of British food that Isabella painted in the first edition was about to change wholesale, and her book was destined to change with it. The aim of this latest book is to reverse those changes: to return to real, wholesome, traditional British food, which Mrs Beeton might be proud to recognise as her own – and to put to rest the matronly image.

SOUPS & STOCKS

SOUPS

Soups can be delicate and light – think of the vegetable soups of spring and summer – or substantial and rich, like the more complex, often meatier, soups of winter. Whatever the type of soup you are making, your aim is to capture the character of the main ingredient, be it a vegetable, meat or fish.

A base for a soup is usually made by stewing some vegetables in oil or butter before adding stock or milk to cook the ingredients. This should give the soup base a deep, intense flavour, which can be reinforced and freshened up with vegetables added toward the end of cooking. Peas or asparagus, however, should only be added at the last minute and cooked for a very short time to preserve their colour and flavour.

It is a common misconception that all soups need to be cooked for a long time. This is only the case when tougher cuts of meat are being used. Generally, a soup is cooked as soon as the vegetables are tender and suitable for pureeing.

When making a puréed soup, a jug blender or liquidiser is essential for achieving the smoothest result. Add the soup in small batches to the liquidiser or jug blender then run the machine for 2–3 minutes between additions. Pass the soup through a fine sieve or chinois (see glossary) into a clean pan before reheating or chilling over ice. The soup can then be finished with a little seasoning to taste and perhaps a small addition of cream or unsalted butter can be whisked in to enrich it. Remember, though, when making soups, to use seasoning lightly. A soup does not require the same level of salt as a sauce, so when tasting, be careful not to over-season.

STOCKS

These words are as true today as when Mrs Beeton wrote them: good stocks are the essence of good cooking. Stocks are the foundation of so many dishes, so it is worth ensuring that they contain only the best ingredients. Take care never to over-season stock. Many recipes call for stocks to be reduced, so a stock that starts off already slightly salty will result in a very salty finished dish.

Unlike in Mrs Beeton's time, ready-made stocks in liquid or powdered form are now widely available. However, they are rarely based on prime ingredients or made with the care you would take when making your own. Ready-made stock almost never has the body of homemade stock – a quality that derives from using gelatinous meat and bones to make the homemade version – so will give a completely different result to the recipes it is used in. Many ready-made stocks are also salty, and so not suitable for reducing.

For all these reasons, it really is worth saving up some bones, setting aside some time, and making your own. Because stock takes some time to cook, it may help to roast any bones and vegetables the day before and chill them overnight before proceeding when you have a full day available.

Adding cold water and a few vegetables and seasoning to raw, roasted or browned meat and bones makes meat stock. Slowly heating the mixture brings fat and scum to the surface. Skimming the impurities and fat away with a large metal spoon or ladle as the stock cooks produces clear, brilliant stock. On no account should stock be allowed to boil until it has been skimmed, strained, and all fat removed. Then, the stock may safely be boiled to reduce it, skimming again to remove any impurities that may rise to the surface.

When stock is finished and cold, any traces of fat that remain on the surface can be removed and discarded and the stock frozen for use later. Freezing stock in re-sealable containers that hold 250ml or 500ml portions will prove useful for most recipes. Alternatively, or to use up any extra, you can freeze stock in ice-cube trays for adding flavour to sauces. Mrs Beeton's original book listed three main meat stocks, each containing a different mixture of meats. However, the use of a mixture of meats in stock can complicate flavours in a way that is not appealing today. Lamb stock, for example, has a very distinct flavour and is not suitable for combining with other meats. It is accepted today that a good stock should give an unmistakable, unadulterated essence of a single type of meat that will complement, not interfere with, the flavour of the finished dish. For this reason, the stocks given in this chapter are modern ones, not taken from or influenced by Mrs Beeton but intended to complement and update her other recipes.

A generic, dark, jellied beef stock is suitable for most red meat dishes, but if you are cooking lamb, pork or game, use a stock made from the bones or meat of the same kind of animal to get the best results. Brown chicken stock will also work well with these meats if you have not got the right bones to hand. The stocks listed in this chapter cover all the requirements for recipes in this book, with versions for poultry, beef, game, fish, shellfish and vegetables.

Stock ingredients

Bones should be fresh and trimmed of any excess fat. Those that have a good proportion of cartilage, such as knuckles, feet and ribs, are excellent for stock as the gelatine they contain gives the stock body. Pigs' trotters and calves' feet should be cut in half so that the gelatine is more easily released – get your butcher to do this.

Vegetables should be good quality and fresh. Wash them well and peel them if necessary before chopping or trimming them. Unless the recipe specifies otherwise always use medium-sized vegetables.

Herbs should be tied together in small bundles (called faggots in Mrs Beeton's day) using kitchen string so they are easy to retrieve from the stock once it has finished cooking.

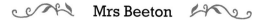
Cold water, rather than hot, should be added to stocks as it encourages fat to rise and solidify, making it easier to skim from the surface.

Wine, if you use it, should be of drinking quality and not dregs or anything past its best.

Salt should only be added at the end. As you reduce the stock it will intensify the natural salts within the ingredients, so you should never add salt until the stock is fully reduced and you have tasted it. You can always add more seasoning at a later stage, if desired, but you cannot repair over-salted stock.

Stockpots

It is most efficient, and worthwhile, to make stock in large quantities, and for this you will need a large, stainless steel stockpot. A pot of 25–30cm in diameter that will hold 17 litres can be accommodated by most domestic hobs.

JELLIED GAME STOCK

✳ Makes 2 litres ✳ Preparation time 1 hour 45 minutes ✳ Cooking time 8 hours

The backbones of game birds can be bitter, so do not use them in stocks. When using giblets, always check them for green or yellow stains. These indicate contamination with bile, and any affected parts should be cut off and discarded.

750g pheasant carcass (backbone discarded) or other game bones and meat

750g pork rib bones

2 tbsp sunflower oil

2 large onions, roughly chopped

1 carrot, roughly chopped

1 stick celery, roughly chopped

1 garlic clove, peeled and sliced in half

2 bay leaves

1 thyme sprig

500ml white wine

special equipment

1–2 roasting tins and a large stockpot

Preheat the oven to 200°C/gas mark 6. Place the bones in a large roasting tin, drizzle with the oil and toss to coat. If you cannot fit the pieces in a single layer use 2 tins. Place in the oven and roast, turning every 20 minutes, until well browned. After 1 hour add the chopped vegetables, garlic and herbs, turning everything occasionally so nothing burns.

After 30 minutes remove from the oven, pour off and discard any fat, and then place the contents of the roasting tin into a stockpot.

Add the wine to the roasting tin or tins and use a wooden spoon to scrape any sediment from the bottom, warming the tins over a low heat to dissolve the juices if necessary, then pour everything from the roasting tins into the stockpot.

Add enough cold water to cover the bones to a depth of 10cm. Bring the stock to a simmer and skim off any fat or scum that rises to the surface. Then turn the heat down to low and leave the stock to simmer very slowly for 6 hours. When cooked, strain the stock through a very fine sieve or chinois into a large bowl, cover and chill.

Once cold, skim any fat from the surface. Pour the stock back into the cleaned stockpot and bring to a boil over a high heat. Reduce to approximately 2 litres, skimming as necessary. Remove the stockpot from the heat and leave to cool. Then chill until cold, pour into re-sealable 250ml containers and freeze for up to 2 months.

To use, allow the stock to thaw out then dilute with an equal quantity of water before using in game soups, braises and casseroles.

JELLIED BEEF STOCK

✳ Makes 2 litres ✳ Preparation time 1 hour 15 minutes
✳ Cooking time 12 hours 30 mintues first day, 4 hours second day

This stock is best started early in the morning so that it has plenty of time to cook. It can then be cooled overnight and reduced the following day to give a rich, unctuous stock.

5kg beef or veal bones

4 tbsp oil

1 large carrot, roughly chopped

1 stick celery, roughly chopped

1 large onion, roughly chopped

3 garlic cloves, peeled

1 bay leaf

100g large mushrooms or mushroom trimmings, roughly chopped

1 tomato, roughly chopped

300ml light red wine

1 pig's trotter, split in half

small bunch thyme

1 small tarragon sprig

1 tsp black peppercorns

special equipment

2 roasting tins and a large stockpot

Preheat the oven to 220°C/gas mark 7. Arrange the bones in the roasting tins and place in the oven. Roast for 1 hour, turning occasionally so that they brown evenly, then remove them from the oven and pour off any melted fat – you can save this to make roast potatoes (see page 179).

Place the oil in the stockpot and set it over a medium heat. Add the carrot, celery and onion and cook, stirring, for about 10–15 minutes, or until well caramelised.

Add the garlic, bay leaf, mushrooms and tomato and continue to cook until the mixture is almost dry and beginning to stick to the pan. Add the red wine and continue cooking until it has reduced by half, scraping all the sediment from the bottom of the pan. Add the trotter to the pan along with 2 litres of cold water, then add half the roasted bones. Give everything a good stir before adding the remaining bones and another 4 litres of cold water, or enough to cover the bones well.

Turn the heat to high and bring the stock to a simmer, but do not allow it to boil. Skim to remove any scum that rises to the surface, and add the herbs and peppercorns. Continue to simmer without boiling for 12 hours, skimming as necessary. Strain the stock through a very fine sieve or chinois into a large bowl and allow it to cool overnight.

The next morning, remove and discard any fat, and pour the stock back into the cleaned stockpot. Bring to a boil and reduce, skimming as necessary, until you are left with 2 litres. Remove the stockpot from the heat and leave to cool. Chill until cold then pour into re-sealable 250ml containers and freeze for up to 2 months.

To use, allow the stock to thaw out then dilute with an equal quantity of water for a full-flavoured beef stock.

CLARIFYING STOCKS

✳ To clarify 2 litres of stock ✳ Preparation time 10 minutes ✳ Cooking time 20–30 minutes

Clarification is a method used to clear stocks that have clouded or need to be refined for use in a consommé. Mrs Beeton noted that, 'when [a stock] is obliged to be clarified it is deteriorated both in quality and flavour', yet she did include a recipe for clarifying stocks, which calls for a simple mixture of egg whites and water, in her book. This updated recipe uses a similar method, but retains the flavour by using a mixture of minced, lean meat of the same type as the stock being clarified, plus vegetables, herbs and spices. You need to start with cold stock so that the egg white solidifies gradually, trapping particles from the stock as it does so.

2 litres cold chicken or beef stock (see pages 22–23 or 19)

120g egg white (about 3 large or 4 medium egg whites)

30g carrot, peeled and roughly chopped

50g onion, peeled and roughly chopped

20g celery, trimmed and roughly chopped

20g leek, trimmed and roughly chopped

200g lean, minced chicken or beef

few thyme sprigs

1 bay leaf

1 garlic clove, peeled

1 tsp black peppercorns

Place the cold stock into a large saucepan. Put the egg white, vegetables and meat in the jug of a food processor and pulse to chop to a coarse paste.

Turn the heat under the saucepan to high and whisk the vegetable and egg paste, the herbs, garlic and peppercorns into the stock. Bring to a gentle simmer over a high heat, whisking again once or twice as it warms. At no point should the stock be allowed to bubble.

As the stock reaches a simmer, the egg and vegetables begin to form a thick scum on the surface. Reduce the heat to low and keep the stock just under a simmer. The surface layer will thicken and set, trapping all of the sediment and debris.

After 10 minutes, remove the pan from heat and break a hole in the egg crust large enough to fit the bowl of a ladle through. Very carefully ladle the stock out through the hole and into a muslin-lined sieve suspended over a large bowl.

Cover and chill immediately and use as required. This will yield approximately 1.8 litres, and can be frozen for up to 2 months.

DARK CHICKEN STOCK

✳ Makes 1.5 litres   ✳ Preparation time 1 hour 15 minutes   ✳ Cooking time 6 hours

This full-flavoured chicken stock is made from browned, roasted chicken bones and pieces. It has an intense flavour and light gelatinous body and is excellent with strongly flavoured poultry and game dishes that can stand up to a robust stock.

1.5kg chicken wings and thighs

2 tbsp sunflower oil

1 large carrot, roughly chopped

2 onions, roughly chopped

2 sticks celery, roughly chopped

2 bay leaves

small bunch thyme

special equipment

a roasting tin and a large stockpot

Preheat the oven to 220°C/gas mark 7. Arrange the chicken wings and thighs in a roasting tin and set in the oven. Cook, turning occasionally, for 1 hour, or until the pieces are deep golden-brown in colour.

When the chicken is nearly cooked, place the oil in a large stockpot over medium heat. Add vegetables and fry until lightly coloured. Add the cooked chicken to the pan. Pour off and discard any excess fat in the roasting tin.

Pour a little water into the roasting tin and stir, scraping up any caramelised juices. Pour these into the pan with the vegetables and chicken.

Finally, add the herbs to the chicken and vegetables and pour enough cold water into the stockpot to cover the chicken and vegetables to a depth of 10cm. Turn the heat to high and bring the stock to a simmer, then reduce the heat. Make sure the stock does not boil at any point and skim off any scum that rises to the surface while it is simmering.

After 5 hours, strain the stock through a fine sieve or chinois into a large bowl. Leave it to cool, then cover and chill.

Once it is completely cold, carefully remove any fat from the top. Pour the stock back into the cleaned stockpot, place over a high heat and bring to a boil. Reduce the stock until you are left with 1.5 litres. Remove from the heat to cool, then chill until cold, pour into re-sealable 250ml containers and freeze for up to 2 months. To use, allow the stock to thaw out.

LIGHT CHICKEN STOCK

✳ Makes 1.5 litres ✳ Preparation time 10 minutes ✳ Cooking time 3 hours

Light chicken stock is used in delicately flavoured dishes, which would be masked by a more intensely flavoured stock. It is also useful for lighter soups, or for braising young vegetables such as turnips or beetroot.

1.5kg chicken wings
and thighs, raw

1 large carrot, roughly chopped

2 onions, roughly chopped

2 sticks celery, roughly chopped

2 bay leaves

small bunch thyme

special equipment

a large stockpot

Place all the ingredients into the stockpot over a medium heat. Cover with cold water to a depth of 5–10cm and bring to a gentle simmer. Continue to simmer for 2 hours, making sure the stock does not boil at any point and skimming as necessary. Strain the stock through a fine sieve or chinois into a large bowl. Leave it to cool, then cover and chill.

Carefully remove any fat from the top of the chilled stock and pour it back into the cleaned stockpot. Bring to a boil over a high heat to reduce the stock until you are left with 1.5 litres. Remove from the heat and cool, then pour into re-sealable 250ml containers and freeze for up to 2 months.

VEGETABLE STOCK

✳ Makes 4 litres ✳ Preparation time 20 minutes ✳ Cooking time 1 hour

This quick, light and fragrant stock is ideal for making vegetable soups and other vegetarian dishes. Vegetable trimmings can be added to the base ingredients, but make sure that they are washed well and that any onion skins you use are free from mould.

4 onions, roughly chopped

2 leeks, roughly chopped

3 carrots, roughly chopped

1 stick celery, roughly chopped

1 large thyme sprig

3 bay leaves

special equipment

a large stockpot

Place all the ingredients into a large stockpot over a high heat. Add 4 litres of water and bring to a gentle simmer, then turn the heat down low and continue to simmer. After 1 hour strain the stock through a sieve into a large bowl, discarding the vegetables and flavourings. Cover and chill.

Once cold, pour the stock into re-sealable 250ml containers and freeze for up to 2 months.

FISH STOCK

✳ **Makes 600ml** ✳ **Preparation time 10 minutes** ✳ **Cooking time 1 hour**

Fish stocks require only light cooking. Cook them too much and you will produce glue. A variety of fish bones can be used, but flatfish bones are the most gelatinous. Sole or halibut bones provide the best flavour and produce the clearest stock.

30g unsalted butter

4 shallots, peeled and finely chopped

250ml light dry white wine such as Muscadet

500g fish bones (preferably sole or halibut), chopped into 4cm pieces

1 carrot, peeled and finely chopped

½ leek, split in half lengthways

1 bay leaf

a few parsley stalks

Place a large saucepan over a medium heat. Add the butter and then the shallots. Cook, stirring, for 4–5 minutes or until they are softened but not coloured.

Add the white wine and cook until it has reduced by half, then add the remaining ingredients. Pour in 700ml cold water and bring the mixture to a gentle simmer. Skim off any scum that rises to the surface.

Cook the stock on a low heat for 45 minutes, then remove from the heat and strain through a sieve into a large bowl. Discard the bones, vegetables and flavourings. Cover and chill the stock. Either use within 3–4 days or freeze in 250ml portions for up to 2 months.

Tip: The boiled meat that you remove from your stock will be very tender and falling from the bone – but it can still be used. Shred it from the bones and chill, then mix with a seasoned mayonnaise for a sandwich filling.

COURT BOUILLON

✳ Makes 1.25 litres ✳ Preparation time 5 minutes ✳ Cooking time 30 minutes

This stock is used for poaching fish and delicate meats. It keeps the flesh moist while adding a lightly piquant flavour and is appropriate when a clean, subtle result is desired. It is only cooked for a short period of time to keep the flavours fresh.

1 carrot, peeled and chopped into chunks

1 stick celery, trimmed and chopped into chunks

1 medium onion, peeled and finely sliced

1 small leek, finely sliced

½ fennel bulb, finely sliced

½ lemon, finely sliced

2 thyme sprigs

2 garlic cloves, peeled and coarsely chopped

2 tsp black peppercorns

2–3 tarragon sprigs

small bunch parsley

200ml dry white wine

special equipment

a large stockpot

Place all the ingredients into the stockpot over a high heat. Add 1.3 litres of cold water, bring to a boil and simmer for 20 minutes. Pass immediately through muslin or a fine sieve into a bowl.

Discard the vegetables, cover the bouillon and chill or freeze in 250ml portions for up to 2 months.

SHELLFISH STOCK & SHELLFISH BISQUE

✳ Makes 2 litres ✳ Preparation time 1 hour 30 minutes ✳ Cooking time 3–4 hours

This richly aromatic stock forms the foundation of delicious shellfish soups, such as bisque. The best shells to use are those left from picking crab and lobster. A fishmonger who sells dressed crabs will usually be happy to save you some shells in the freezer. Roasting the shells intensifies their flavour.

2kg crab, lobster or prawn shells

2 tbsp sunflower oil

1 stick celery, roughly chopped

1 large onion, peeled
and roughly chopped

1 medium carrot, peeled
and roughly chopped

1 large tomato, roughly chopped

50ml brandy

300ml dry white Vermouth

500ml dry white wine

1 garlic clove, peeled and halved

2 bay leaves

1 large thyme sprig

for the bisque

50g onion, peeled and chopped

50g leek, chopped

50g carrot, peeled and chopped

50g celery, chopped

250ml double cream

500g fresh crab or lobster meat
(optional)

salt, to taste

special equipment

a roasting tin and a stockpot

Preheat the oven to 200°C/gas mark 6. Place the shells in the tin, drizzle over the oil and toss to coat, then set in the oven to roast. Stir occasionally until beginning to brown.

After 1 hour add the celery, onion, carrot and tomato, and mix well. Roast for a further 30 minutes, stirring occasionally. Remove the tin from the oven and set on the cooker top.

Add the brandy to the tin and carefully set the mixture alight at the side of the tin using a match, tipping the liquid around the tin to catch all of the alcohol. Allow the flames to die down then add the wine and Vermouth. Stir the mixture together and scrape into the stockpot.

Pour in enough cold water to cover the shells to a depth of 10cm, then add the garlic and herbs to the pan and set over a high heat. Bring to a simmer, turn the heat down to low and cook for 3 hours. Strain the mixture into a bowl then pour it back into the cleaned stockpot and simmer until it is reduced to about 2 litres.

For the bisque, add the chopped vegetables to the stockpot and simmer for 5 minutes, then strain to remove the vegetables. Measure the stock, and for every 400ml, add 50ml double cream.

Return the bisque to a clean pan and set on a medium heat. Warm the soup to a very gentle simmer, then taste for seasoning, adding a little salt if necessary. Stir through the fresh crab or lobster meat (if using), heat for another 2 minutes without boiling and serve immediately.

CHANTILLY SOUP

✳ Serves 4 ✳ Preparation time 10 minutes ✳ Cooking time 20 minutes

Mrs Beeton features another green pea soup recipe in her book, which is much as you might expect a Victorian soup recipe to be. The peas are boiled for upwards of 2 hours, ham is added, presumably to give the soup some flavour after all that boiling, and the green colour comes from 2 handfuls of spinach thrown in just before serving. Her Chantilly soup, by contrast, is refreshingly clean. Other than refining Mrs Beeton's onions to a combination of shallots and leeks and varying the herbs, very little has been changed in this recipe. It is important to use young, tender peas, but we are fortunate today in that we have the option of using frozen, which are a good alternative.

30g unsalted butter

50g leek, finely chopped

1 small shallot, peeled
and finely sliced

½ bay leaf

700ml light chicken stock
(see page 23)

500g fresh or frozen young
peas few mint leaves

salt and freshly ground
black pepper

Melt the butter in a saucepan over a low heat. Add the leek, shallot and bay leaf and cook gently for 10 minutes, ensuring that the vegetables do not colour. If they begin to brown, add a little water and, if necessary, turn the heat down.

Add the stock and turn the heat up to bring it to simmering. Then turn the heat to high, add the peas and bring to a boil.

Remove from the heat, leave to stand for 5 minutes then season to taste with salt and black pepper. Transfer the soup to the jug of a liquidiser and add the mint. Run the machine for 2–3 minutes to purée the soup to a very smooth consistency. Pass the soup through a fine sieve into a pan, heat gently, check the seasoning and serve immediately – or chill as quickly as possible to preserve the colour if using later.

LEEK & POTATO SOUP

✳ **Serves 4** ✳ **Preparation time 10 minutes** ✳ **Cooking time 15 minutes**

Surprisingly, given her usual approach to household economy, Mrs Beeton only uses the white part of the leek for this soup. Perhaps she saved the green part for something else. Because the leeks we buy today are almost always young and tender, this recipe uses the whole thing. The cooking time here has been reduced from the hour required in the original recipe to just a few minutes. However, to obtain the silkiest texture you will need to slice the leeks very finely and purée the soup very well.

40g unsalted butter

400g trimmed leeks, green and white parts separated, both finely shredded

2 bay leaves

1 thyme sprig

300g potatoes, peeled and cut into 3–4cm cubes

500ml vegetable stock (see page 23)

200ml whole milk

2 tbsp chopped parsley

50ml single cream

grating of nutmeg, to taste

salt and freshly ground black pepper

Place a saucepan over low heat and add the butter. When it has melted add the finely shredded white part of the leek, the bay leaves and the thyme.

Cook, stirring, over a low heat for 5–10 minutes, until the leeks begin to sweat and release their juices. They should sizzle gently but not brown. Add the cubed potatoes, stock and milk and bring to a rapid simmer.

Cook until the potato is tender, then add the finely chopped leek greens and parsley and continue to simmer for 4–5 minutes, until the leek greens are just tender.

Transfer the soup to the jug of a liquidiser and purée for 2–3 minutes, then pass through a fine sieve into a clean pan over a medium heat. Pour in the cream and reheat gently, stirring constantly.

Season with salt and black pepper, and grate over some fresh nutmeg to taste before serving.

FISH & SHELLFISH

COOKING TECHNIQUES FOR FISH

M ost fish flesh is delicate and only needs light cooking. It should, however, be cooked fully to 60°C to kill off any parasitic worms the fish may be carrying. If you intend to eat fish raw, for example as sushi, freezing it for a minimum of 1 week will also kill off any parasites.

Poaching: This is a gentle technique where fish are lightly cooked in court bouillon at around 80–90°C. This allows heat to penetrate gradually so that the outer layers do not overcook. After poaching, the fish is drained and served with a sauce.

Baking: This is a good method for cooking a whole fish, particularly salmon. The fish is delicately seasoned and sometimes stuffed, wrapped in a foil parcel and baked in a low to medium oven.

Roasting: This is a robust method of cooking that suits highly flavoured fish. This technique is used for small, whole fish or shellfish that can be cooked through quickly without the outer layers becoming overcooked. Roasting is suitable for herring, mackerel and scallops. Fish are roasted in a hot oven with fat, the intention being to brown the outside of the flesh.

Grilling: This versatile method can be used for cooking many kinds of fish, either as fillets or whole. Shellfish, such as half lobsters and oysters, can also be cooked under a grill.

Frying: Fish fillets, shellfish and small fish are suitable for frying either in oil or butter. The flesh develops a tasty brown crust and a delicious, savoury aroma. To protect it and add texture some fish benefit from being given a coating of oats or flour before frying.

SEASONALITY

F ish varies in quality depending on when it is harvested in relation to its life cycle. Fish that are preparing to spawn will have weak and soft flesh. This means most white fish are at their best in the winter months when they do not breed.

The cold waters off the UK provide an environment that enables shellfish to grow slowly and develop a rich deep flavour but, like fish, if they are harvested when they are spawning the flavour and texture will not be as good. Avoid buying fresh shellfish in the late spring and summer months. Local bylaws affect what types of shellfish you are legally allowed to collect. If you are in any doubt, contact your local authority for advice. Britain's native oyster is protected from fishing during its summer breeding cycle, which is why it is illegal to fish for it during months without an 'r' in the name. Pacific oysters can be sold year-round because, in UK waters, they are mostly farmed.

POACHED BRILL
WITH BROWN SHRIMP BEURRE BLANC

✳ **Serves 4 as a starter or 2 as a main course** ✳ **Preparation time 5 minutes**
✳ **Cooking time 30 minutes**

This recipe strikes a marvellous balance of delicacy and richness. Fishmongers sell brown shrimps ready-peeled in small packets. At a pinch, you can buy potted shrimps and melt them out of their lovely butter and use them instead. Alternatively, as Mrs Beeton suggests, if you are lucky enough to have a lobster to hand, some of the coral head meat can be blended into the sauce to flavour it.

**1 quantity court bouillon
(see page 25)**

**1 quantity beurre blanc
(see page 336) or fish cream
sauce (see page 335)**

**1 whole brill weighing 1kg,
skin and head removed**

10g unsalted butter

100g peeled brown shrimps

lemon halves, to serve

special equipment

a temperature probe

Prepare the court bouillon and set it aside. Make the beurre blanc or fish cream sauce and keep it warm. If you are using beurre blanc place it in a bowl suspended over a pan of warm water. Cover it with a thick tea towel, and stir occasionally to ensure that it does not split.

Turn the oven on to low and set five plates inside to warm. Place the brill into a large, deep frying pan just big enough to hold it. Pour over the bouillon and bring to a simmer over a medium heat. Leave to cook gently for 12–15 minutes, then turn the heat off under the pan but leave the pan on the hob for a further 6–7 minutes. If you have a temperature probe, the fish should register 60°C at its thickest part. If for any reason the fish is colder than 55°C, leave it in the hot bouillon for another 5 minutes.

When the fish is cooked lift it from the pan, allow it to drain and transfer it to a warmed dish to rest for 5 minutes. Meanwhile, melt the butter in a small saucepan over a medium heat. Add the shrimps and cook until they begin to sizzle. Drain in a sieve and add to the beurre blanc or fish cream sauce, stirring to combine. Carefully remove the cooked fish to a board and, using a palette knife, remove each of the top 2 fillets that run lengthways along the backbone. Set each fillet onto a warmed plate. Repeat with the bottom 2 fillets and set them onto the other 2 plates. Pour over the sauce and serve with the lemon halves, accompanied by steamed green vegetables.

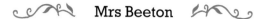

ANCHOVY BUTTER

✳ Makes 100g ✳ Preparation time 5 minutes

This savoury butter is a good standby to have in the fridge and makes an excellent snack served spread over hot, white toast or over steamed vegetables with a squeeze of lemon juice on top.

60g anchovy fillets in oil

40g unsalted butter, softened

1 pinch each ground ginger, mace, cinnamon and freshly ground black pepper

10 drops Tabasco or other chilli sauce

Drain the anchovy fillets, then place all the ingredients in a mortar and pestle or into the jug of a small blender and blend to a smooth paste. Place in a dish or ramekin, cover with cling film and chill until required.

SMOKED HADDOCK COCOTTES

✳ Serves 4 ✳ Preparation time 10 minutes ✳ Cooking time 13–20 minutes

The best smoked haddock is only lightly cured so that the sweet perfection of the flesh is not lost. Finnan haddock, which originates in the Aberdeenshire village of Findon, was named by Mrs Beeton as the finest expression of this particular fish, and it can still be found today. She cooked it in water with herbs, but to make a little go a long way it is paired here with cream and eggs and served in ramekins.

120g undyed smoked haddock, skinned and cut into small chunks

freshly ground black pepper

8 tbsp double cream

4 medium eggs

4 tsp grated Parmesan

special equipment

4 ramekins and a roasting tin

Preheat the oven to 160°C/gas mark 3. Divide the fish equally between the ramekins, grind over a little black pepper and add 1 tbsp of double cream to each ramekin.

Fill and boil the kettle. Place the ramekins in the roasting tin and pour boiling water around them to a depth of 2.5cm. Carefully transfer to the oven and cook them for 5 minutes. Remove the tin from the oven and crack a fresh egg into each ramekin. Add another tablespoon of double cream, a grinding of black pepper and a little Parmesan to each. Return to the oven for 13–15 minutes for a soft egg or 16–20 minutes for a set one. Serve immediately.

CRAB FRESHLY BOILED WITH MAYONNAISE

✳ Serves 2 ✳ Cooking, cooling and preparation time 3 hours

A freshly cooked crab is one of the delights of the British seaside. A light white wine and good bread is the only accompaniment you need for a memorable summer lunch. You can buy crabs already cooked from good fishmongers, or if you have a live crab that you would like to cook yourself, see the instructions on page 47.

½ **quantity mayonnaise (see page 341), to serve**

1 **fresh cooked crab weighing 1kg**

½ **tsp Worcestershire sauce**

½ **tsp brandy**

6 **drops Tabasco sauce**

lemon juice, plus lemon wedges, to serve

salt and freshly ground black pepper

special equipment

a small hammer

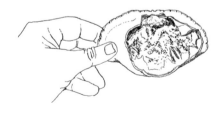

Make the mayonnaise a little ahead of time and chill until ready to serve. Place the crab upside down and facing away from you. Pull the claws gently towards you to remove them from the body. Crack them carefully with a small hammer and remove the white meat to a small bowl.

Using a blunt knife, prise the body part of the shell away from the top part. The body contains white meat and a little dark, and has a number of pointed grey gills running up its sides, known as dead men's fingers. Remove these and discard them. Using a metal skewer, ease the meat from the tunnels in the body and spoon the dark meat and the light meat into separate bowls, being sure to discard any bits of shell. Spoon the brown meat from the upper shell.

A 1kg crab should yield 240g claw meat, 80g white meat and 130g brown meat. Hen crabs will yield more body meat; cocks more claw meat. The amount of brown meat will depend on what moulting stage the crab was at. If a soft new shell is forming within the body cavity, there will be more. Soft new shell is edible – simply mash it with the remainder of the brown meat.

To present the crab, clean the upper shell then make the cavity larger by pressing against the rim of the hole until a segment of shell breaks cleanly away (see illustration). Do this on both sides of the shell. Pile the white meat back into the shell, leaving a space in the middle. Season the brown meat with the Worcestershire sauce, brandy and Tabasco sauce, adding black pepper and lemon juice to taste. Mash to a rough paste and pile into the space in the centre. Serve with the lemon wedges and mayonnaise.

FISH PIE

❋ Serves 4–6 ❋ Preparation time 1 hour ❋ Cooking time 25–30 minutes

Mrs Beeton used cod and oysters in her fish pie, a delicious mixture but one that is now rather expensive for a kitchen-supper dish. The smoked haddock used here instead adds piquancy to the delicate pollock or coley, with a few prawns added for succulence.

1 quantity mashed potatoes (see page 182)

500ml milk

1 bay leaf

1 small carrot, cut in half

½ onion, cut into large chunks

1 tsp black peppercorns

400g pollock or coley fillet

100g smoked undyed haddock

approx. 150ml double cream

50g unsalted butter

50g plain flour

freshly grated nutmeg, to taste

50g prawns

1 tbsp melted unsalted butter

salt, to taste

to garnish

small bunch fresh parsley, tough stems discarded, leaves chopped

1 tarragon sprig, stem discarded, leaves finely chopped

special equipment

1.5-litre ovenproof dish and a temperature probe

Make the mashed potatoes and set aside.

Place the milk, bay leaf, carrot, onion and peppercorns in a saucepan and bring to a boil. Turn off the heat and allow to infuse for 15 minutes. Strain the milk into another pan that is large enough to hold the fish, and discard the other ingredients. Bring the liquid to a simmer over a medium heat. Add the fish and simmer for 2 minutes, then turn the heat off and leave to sit for 10 minutes. Set the fish aside, strain the milk into a measuring jug and make up to 500ml with the double cream. Pour the milk and cream mixture into a saucepan over a low heat and bring to a simmer.

Meanwhile, make a roux by melting 50g butter in a small pan over a medium heat. Add the flour and cook, stirring, for 3–5 minutes, or until the mixture begins to foam, taking care that it does not burn. Turn the heat to low and whisk the milk mixture into the roux a little at a time, then simmer for 3–4 minutes, or until the sauce is glossy, silky and free of lumps. If it tastes floury, cook it for another 1–2 minutes. Season to taste with nutmeg and a little salt.

Preheat the oven to 180°C/gas mark 4 and line a baking tray with foil. Flake the cooked fish into the ovenproof dish, scatter over the prawns and pour over the sauce. Spoon the mashed potatoes on top, starting at the edge of the dish and working inwards.

Brush the pie with the butter, place it on the baking tray and bake in the centre of the oven for 25–30 minutes. The pie is cooked when it is bubbling around the edges, or when a temperature probe inserted in the centre reads 85°C. If the surface of the pie is still pale in colour at this stage, place it under a hot grill to brown the top. Serve immediately, sprinkling the herbs over each portion as you hand it round.

DOVER SOLE GRILLED WITH WHITE WINE & LEMON

✳ **Serves 2** ✳ **Preparation time 5 minutes** ✳ **Cooking time 8–10 minutes**

Here is a very smart yet simple way to serve this meaty and delicious flatfish. Mrs Beeton often advised her readers to blanch fish first in boiling water to remove impurities. This can result in overcooked fish if you are not careful, so it is best to cook the fish as suggested here.

40g softened unsalted butter, plus extra for greasing

1 Dover sole weighing 600g, skinned, head removed if preferred

juice of ½ lemon

70ml light fruity white wine such as Muscadet

salt and freshly ground black pepper

special equipment

a large, ovenproof serving dish

Preheat the grill to hot, and set the top shelf 10–15cm from the grill element. Place a large serving dish below the rack to warm. Line a baking tray with foil and grease with a little butter.

Season the fish lightly on both sides with salt and black pepper and place on the baking tray with the thickest side uppermost. Dot the butter onto the fish and pour over the lemon juice and white wine. Grill for 4–5 minutes on one side, then turn carefully with a fish slice and grill on the other side until lightly browned and cooked through. The fish is cooked when the meat pulls away from the bones eaily with a fork.

Transfer to the serving dish, pour over the cooking juices and serve immediately.

LEMON SOLE GRILLED WITH CREAM & MACE

✳ **Serves 4 as a starter or 2 as a light main course** ✳ **Preparation time 10 minutes**
✳ **Cooking time 15 minutes**

This is a very simple, absolutely delicious, way of cooking sole but it also works with other small flatfish like dabs and plaice. Mrs Beeton clearly liked to use mace as a fish seasoning: its sharp piquancy adds a spicy note to the delicate flavour of the fish and cream.

30g butter

300ml double cream

1 large pinch ground mace

zest of ¼ lemon

½ tsp salt

2 x 400g whole lemon sole, skinned and heads removed

special equipment

a large, oval flameproof dish

Melt the butter in the dish, rolling it around to thoroughly coat the inside surface, then set aside. Preheat the grill to high and position the shelf 10–15cm from the element.

Warm the cream in a small pan over a medium heat. Stir in the mace, lemon zest and salt.

Place both fish, thickest side uppermost, on the prepared dish and pour the cream sauce over them. Grill for 5–7 minutes on one side, spooning the sauce over occasionally. Turn the fish carefully and grill on the other side for a further 3–4 minutes. The sauce will reduce to a thick savoury cream. The fish is cooked when the flesh pulls away from the bone cleanly with a fork. At this point, turn the grill off and let the fish rest for 3–4 minutes before serving.

RAY WITH BROWN BUTTER, CAPERS & PARSLEY

* **Serves 4** * **Preparation time 10 minutes** * **Cooking time 20 minutes**

Mrs Beeton gives a recipe for skate with capers, but since skate is rare today, this recipe has been modified for use with ray. This classic method of poaching ray is beautiful and here a court bouillon is used to flavour the flesh delicately, rather than the basic water and herb mixture that Mrs Beeton used. Look for thick portions of ray wings because they cook more evenly in their poaching liquor. The capers add a tangy flavour to the browned butter, with lemon adding a fresh citrus note as the fish is served.

1 quantity court bouillon
(see page 25)

4 x 200g portions ray wings

bunch parsley, stalks removed
and reserved, leaves finely
chopped

100g unsalted butter

4 tbsp baby capers,
finely chopped

100g unsalted butter

1 lemon, quartered

salt and freshly ground
black pepper

special equipment

a large, ovenproof serving dish
and a temperature probe

Make the court bouillon and chill until needed. Remove the fish from the fridge and leave, covered, at room temperature for half an hour before cooking.

Place a large serving dish in a low oven. Place the parsley stalks in the bottom of a large frying pan and arrange the fillets on top. Pour over the cold court bouillon, cover with a lid and place on a medium to high heat. Bring up to almost simmering, which should take about 8 minutes, then turn the fish and remove from the heat. Leave, covered with a lid, for a minimum of 5 minutes, to allow the fish continue to cook. A probe inserted in the fish should read about 60°C. If it is less than 50°C, leave the fish in the warm water for a further 5 minutes.

Once cooked, remove the fish from the liquid and drain. Place on the warm serving dish, sprinkle with a little salt and black pepper and keep warm in the oven while you make the butter sauce.

Place the butter in a small pan over a high heat until it sizzles, foams, turns brown and smells nutty. Just before it burns, toss in the capers and parsley and remove from the heat. Pour the foaming butter over the fish and serve immediately with the lemon wedges.

WHOLE BAKED SALMON

✳ Serves 10–15 ✳ Preparation time 10 minutes
✳ Cooking time 1 hour 30 minutes–2 hours plus 30 minutes resting time

A whole salmon makes an impressive party centrepiece. Mrs Beeton boils hers in a fish kettle, but this method for baking the fish on an oven tray achieves a similar result. You will need a wide roll of foil to parcel it up.

1 whole salmon weighing 4kg, head and tail removed

sunflower oil, for brushing

1 tbsp Maldon or other flaky sea salt or 2 tsp fine salt

1 small, unwaxed lemon, thickly sliced

special equipment

wide foil, a very large, deep baking tray and a temperature probe

Preheat the oven to 140°C/gas mark 1. Place the salmon on a large sheet of foil and brush the skin with the oil. Season inside the body cavity with a few pinches of salt and insert the lemon slices, then place the salmon on its belly on the foil and sprinkle it all over with salt. Seal the foil well around the fish, pinching the edges together to ensure there are no gaps, then place in a large roasting tin, curving the salmon slightly to fit if necessary.

Pour enough boiling water into the tin to come 2.5cm up the side and place in the oven for 1½–2 hours. After this time a temperature probe inserted into the thickest part of the fish should register 45–50°C. If not, cook for a further 15–20 minutes and retest. Remove from the oven and leave parcelled up in a warm place to rest for 30 minutes.

If you are planning to eat the salmon hot, open the parcel and skin the fish. Using a small knife, scrape the brown meat from the sides and discard. Slip the salmon onto a serving dish and serve with a double quantity of hollandaise sauce (see page 338) or fish cream sauce (see page 335) and perhaps some roasted beetroot and a potato & cream gratin (see page 181).

If you are planning to eat the salmon cold, chill it briefly after resting. Then remove the skin and scrape the brown meat from the sides of the fish. Discard all the debris and transfer to a serving dish. If you are preparing this a day ahead, cover with cling film and chill overnight, but allow it to come up to a cool room temperature for an hour before eating. Dress the fish with a large heap of watercress salad (see page 175) and serve with a double quantity of homemade mayonnaise (see page 341) or soured cream.

POACHED LOBSTER

✳ **Serves 2 as a starter** ✳ **Preparation time 5 minutes** ✳ **Cooking time 15 minutes per kg**

If you come across really lively fresh lobsters, buy one and cook it for yourself – you will appreciate why people prize them so highly.

1 live lobster weighing 650–750g

1½ tsp salt

Calculate your cooking time at 15 minutes per kg – a 750g lobster, for example, needs 12 minutes. If you plan to cook more than 1 lobster you can either use 2 pans or you can cook up to 2 in a pan. Cooking more than 2 together will affect the cooking times.

Place 4 litres of water in a large pan over a high heat. Add the salt and bring to a rapid boil with the lid on. Kill the lobster according to the instructions on page 47 and then transfer it to the boiling water. Cover the pan but don't let it boil over. Once it returns to a rapid boil, adjust the heat to a simmer. Time the cooking of the lobster from the moment the water begins to simmer. While it is cooking fill a large bowl with ice and water.

When the lobster is cooked remove it from the pot using long-handled tongs and plunge it into the bowl of iced water for 10 minutes. Drain the bowl, rinse the lobster briefly under cold water then chill until required.

To prepare the lobster for the table, cut it in half lengthways with a large, sharp knife. Open up the halves. You will notice that the head cavity contains some brown meat. This is delicious. It also contains a clear stomach sac that may have some contents depending on when the animal last ate. Remove any parts of this from both halves. Next look at the lobster's tail meat. Just under the outer rim of the shell you should see a long narrow intestinal tube extending the full length of the tail. Remove this carefully and discard it. Wipe the white tail meat with a damp piece of kitchen paper to remove any particles of debris. The lobster is now ready to eat. You can serve it with homemade mayonnaise (see page 341), clarified butter (see glossary) or lemon wedges, and a light fruity Muscadet or perhaps a dry Riesling or Chablis to drink.

GRILLED LOBSTER

WITH PARSLEY & GARLIC BUTTER

✳ **Serves 4** ✳ **Preparation time 15 minutes** ✳ **Cooking time 15 minutes**

Lobster was relatively expensive even in Mrs Beeton's day but nonetheless she gave many recipes for it. Then, as now, it made an impressive dish. It is best treated carefully and not overcooked otherwise the flesh will be tough and rubbery. Mrs Beeton often chops or pounds the flesh then cooks it with cream or flavoured mixtures. Here, her version of maître d'hôtel butter is used to baste the flesh as it cooks.

100g parsley & garlic butter (see page 336)

2 tbsp melted unsalted butter, for greasing

½ tsp salt

2 lobsters weighing 650–750g each, freshly killed (see page 47 or ask your fishmonger to do this for you)

4 slices crusty bread

lemon wedges, to serve

special equipment

a small hammer

Make the parsley and garlic butter and chill until needed. Line the baking tray with foil, grease and set aside.

Place a pan over a high heat and add 1 litre of water. Bring to a boil, turn down to a simmer then add the salt, stirring to dissolve. Remove the claws from the lobsters by pulling them backwards gently until they come away from the body. Add these to the pan and simmer for 5 minutes. Meanwhile, fill a large bowl with ice and water. Remove the claws from the pot using long-handled tongs and plunge them into the icy water for 5 minutes. Once the claws are cool, rinse them under cold water, then crack them open using a large spoon or small hammer. Remove the meat, preferably in whole pieces, and set aside.

Preheat the grill to high and place the shelf 10–15cm from the element. Cut the lobsters in half lengthways and remove the stomach sacs from the head cavities. Leave any pale brown and dark green matter in place – this is edible and will turn red when cooked. Place the lobster halves cut-side down on the prepared baking tray and grill for 5 minutes.

Turn the halves over. Fill the head cavities with the claw meat and spread the parsley and garlic butter all over. Grill for a further 3–4 minutes, until browned and sizzling.

Place a piece of crusty bread on each plate and top with half a lobster. Drizzle over the cooking juices and serve immediately with lemon wedges and a simple green salad.

GRILLED MACKEREL
WITH GOOSEBERRY SAUCE

✳ **Serves 4** ✳ **Preparation time 15 minutes** ✳ **Cooking time 25 minutes**

Inspired by Mrs Beeton's gooseberry sauce for boiled mackerel, this is an unusual combination, but a good one: the sharpness of the gooseberries cuts through the richness of the fish. In the early summer, both mackerel and gooseberries appear in our markets, though you could easily go and catch a mackerel yourself just by trailing a line off a pier. Mackerel must be cooked as soon as possible because it deteriorates more quickly than any other fish.

300g green gooseberries, topped and tailed

½ tbsp white wine vinegar

3 tbsp sugar

½ shallot, finely chopped

4 whole mackerel, gutted

4 tbsp light olive oil

salt and freshly ground black pepper

Put four plates into a low oven to warm. Line a baking tray large enough to hold all the fish in one layer with foil and set aside.

Put all of the ingredients except for the fish, olive oil and seasoning into a small saucepan over a low heat along with 4 tbsp water. Simmer gently, stirring occasionally, for 15–20 minutes, or until the berries are broken down and tender. Crush any whole berries with a fork and remove the sauce from the heat. Cover and keep warm until needed.

Meanwhile, preheat the grill to high and arrange the shelf about 15cm from the element. Dry the mackerel well with kitchen paper and make 3–4 diagonal slits in each side of the fish. Rub the skins lightly with the oil and season all over with salt and black pepper. Arrange the fish on the prepared tray and grill for 5 minutes, then turn the fish over and grill for a further 3–5 minutes.

The fish is ready when the flesh is firm to the touch and can be eased away from the bone with a fork, or when a temperature probe inserted into the fattest part reads 60°C or more. Serve the fish with the sauce on the side.

SOUSED MACKEREL

✳ Serves 8–12 ✳ Preparation and cooking time 3–4 hours plus cooling overnight
✳ Pickling time 3 days

Many of the fish Mrs Beeton wrote about are simply not available to us today in quantity, but mackerel are still caught in large numbers in the summer from many small day boats around our coastline. If you come across a glut of fish, this recipe will preserve them for up to one month. You will need to make the brine on one day, and then allow it to cool before brining and pickling the fish the following day. Mrs Beeton's pickled mackerel recipe uses boiled fish, but today we are accustomed to the softer, fresher texture of uncooked fish in delicacies ranging from smoked salmon to sushi. If you are concerned about safety, the fish can be frozen for a week before pickling to kill off any parasites.

120g Maldon or other flaky sea salt

4 bay leaves

1 tbsp coriander seeds

½ tbsp allspice berries

1 tbsp juniper berries

1 tsp black peppercorns

1 tbsp sugar

zest of ½ lemon, sliced into strips

500ml cider vinegar

120g shallots, finely sliced

16 mackerel fillets

special equipment

a ceramic or glass baking dish large enough to hold all the fish and the pickling liquid

To make the brine, place 600ml water in a large pan over a high heat and add the salt. Bring to a simmer for 2 minutes, then cover and cool to room temperature.

To make the pickle, add 250ml cold water to a large pan over a high heat. Stir in all the remaining ingredients except the shallots and the mackerel and bring to a boil. Remove from the heat, leave to cool then add the shallots. Cover and reserve.

When the brine is cold, arrange the fish in the baking dish and pour over the brine. Leave for 2–3 hours to allow the fish to firm up, then remove the fish and pat it dry on kitchen paper. Discard the brine.

Rinse out the dish and arrange the fish in it in a double layer. Pour over the pickle and cover with cling film. Chill and keep in the fridge for at least 3 days before using. Use within 1 month of making. Serve with a salad of cucumber and Granny Smith apples or soured cream and malted bread.

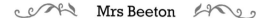
OYSTERS

Native oysters were once cheap and plentiful enough to use as a filler in fish pies and other recipes, where their flavour blended well with the other ingredients and their juices added body. The pollution caused by the Industrial Revolution put paid to this because oysters tend to accumulate toxic compounds in polluted waters. Today, the larger Pacific oyster is the most commonly available species because it is farmed widely. Native oysters can still be found, however, and are worth searching out. Although Mrs Beeton always cooked oysters, they are widely appreciated today served raw on the half shell. A modern serving suggestion of shallot vinegar is included with this selection of recipes.

GRILLED OYSTERS WITH DOUBLE CREAM

❋ **Serves 4** ❋ **Preparation time 15 minutes** ❋ **Cooking time 5 minutes**

12 large oysters

juice of ½ lemon

freshly ground black pepper

60ml double cream

1 slice white bread, made into fine breadcrumbs

special equipment

an oyster knife

Preheat the grill to high and arrange a grill shelf about 10cm from the element.

Open the oysters according to the instructions on page 47, loosen them from their shells and arrange them, still in their shells, on the baking tray. Sprinkle over the lemon juice and grind some black pepper over each oyster. Then place 1 tsp double cream and a sprinkling of breadcrumbs into each oyster.

Place the oysters under the grill. Be watchful, as the shells occasionally crack and explode. Grill for 3 minutes, or until the crumbs are just brown and the oysters are bubbling. Serve immediately.

OYSTERS FRIED IN OATMEAL

✳ **Serves 4** ✳ **Preparation time 15 minutes** ✳ **Cooking time 2 minutes**

This dish is a treat to make for good friends who are happy to graze in the kitchen, and it requires little formality.

12 top size oysters

50g medium oatmeal

**50g clarified butter
(see glossary)**

freshly ground black pepper

lemon wedges, to serve

Tabasco sauce, to serve

special equipment

an oyster knife

Shell the oysters following the instructions on page 47.

Remove the oysters in whole pieces from their shells and pat dry with kitchen paper. Season each one lightly with a grinding of black pepper. Spread the oatmeal on a plate and line another plate with kitchen paper. Roll the oysters in the oats to coat them completely.

Place a frying pan over a high heat, add the butter and, when it is foaming, add the oysters one at a time. By the time the last is in the pan the first should be ready to turn. Continue cooking and turning them until the oatmeal is a golden brown. Remove to the lined plate for a moment to drain, then serve on the shell with a squeeze of lemon or a few drops of Tabasco sauce.

SHALLOT DRESSING FOR OYSTERS

✳ **Makes enough for 24 oysters** ✳ **Preparation and chilling time 1 hour 5 minutes**

**1 medium shallot, peeled
and very finely diced**

20ml red wine vinegar

30ml cider vinegar

Mix all the ingredients together in a bowl. Cover with cling film and and chill for a minimum of 1 hour or up to 24 hours before using. Serve with raw oysters.

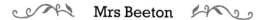
GRILLED KIPPER

✳ **Serves 1** ✳ **Preparation time 2 minutes** ✳ **Cooking time 5–7 minutes**

The migratory herring carried with it the fortunes of many eastern coastal towns, with large numbers of men and women catching and processing the huge shoals in difficult conditions until gradually fish numbers declined and the value of the harvest no longer made it worthwhile. These 'silver darlings' were more often salted or smoked than eaten fresh simply because of the sheer numbers caught. Split and smoked, they are called kippers, while those with their guts intact and lightly smoked are known as bloaters, famously produced in Great Yarmouth. Mrs Beeton included a recipe for Yarmouth bloaters, but today it is the kipper that is most popular and widely available, hence the substitution.

1 kipper on the bone weighing 250g, head and tail removed

10g unsalted butter, softened

1 lemon wedge, to serve

Preheat the grill to medium. Position the top shelf about 10–15cm from the grill element and place a serving plate under the top shelf to warm. Line a baking tray with foil.

Place the kipper skin-side down onto the lined tray. Spread the butter over the fish and place under the grill for 5–7 minutes. Serve on the warmed plate with the lemon wedge.

JUGGED KIPPER

❋ Serves 1 ❋ Preparation time 5 minutes ❋ Cooking time 10 minutes

This method, an alternative to grilling, allows you to enjoy a kipper without filling your house with the smell of smoked fish.

1 kipper on the bone weighing 250g, head and tail removed

10g unsalted butter, softened

1 lemon wedge, to serve

special equipment

a large freezer bag and a 2-litre jug tall enough to hold the length of the kipper

Warm a plate in a low oven. Place the kipper head first into the freezer bag, then place the sealed bag into the jug, with the end sticking out beyond the rim of the jug.

Fill and boil the kettle. Pour boiling water into the jug around the outside of the bag so that the kipper is immersed but does not actually get wet. Leave for 10 minutes, then transfer the kipper onto the warmed serving plate and spread the softened butter on top. Serve with the lemon wedge.

POTTED FISH AND SHELLFISH

Potting meat and fish is a lovely way of making something special with leftovers, and the methods we use today are still identical to those used by Mrs Beeton. When potting meat it is often cooked immersed in fat, which acts to preserve the flesh for some time in the same manner as a confit of duck or pork. Fish, on the other hand, is more usually mixed with a seasoned butter, which is used to season the flesh rather than to preserve it. The result is an assertively flavoured delight that is perfect for a supper, lunch or picnic.

POTTED SHRIMPS

✳ **Serves 4** ✳ **Preparation time 35 minutes** ✳ **Cooking time 10 minutes**

200g unsalted butter

6 blades mace

¼ fresh nutmeg, grated

1 bay leaf

zest of ½ lemon, cut in strips

250g peeled cooked brown shrimps

2 tsp lemon juice

salt and freshly ground black pepper

Place the butter, mace, grated nutmeg, bay leaf and lemon zest in a small pan over a medium heat and warm until the butter begins to bubble. Remove from the heat, cover and leave to infuse in a warm place for 30 minutes. Once infused, pour the butter through a sieve into a bowl, being careful to leave behind the milky liquid, known as solids, in the pan. Stir gently to distribute the butter evenly.

While the butter is infusing, place the shrimps snugly in a bowl and season with the lemon juice and black pepper. Check for saltiness. If the shrimps have not been salted add ½ tsp salt. Mix well to combine. Pour over the butter, stir to coat the shrimps, then press down. Cover and refrigerate until required. Eat within 4 days, served with bread.

POTTED SALMON

❋ Serves 4 ❋ Preparation time 35 minutes

1 quantity potting butter
(see potted shrimps recipe
opposite)

375g poached salmon

1 tsp lemon juice

salt and freshly ground
black pepper

warm toast and lemon
wedges, to serve

Make the potting butter and leave it to infuse for 30
minutes. When it has nearly finished infusing, flake the
salmon into a small serving dish with the lemon juice,
½ tsp salt and some black pepper and mix gently to
combine.

Pour the potting butter over the salmon, pressing the fish
to keep it under the surface of the butter. Cover and chill
for up to 4 days. It is delicious served with warm toast and
lemon wedges.

POTTED KIPPER

❋ Serves 4–6 ❋ Preparation time 35 minutes ❋ Cooking time 10 minutes

1 quantity potting butter
(see potted shrimps recipe
opposite)

375g jugged kipper meat –
about 2 kippers (see page 73)

½ tsp lemon juice

freshly ground black pepper

warm toast and lemon
wedges, to serve

Make the potting butter and leave it to infuse for 30
minutes. When it has nearly finished infusing, flake the
kipper into a small serving bowl, carefully removing any
small bones. Add the black pepper and lemon juice. Taste
and add a little more of either ingredient if you would like.

Pour over the potting butter and mix it in, pressing the
fish down into the butter. Cover and chill for up to 4 days.
Serve this with toast and lemon wedges.

POULTRY
& GAME

The main difference between poultry and game is that poultry is farmed and available all year round. Game can be either reared or wild, and for everything other than farmed venison there are fixed seasons when it may be hunted. Most game can now be bought from butchers and even supermarkets in the winter months, and some suppliers are recommended at the back of the book.

POULTRY

In recent years, the wide availability of chickens and turkeys raised in factory-like conditions has turned what was once highly prized meat into something cheap and largely flavourless, not to mention what it has done to the quality of life of the animals. Free-range or organic poultry, which is more likely to be produced on a smaller scale and from a variety of breeds, is much more likely to taste authentic. Among fowl, British geese are almost always free-range or organic.

Indoor-reared: Most birds produced in the UK are reared indoors. They are densely stocked, with up to 15–16 mature birds per square metre. Additionally, they are bred to mature very quickly, reaching full size in 6–7 weeks. This results in a cheaper chicken, but it has little flavour. Indoor-reared chickens that bear the RSPCA's Freedom Food logo are still produced in large flocks in closed-barn systems, but they are kept at a slightly lower density, and allowed some natural light.

Free range: A growing number of large-scale producers use free-range systems, but these are not always as you might imagine. Many of the larger free-range systems are essentially barn systems with small exits that allow (but do not encourage) birds outside. Smaller free-range producers usually have more open systems in which birds do roam freely out-of-doors. However, these only account for a small percentage of the free-range poultry available in the shops.

Organic: Organic chickens are reared in smaller flocks than those in the other systems – under Soil Association rules, there must be no more than 1000 birds per flock. Producers are also encouraged to use traditional breeds that grow and mature at a natural rate. The longer growing time means that organic birds are more expensive to produce, and the cost must be passed on to the consumer, but the chickens are generally of superb flavour. Organic chickens also do not have their movements restricted like caged birds and are more likely to be produced in good conditions with more access to the open air than even free-range birds. For those concerned with animal welfare, an organic bird is the best option.

GAME BIRDS

If you have never tried the many game birds and wildfowl (ducks and geese) available in this country, do so as soon as you can. They are truly delicious, a healthy source of protein, and you will find that most can be bought easily from butchers or supermarkets during the winter months.

Game birds divide roughly into those reared for shooting and those that are truly wild. Game birds that are reared – usually the pheasant, French (red-legged) partridge and, occasionally, the mallard – can be shot in a variety of ways. At one end of the scale is the small, country shoot, which usually consists of groups of friends meeting on farmland to shoot birds for their own consumption. Any excess may be sold to game dealers, but generally the numbers shot are in the dozens rather than the hundreds. At the other extreme is the large, formal driven-game shoot. This is where birds, such as pheasant and partridge, are 'driven' out of cover by a row of beaters with dogs to a line of standing guns. These shoots take place on farms and country estates and may bring down many thousands of birds during a season. The landowner sometimes sells the birds on to game dealers or directly to the public. However, there is a risk, when hundreds of birds are shot in a single day, that supply will exceed demand and many will go to waste.

Conservation plays a large part in a shoot. The types of birds targeted are often restricted so that, for example, only male birds may be shot later in the season. Wild birds that are not common, such as the English (grey) partridge, are usually left alone. Very large shoots must be managed carefully to limit their impact on local wildlife, and, sadly, this often does not happen. As an alternative to rearing game for shooting, an increasing number of estates manage habitats to encourage wild game birds to breed on their land. This is usually done with birds that are not reared and is particularly the case with red grouse.

Preparing birds

Birds can all be jointed in the same way. Knowing how to do this is good for kitchen economy as it is invariably cheaper to buy a whole bird than it is to buy all the pieces separately – and you are then also left with the carcass, which can be used to make stock (see pages 17, 22 and 23).

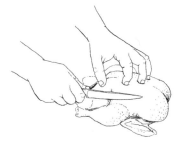

Place the bird breast side up. To remove a leg, first cut through the skin where the thigh joins the body to reveal the joint. Bend the leg back until the joint pops out of its socket. Holding the bone out of the way, cut through the tendons to detach the leg from the backbone. Repeat with the other leg. To detach the wings and to separate the thigh from the drumstick simply bend the joints backwards in the same way and cut neatly around the bone.

Finally, remove the breasts. Feel for the raised bony ridge of the breastbone and insert the full length of your knife to one side of it. Cut down until you feel resistance, then turn your knife out away from the breastbone and continue to slice around and underneath the breast, staying as close to the carcass as possible. Repeat on the other side.

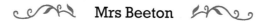
GAME MAMMALS

Hare and deer are game mammals. The hare has splendid, rich, dark meat, and a large specimen will easily feed six people. The quality of meat of the various deer species, collectively known as venison, depends on the age and gender of the animal. Venison from a male under two years of age will usually be tender. The texture of venison from an older animal will be firmer, but it will taste better. Venison from mature males should be avoided, especially during the rut, because it can have an overly strong flavour.

Farmed venison: Red deer are farmed for the flavour and quality of their venison (females are tender and flavoursome up to six years; males up to two years). Wild red deer meat is available, but as it is often produced as part of land management practices, the meat quality is variable. Well-farmed red deer is therefore more likely to offer consistently high quality.

Wild venison: Roe deer are never farmed, and if they are shot, most of their meat goes into the catering trade. Fallow deer are larger than roe, and are mostly to be found in deer parks in the UK. They are considered to be a wild managed herd in this instance, and so have a fixed season. Sika and muntjac deer are also common in the UK, but their meat rarely appears on the market.

Preparing game mammals

To joint a rabbit or hare, lay it on a chopping board with the hind legs towards you. Make a cut across the pelvis just above the hind legs, and then cut each leg off, keeping your knife close to the bone. Twist the legs to free the joint. Then, remove the forelegs, keeping your knife close to the rib cage. Cut the thin belly flaps off, ribs and all, and discard – the ribs are sharp so be careful. Finally, cut the saddle into two even parts.

Hanging game

To develop the fullest flavour and improve tenderness, all game can benefit from being hung for a week in a cool and airy place. It must be hung under such conditions as soon as possible after being shot because in damp or warm weather it will deteriorate quickly and may attract flies or pests.

COOKING POULTRY AND GAME

It is important that chicken and turkey are cooked through. All game, however, can be eaten rare or medium, which ensures it remains tender. Thoroughly cooked game will be dry unless it is braised for several hours – for example in the venison casserole (see page 110).

Frying: This method is suitable for the breast of game birds and venison, hare or rabbit loin. Trim the meat of any silver skin, sinew or fat then season with salt and freshly ground black pepper. Brown the pieces on all sides in a roomy frying pan over a medium-high heat, usually in oil or clarified butter. Don't crowd too much meat into the pan or it will steam and not fry.

Braising: This moist, slow method suits older game birds, shoulder of venison or hare legs. Brown the meat first then add the vegetables and liquid and cook, covered, over a low heat or in a low oven.

Roasting: A rapid method of cooking that suits all poultry and game birds, and joints of venison loin and haunch. Small birds roast very quickly, usually in less than 30 minutes, and so need to be browned in oil and butter before they go into the oven to enhance the flavour and add colour.

Pot roasting: This is a useful way of cooking game, especially older animals. Joints of venison or whole birds can be browned and then roasted in a covered pot with aromatics, vegetables and a small amount of stock to prevent the meat drying out.

Resting poultry and game

After roasting any meat it is important to rest it in a warm place. During cooking, moisture is pushed away from the hot surface of the meat and retained in the cooler centre. During resting, the heat equalises and the juices are reabsorbed. This means that less juices are lost when the meat is carved, leaving it more succulent. The length of time that meat should be rested for varies according to its size. Each recipe in this book gives an indication of the resting time needed.

Because the centre of the meat continues to heat up during the resting time, it is necessary to remove it from the oven before the serving temperature has been reached. If you test the meat after resting and find that it has not reached the required temperature, put it back into the oven for 5 minutes per 500g initial weight and then retest.

Carving birds

To carve a bird, first cut down in between the leg and breast, pushing the leg outwards with the knife to reveal the joint and then slicing through it to remove the leg. Separate the drumstick from the thigh by cutting through the elbow joint. Now that the breast is exposed, you can easily carve the meat into long, even slices. Alternatively, remove the breast as a whole piece in the same way as you would when jointing a raw bird (see page 79) and slice it into long even slices on a board. Repeat the same process on the second side.

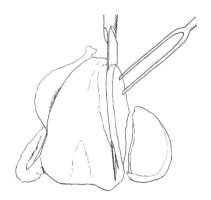

CHICKEN PIE

✳ Serves 6 ✳ Preparation time 2 hours 30 minutes ✳ Cooking time 45 minutes

Mrs Beeton used a mixture of chicken with ham, eggs and forcemeat in her fowl pie, in a complicated mixture that would mask the delicate flavours of a modern chicken. In this simplified recipe, the carcass is browned to flavour the stock, making use of every part of the bird. The meat, sauce and pastry can all be made a day ahead, if you like.

1 quantity flaky shortcrust pastry (see page 216)

2kg whole chicken, jointed, carcass reserved

1 tbsp sunflower oil

1 onion, peeled and roughly chopped

1 carrot, peeled and roughly chopped

1 bay leaf

1 thyme sprig

150g ham, cut into small chunks

15g unsalted butter

150g mushrooms, chopped roughly if large

2 medium leeks, trimmed and cut into 1cm slices

200ml double cream, plus extra to glaze the pie

plain flour, for dusting

salt and freshly ground black pepper

special equipment

a roasting tin, a deep 22–25cm pie dish and a temperature probe

Make the shortcrust pastry and keep it covered and chilled until ready to use. Preheat the oven to 200°C/ gas mark 6. Toss the chicken joints and carcass in the sunflower oil in a large roasting tin to coat and season with a little salt. Roast for 30 minutes, then remove the breasts. Continue to cook legs, wings and carcass for 15 minutes, or until well browned, then remove from the oven.

Chill the breast pieces while you make the stock. Place the onion, carrot, bay leaf, thyme and chicken legs, wings and carcass into a large saucepan. Add 800ml cold water and place over a medium heat. Bring to a simmer and cook for 30 minutes.

Once cooked, strain the chicken stock and spoon off any fat from the surface. Pull the meat from the bones and place it in a large bowl, adding the breast meat pulled into chunks. Add the ham.

Heat the butter in a frying pan over a medium heat. Add the mushrooms and fry until lightly browned. Add the leeks and enough stock to cover. Simmer for 2–3 minutes until the leeks are tender. Add the mushrooms and leeks to the chicken, leaving the liquid in the pan. Pour in the remaining stock and cream. Season to taste with salt and black pepper, then pour over the chicken and mix thoroughly. Cool the pie filling while you prepare the pastry, or chill and finish the pie the following day.

Preheat the oven to 200°C/gas mark 6. Place the filling in the pie dish, piling it up in the middle. Flour your work surface and roll the pastry into a neat circle 10cm larger than your pie dish and around 4–5mm thick. Any offcuts can be used to decorate the lid of the pie.

Moisten the edge of the dish with water. Trim 4mm from around the edge of the pastry, moisten it and attach it to the rim of the pie dish. Moisten the top of the strip with a little water, then take the circle of pastry and drape it over the pie dish, pinching around the edge to make a seal. Trim the edges of any surplus pastry and reserve for decorating the pie. Cut a small hole in the top of the pie to let the steam escape and decorate the lid with pastry leaves made from the surplus pastry, sticking these down with water.

Brush the pie with a little cream and bake for 45 minutes, or until the pastry is well browned and crisp. When a temperature probe placed in the centre of the pie reads 80°C the pie is ready. If not, turn the heat down to 150°C/gas mark 2 and continue cooking until the insides come up to temperature. If the pastry begins to burn, cover it with foil.

Note: A large rabbit can be treated in the same fashion – simply joint the animal and braise all of the parts as the above recipe does for the chicken legs, ensuring it is tender before making the sauce. If you like, you can slice the liver and add it to the mushrooms to cook briefly before adding the leeks.

ROAST CHICKEN

✳ **Serves 4** ✳ **Preparation time 5 minutes**
✳ **Cooking time 1 hour plus 20 minutes resting time**

Mrs Beeton gives a nice recipe for roast fowl or chicken, and many for using up the leftovers. If you are using a larger or smaller chicken, calculate the cooking time at 20 minutes per 500g. Cook at 200°C/gas mark 6 for the first 25 minutes, and then lower the temperature to 150°C/gas mark 2 for the remainder of the cooking time.

1.5kg whole chicken

15g softened unsalted butter

½ small, unwaxed lemon

small bunch thyme

1 bay leaf

salt and freshly ground black pepper

special equipment

a roasting tin and a temperature probe

Preheat the oven to 200°C/gas mark 6.

Rub the chicken all over with the butter. Put the lemon, thyme and bay leaf inside the cavity of the bird, and then season the outside with salt and a few grindings of pepper. Place the bird in a roasting tin.

Roast for 25 minutes, then turn the oven down to 150°C/gas mark 2 for a further 30–35 minutes until a probe inserted into the thickest part of breast reads 65°C and into the thigh reads 70°C. Otherwise pierce the thigh with a skewer. If the juices run clear and are not pink, the chicken is cooked. If it is not quite cooked, leave it in the oven for another 10 minutes, and then retest.

Remove from the oven and cover loosely with foil. Leave the chicken to rest for 20 minutes in a warm place before carving and serving.

ROAST & BRAISED TURKEY

✳ Serves 12 ✳ Preparation time 30 minutes
✳ Cooking time 3 hours for legs, 2 hours 15 minutes for crown including resting time

This dish takes its inspiration from Mrs Beeton's roast turkey, but since it is difficult to roast a large bird evenly, the legs of the turkey are braised slowly to soften them, and to give a wonderful gravy. The crown is then roasted to a perfect moistness without the worry that the legs will be underdone. Ask your butcher to remove the bird's legs and trim the backbone to neaten the crown. The wings can also be cut to the first joint and put in with the legs and giblets. The legs can be cooked the day before you roast the crown, which gives you a head start on your gravy if you are making this for Christmas lunch. Alternatively, if you have two ovens, they can be cooked simultaneously.

for the braise

legs and wings from a 6.5kg turkey

giblets from turkey

1 carrot, peeled and cut into large chunks

1 onion, peeled and roughly chopped

1 stick celery, roughly chopped

2 bay leaves

small bunch thyme

100ml dry white wine

800ml dark chicken stock (see page 22)

salt and freshly ground black pepper

for the crown

3kg crown, trimmed, at room temperature

25g salted butter

Preheat the oven to 220°C/gas mark 7.

Season the legs well with salt. Place them in a roasting tin with the wings and cook for 15 minutes. Add the giblets and cook for another 15 minutes.

Remove from the oven and pour away any excess fat then add the vegetables, bay leaves and thyme and a few grindings of black pepper. Pour in the wine and stock. Cover the tin with a layer of greaseproof paper, and then a layer of foil. Turn the oven down to 150°C/gas mark 2 and return the roasting tin to the oven.

After 2½ hours remove the tin from the oven and pour off the liquid (you should have at least 600ml) into a large bowl. Allow it to cool, then skim off any fat. Discard the giblets, herbs and vegetables, but if you are preparing the legs ahead of time, wrap them in foil and chill.

To cook the crown, preheat the oven to 200°C/gas mark 6. Rub the butter all over the skin of the crown and season with 1 tsp salt and a few grindings of pepper. Set it on a roasting tin and place in the oven. After 30 minutes turn the oven down to 160°C/gas mark 3 for a further 1 hour 15 minutes.

for the gravy

15g unsalted butter

15g plain flour

600ml stock from the braised legs (see opposite)

special equipment

2 large roasting tins and a temperature probe

(If the legs need reheating, return them to a roasting tin and pour over the stock. Place in the oven underneath the crown and allow cook for 1 hour until they reach at least 73°C.)

To check the crown for doneness, insert a probe into the thickest part of the breast, right down to the bone. It should read at least 65°C. If not, leave the crown in the oven for a further 20 minutes and retest.

Remove from the oven and cover with a sheet of foil and several tea towels. Allow it to rest in a warm place for 30 minutes, by which time the heat at the thickest part will have reached at least 73°C.

To make the gravy, heat the butter in a saucepan over medium heat and stir in the flour. Let it bubble and when the mixture smells nutty and begins to turn brown add the stock from the legs a little at a time and cook, stirring, until you have smooth gravy. Boil for 3–4 minutes then season to taste and strain into a warmed sauceboat.

To serve, slice the meat from the legs and arrange at one end of a large serving dish. Place the crown alongside and take to the table. For notes on carving, see page 81.

Note: You should always ask for giblets when buying a turkey, as they are a valuable source of flavour. Inspect them carefully and cut away any dark green parts – these are contaminated with bile and will make your stock bitter.

ROAST GOOSE

✳ **Serves 6–8** ✳ **Preparation time 5 minutes**
✳ **Cooking time 4 hours 15 minutes including resting time**

Mrs Beeton stuffs her goose with a typical sage, breadcrumb and onion stuffing. We tend not to stuff geese today as they cook more evenly without stuffing – so here, the stuffing is baked alongside the bird. Mrs Beeton serves this dish with apple sauce (see page 331).

5kg whole goose

for the gravy

giblets from the goose, checked over and any green gall stains removed

2 shallots, peeled and roughly chopped

1 tbsp sunflower oil

100ml white wine

800ml dark chicken stock (see page 22)

1 large thyme sprig

1 bay leaf

15g unsalted butter

15g plain flour

for the stuffing

40g salted butter

300g onions, peeled and finely chopped

10 sage leaves, finely chopped

140g fresh white breadcrumbs

1 medium egg, beaten

salt and freshly ground black pepper

special equipment

2 roasting tins

Preheat the oven to 220°C/gas mark 7. Place the giblets and the shallots in a roasting tin, pour over the oil and toss to coat. Sprinkle the goose with salt and set in another roasting tin. Place the tin containing the giblets on the bottom oven shelf, and the goose on the shelf above. After 30 minutes, remove the giblets and turn down the temperature to 150°C/gas mark 2. Set the timer for 2 hours.

Transfer the roasted giblets and shallots to a medium saucepan. Add the white wine, stock, thyme and bay leaf and simmer gently for 2 hours. After this time, remove the goose from the oven, pour off any excess fat from the tin and cover with foil. Turn the oven down to 140°C/gas mark 1 and return the goose to the oven for a final 1½ hours.

Now make the stuffing. Melt the butter in a saucepan over a medium heat. Add the onions and a pinch of salt and cook, stirring, for 5–7 minutes, until the onions are soft, but not brown. Remove from the heat and stir in the sage leaves and the breadcrumbs. Add the beaten egg, mixing it in well. Season with salt and pepper and transfer to a baking dish. Cover with foil and bake alongside the goose for 30 minutes, then take off the foil and allow the stuffing to brown in the oven for another 15 minutes. Remove the stuffing from the oven and keep warm.

Remove the goose from the oven and place on a warmed serving dish. Cover with foil and then a towel and leave to rest. For the gravy, melt the butter in a saucepan and stir in the flour. Let it bubble and, when the mixture smells nutty and begins to turn brown, add the stock a little at a time and cook, stirring, until you have a smooth gravy. Boil for 3–4 minutes, then season and strain into a warmed sauceboat.

CHICKEN BRAISE WITH MUSHROOMS

✳ Serves 4 ✳ Preparation time 15 minutes ✳ Cooking time 35 minutes

A quick way to cook a slowly reared chicken. Today's best equivalent would be an organic bird. Mrs Beeton's original recipe called for gravy, but you can use good chicken stock. Combined with the vegetables, the stock makes the dish rich and satisfying.

2kg whole chicken

3–4 tbsp sunflower oil

4 large field mushrooms, chopped into large chunks

1 onion, peeled and cut into large chunks

1 carrot, peeled and cut into 2cm chunks

2 garlic cloves, peeled

small bunch thyme

1 bay leaf

300ml light chicken stock (see page 23)

100ml double cream (optional)

salt and freshly ground black pepper

special equipment

a flameproof casserole or a large saucepan

Cut the chicken into pieces. Remove the legs and separate the drumsticks from the thighs, then cut each breast into two equal chunks. Season all over with a little salt.

Heat 3 tbsp oil in a large frying pan over a medium heat. Add the chicken pieces and fry until golden brown on all sides. Set aside the breast pieces and place the leg pieces into a flameproof casserole dish or large saucepan.

Turn up the heat under the frying pan and pour in a further 1 tbsp oil if needed. Add the mushrooms and cook, then transfer the cooked mushrooms into the casserole with the chicken legs. Now fry the onion and carrot with a pinch of salt for 2–3 minutes, until the onion begins to brown at the edges. Add the garlic, thyme, bay leaf and a grinding of black pepper and stir, then transfer the vegetables to the casserole.

Finally, stir the stock into the frying pan, scraping up any sediment with a wooden spoon to dissolve it into the sauce. Pour this over the chicken legs and other ingredients in the casserole, then cover with a lid and set on a medium heat. Simmer for 20 minutes, then add the chicken breasts, replace the pan lid and cook for a further 10 minutes, or until the chicken is cooked.

Strain the liquid into a small pan and simmer over a medium heat – it should taste richly of chicken but should not be reduced too much. Taste for seasoning and add a little salt and black pepper if necessary. Pour the sauce back over the chicken pieces and reheat. Add the cream, if desired, and simmer for 2–3 minutes.

Serve in deep soup plates with stoved potatoes (see page 183) and a green salad or steamed green beans.

DUCK LEGS BRAISED WITH SUMMER VEGETABLES

✳ **Serves 4** ✳ **Preparation time 30 minutes** ✳ **Cooking time 2 hours**

Mrs Beeton's lovely recipe for duck with turnips was made from cold, leftover duck. This version uses raw duck legs, which are a flavourful and inexpensive alternative to using a whole duck. You can substitute other vegetables for the turnips if you prefer.

4 duck legs

1 tbsp sunflower oil

100g streaky bacon, cut into 1cm chunks

1 medium onion, peeled and finely chopped

1 stick celery, finely chopped

1 garlic clove, peeled and sliced

2 bay leaves

1 large thyme sprig

100ml dry white wine

200ml dark chicken stock (see page 22)

200g white turnips, peeled and cut into large chunks

80g peas

salt and freshly ground black pepper

Preheat the oven to 180°C/gas mark 4. Season the duck legs lightly with salt and black pepper. Place the oil in a large non-stick frying pan over a medium heat. Add the duck legs, skin-side down and brown on both sides. Transfer to a baking tray that will fit them snugly.

Pour away most of the fat from the pan and add the bacon, onion and celery. Cook over a low heat, stirring, until the vegetables have picked up a little colour, then add the garlic, bay leaves, thyme and white wine. Turn up the heat and bring to a boil. Reduce the liquid by half, and then stir in the stock. Pour the mixture over the duck legs and top up with enough boiling water to almost cover them.

Cook for 1 hour in the oven then test by inserting a knife into the joint. If the juices run clear, they are cooked. If not, allow another 10–20 minutes. Add the turnips, making sure that they are tucked into the liquid, and return to the oven for a further 20 minutes.

Remove the duck legs from the liquid and place them on a baking sheet. Turn the oven up to 200°C/gas mark 6, and put the legs back into the oven to crisp up for 10–15 minutes.

Meanwhile, skim the fat from the liquid in the baking tray and then strain it into a saucepan (reserving the vegetables) placed over a medium heat. Boil until the liquid has reduced by half. Skim the surface again to remove any fat or scum and then add the peas. Taste the liquid at this stage and correct the seasoning if required. Add the vegetables and warm through.

To serve, divide the vegetables and liquid among 4 serving bowls and place a duck leg on top of each.

ROAST WILD DUCK

* Serves 4 * Preparation time 10 minutes
* Cooking time 45 minutes including resting time

Mrs Beeton recommends serving a piquant accompaniment to roast duck, and her raspberry vinegar (see page 375) livens up the simple gravy perfectly. Serve this dish with steamed and buttered kale. This recipe can also be made with red grouse, in which case cook the birds for 20–25 minutes.

2 wild ducks, weighing around 1.3kg in total

1 tbsp sunflower oil

30g butter

300g red onions, peeled and very finely sliced

50ml red wine

150ml dark chicken or jellied game stock (see page 22 or 17)

1 tbsp raisins

2 tbsp raspberry vinegar (see page 375) or sherry vinegar

salt and freshly ground black pepper

special equipment

a roasting tin

Preheat the oven to 200°C/gas mark 6.

Season the ducks inside with salt and black pepper. Place the oil and 10g of the butter in a large frying pan over a medium to high heat. Add the ducks and brown them on all sides. Transfer the ducks to a roasting tin and place in the oven for 25 minutes.

Meanwhile, turn the heat under the pan to low and add another 10g of butter. Place the sliced onions and a pinch of salt in the pan. Once they begin to brown, add the wine and simmer until it has reduced to almost nothing. Then add the stock and raisins, stirring until the onions are soft and there is very little liquid left. Remove the pan from the heat and stir in the remaining 10g of butter and the raspberry vinegar.

Once the duck is cooked, cover it with foil and allow it to rest for 15 minutes in a warm place. Remove each breast in one piece and cut into 3 or 4 long slices. Drizzle some raspberry vinegar over each portion and serve with onions on the side.

Note: A bird shot in September will be fat from the late summer corn. A bird shot later in the season will be less fat but have a deeper flavour. Either bird would benefit from being roasted. You can also use the leftover legs for the wild duck & mushroom broth (see page 39).

PIGEONS & MUSHROOMS ON TOAST

✳ Serves 4 ✳ Preparation time 15 minutes
✳ Cooking time 20 minutes including resting time

Mrs Beeton suggested serving mushrooms with pigeon and the two make a winning combination either as a sauce or, as here, simply pan-fried and served on toast to absorb the lovely cooking juices.

85g unsalted butter

8 skinless pigeon breasts

4 small shallots, peeled and finely sliced

2 thyme sprigs

1 bay leaf

200g Portabella mushrooms, cut into 1cm chunks

2 garlic cloves, peeled and chopped

50ml white wine

100ml dark chicken stock (see page 22)

small bunch flat-leaf parsley, stems discarded, leaves chopped

lemon juice, to taste

salt and freshly ground black pepper

to serve

4 slices good white bread for toast

salted butter

Preheat the oven to 105°C/gas mark ¼.

Place 50g of the butter in a large frying pan set over a medium to high heat. Season the breasts with ½ tsp salt and then fry in the butter for 1–2 minutes on each side, or until golden brown on the outside and still rare in the centre. Set the breasts on a plate in the oven, covered with foil, to rest while you finish the recipe.

Return the pan to the heat and turn down to medium. Immediately add the shallots, thyme, bay leaf and a few grindings of black pepper. Cook until the shallots are soft and beginning to colour. Add the mushrooms, garlic and another 25g of the butter and cook for 5 minutes.

Add the white wine to the pan and, using a wooden spoon, stir to dislodge any caramelised bits sticking to the bottom of the pan. Stir in the stock then return the breasts to the pan, cook for 5 minutes, and add the remaining butter and parsley. Meanwhile, toast the bread. Adjust the seasoning and stir in a squeeze of lemon juice to freshen up the sauce.

To serve, set a piece of buttered toast on each plate. Place some sauce and mushrooms and 2 breasts on top of each and serve immediately with a simple salad.

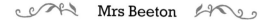
PIGEON & BLOOD ORANGE SALAD

✳ Serves 4 ✳ Preparation time 15 minutes ✳ Cooking time 10 minutes including resting time

Mrs Beeton commonly used citrus fruit (which is, of course, easily available today), with poultry and game bird recipes. However, many of the birds she used are now protected and no longer available for cooking. We can use pigeons, however, which are shot in large numbers in early spring, just when the best citrus fruit is arriving in our shops. Mrs Beeton usually broiled or grilled her birds and served them quite plain, but the breasts can be pan-fried and make a delicious salad.

160g green beans, trimmed

1 blood orange

8 skinless pigeon breasts

30g unsalted butter

1 small shallot, peeled and finely chopped

60g hazelnuts, roasted, peeled, and coarsely chopped (see note)

small bunch flat-leaf parsley, stems discarded, leaves finely chopped

small bunch chervil, stems discarded, leaves finely chopped

60g watercress, thick stems removed

salt and freshly ground black pepper

for the dressing

2 tsp sherry vinegar

3 tsp extra virgin olive oil

1 tsp Dijon mustard

Boil the green beans in slightly salted water for 5 minutes until just tender, then drain and plunge into a bowl of iced water. Leave for 2 minutes, drain and set aside.

Using a sharp knife cut the top and bottom off the orange. Cut the skin off, taking the white pith off as well. Cut out each segment and set aside in a small bowl with any spare juice.

Season the pigeon breasts with salt and black pepper. Place a large frying pan over a high heat and add the butter. Add the breasts to the pan and fry for 2 minutes on each side until well browned. Transfer to a plate, cover with foil and leave to rest in a warm place.

Meanwhile, whisk all the dressing ingredients together in a large bowl. Add the beans, orange segments, shallot, nuts and herbs. Toss together, and then add the watercress, mixing the leaves in thoroughly.

Cut the pigeon breasts in half horizontally and place 4 halves on each plate. Serve the salad alongside the breasts and drizzle over any dressing left in the bowl.

Note: To roast hazelnuts, preheat the oven to 180°C/gas mark 4 and place the nuts in a single layer on a baking sheet. Bake for 10–15 minutes, watching them closely, as they will burn quickly. While the nuts are warm, loosen the skins by rubbing the nuts between two tea towels. Discard the skins, spread the nuts out on a cutting board to cool completely then chop them to the desired texture.

ROAST PARTRIDGES

✳ **Serves 4** ✳ **Preparation time 25 minutes**
✳ **Cooking time 35–40 minutes including resting time**

This is a simple yet mouth-watering way of cooking partridges. Serve them with a potato & cream gratin (see page 181) and roast chicory cooked pears (see page 172).

4 oven-ready partridges

2 tbsp sunflower oil

60g unsalted butter

2 shallots, peeled and finely chopped

4 large thyme sprigs

2 tbsp brandy or cognac

salt and freshly ground black pepper

special equipment

a large roasting tin and a temperature probe

Preheat the oven to 200°C/gas mark 6.

Place a large frying pan over a medium to high heat and add the oil and 15g of the butter. When it sizzles, add the birds and fry them on all sides for 5 minutes, or until they are a golden brown.

Divide the shallots, thyme and the remaining butter between the body cavities of the birds and put all the birds into a roomy roasting tin. Season with salt and pepper and pour ½ tbsp brandy into the body cavity of each bird.

Roast for 15 minutes for rare or 20–25 minutes for medium to well done, then remove from the oven and place on a serving dish in a warm place. Cover with foil and leave for 10 minutes. A temperature probe pushed into cooked and rested birds at the thickest part of the breast just above the wing joint should read 55°C for medium rare.

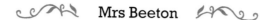

PHEASANT BREASTS WITH CIDER & CREAM

✳ Serves 2 ✳ Preparation time 5 minutes ✳ Cooking time 15 minutes including resting time

This recipe shows how versatile game can be, and that you do not always have to cook a whole bird. Pheasant breasts are widely available now and they cook quickly. This dish is an amalgam of two of Mrs Beeton's recipes, and a modern version of a fricassee (which traditionally was leftover cooked meat with piquant seasoning and cream). If you can't get Hertfordshire cider, any good cider will do.

2 cock pheasant breasts or 3 hen pheasant breasts, weighing 400g in total

1 tbsp sunflower oil

20g cold, unsalted butter

2 shallots, peeled and finely sliced

1 thyme sprig

1 Cox's apple, peeled, cored, and cut into 12 slices

150ml dry Hertfordshire cider

45ml cider brandy or Calvados

150ml double cream

1 tsp green peppercorns, drained

Preheat the oven to 120°C/gas mark ½.

Season each breast with salt and black pepper on the flesh side. Place the oil in a frying pan over a medium to high heat and fry the pheasant skin-side down until it is well browned, then turn over and brown the other side. This should take 2–3 minutes on each side. Remove the breasts to a plate, cover with foil and keep warm.

Place half the butter in the pan over medium heat. Add the shallots and thyme and cook, stirring, for 2 minutes. The shallots will pick up colour from the caramelised juices. When they are lightly browned, add the apple slices. Cook for 30 seconds, turning them once.

Add the cider and return the pheasant breasts to the pan. Cook until all the liquid has evaporated, turning the breasts once or twice to heat through. When the sauce is reduced and sticky, remove it from the heat (and keep it away from any overhanging curtains or blinds), add the Calvados and flame by holding a match to the edge of the pan.

When the flames die down, add the cream and peppercorns. Shake the pan to amalgamate the sauce and simmer for 2–3 minutes. Add the remaining butter to the pan, shake again and serve immediately with buttered noodles and a watercress salad (see page 175).

POT-ROAST PHEASANT WITH CELERY

✻ Serves 4 ✻ Preparation time 15 minutes ✻ Cooking time 1 hour including resting time

Pheasants can be abundant in rural areas in the winter, and butchers often sell them very cheaply indeed, making them accessible to us in a way they would not have been to Mrs Beeton. She roasted her pheasant, but this updated one-pot recipe prevents the birds from drying out and provides a no-hassle gravy. The combination of pheasant with celery is a classic English pairing. If you can find it, use white blanched celery. Mrs Beeton would have been familiar with this, and it has the finest flavour. Any leftover legs can be used for the pheasant & chestnut soup (see page 36).

1 pheasant brace
(a 1kg cock and a 600g hen)

2 thyme sprigs

1 tbsp sunflower oil

50g unsalted butter

6 shallots, halved

4 sticks white blanched
celery, cut into 5cm lengths

2 carrots, peeled and cut into
3cm lengths

1 bay leaf

300ml dry white wine

150ml dark chicken or jellied
game stock (see page 22 or 17)

4 very thin rashers
dry-cure streaky bacon

2 tbsp finely chopped
celery leaves, to garnish

special equipment

a large flameproof casserole
with a lid and a temperature
probe

Preheat oven to 160°C/gas mark 3.

Insert a sprig of thyme into the cavity of each bird.

Place a large casserole on a medium to high heat. Add the oil and half the butter and when it sizzles, add the birds and fry them until they are well coloured on all sides. Remove to a large plate. Add the vegetables to the casserole and fry until well browned. Then add the bay leaf, wine and stock.

When the liquid is simmering, return the birds to the casserole, grind some black pepper over them and lay the bacon over the birds. Cover with a lid and place in the oven for 20 minutes. For medium or medium-rare, the hen should be ready in 20 minutes, the cock in 30 minutes. A temperature probe inserted into the breast just above the wing joint should read 45–50°C. If you like your birds well done, cook for a further 10 minutes until the breasts are firm.

Once the birds are done remove the pot from the oven and put it in a warm place to rest with the lid on for 15 minutes. Then carve the breasts from the carcass and cut each one into 2–3 pieces. Place on a platter alongside the vegetables and sprinkle the finely chopped celery leaves over. The sauce should simply be skimmed to remove any fat, poured into a sauceboat and served alongside.

GAME TERRINE

❋ Serves 8 ❋ Preparation time 1 hour
❋ Cooking time 1 hour 40 minutes plus 2–3 days chilling time

This recipe makes a lovely lunch or supper dish from just one bird, either a wild duck or small (hen) pheasant, or the equivalent weight of any game meat. Mrs Beeton used forcemeat in her recipe; here, minced pork and seasoning are used instead, as they are more easily available today. Just ask your butcher to coarsely mince some fatty pork, which will baste the meat as it cooks. The terrine is best made a few days before you are planning to serve it.

1 quantity rich shortcrust pastry (see page 217)

1 large wild duck
(to yield 225g breast meat and 120g leg meat)

750g coarsely minced fatty pork, such as belly

1 medium egg, beaten

for the seasoning

1 garlic clove, crushed

2 tsp salt

1 tsp ground mace

½ tsp black pepper

1 tbsp chopped fresh thyme

for the jelly

2 leaves gelatine

200ml jellied game stock (see page 17)

50ml Marsala

special equipment

a 1kg terrine dish or loaf tin

Make the shortcrust pastry and keep it covered and chilled until ready to use.

Line a 1kg terrine dish or loaf tin with a strip of non-stick baking paper, leaving a 2cm overhang along the long sides of the tin to help you lift the terrine from the tin for serving.

Remove the breasts from the duck, discard the skin and slice into strips. Set aside.

Remove the meat and skin from the legs, scraping the flesh from the bones with a small knife. Pull out any hard white tendons from the drumstick meat as you cut. Put the leg meat into the bowl of a food processor and pulse to reduce it to a fine paste. Add the minced pork.

Combine the seasoning ingredients together in a bowl and sprinkle 2 pinches of the mixture over the breasts. Mix the rest of seasoning in with the leg meat mixture.

Preheat the oven to 200°C/gas mark 6.

Roll out 300g of the shortcrust pastry and use it to line the base and sides of the loaf tin in one piece, allowing it to overhang the sides a little so that you can create a good seal when the lid is on.

Fill the pastry case with alternating layers of leg meat mixture and breast meat, ending with a layer of leg meat mixture.

Roll out the remaining pastry to make a lid. Place it on top of the pie and seal it by tightly crimping the pastry edges, folding the bottom layer over the top and pinching the two together with your fingertips. Shape any trimmings into leaves to decorate the top, sealing them in place with a little water, then brush the lid with the beaten egg. Finally, cut a small hole in the top of the pie and insert a rolled-up piece of greaseproof paper to act as a funnel.

Bake the pie for 25 minutes then turn the oven down to 180°C/gas mark 4. After 45 minutes turn the oven down to 160°C/gas mark 3 and bake for a final 30 minutes, then cool in the tin.

When the pie is almost cold, prepare the jelly. Soak the gelatine sheets in a small bowl of cold water for 10 minutes. Meanwhile place a small pan over low heat. Add the stock and Marsala and let it warm until it is hand-hot. Squeeze the water from the gelatine leaves and add them to the warm stock, stirring to dissolve. Very slowly and carefully pour the jelly through the hole in the top of the pie, allowing it time to filter into the terrine. Chill, in the tin, ideally for 2–3 days before serving. When you are ready to serve, dip the terrine tin into a bowl of hot water for 1–2 minutes. Holding on to the overhanging baking paper, lift the pie from the tin, peel away the paper and place on a serving dish. The terrine is delicious served sliced with apple chutney and a salad of chicory leaves dressed with a little oil and either raspberry or sherry vinegar, or simply with pickles.

WOODCOCK ON TOAST

✳ **Serves 4** ✳ **Preparation time 15 minutes**
✳ **Cooking time 12–15 minutes plus 10 minutes resting time**

Woodcock make an excellent quick meal or shooting breakfast. Serve with a good bottle of Claret for a real treat. Small birds have traditionally been served on toast or buttered breadcrumbs to absorb the juices, as Mrs Beeton recommended doing with larks.

2 tbsp sunflower oil

60g unsalted butter

4 woodcock (see note below)

2 shallots, peeled and finely chopped

4 large thyme sprigs

2 tbsp brandy or cognac

salt and freshly ground black pepper

to serve

200ml jellied game or chicken stock

4 slices good bread

salted butter, for spreading

special equipment

a large roasting tin and a temperature probe

Preheat the oven to 200°C/gas mark 6. Heat a large frying pan over a medium to high heat, add the oil and a knob of the butter and, when it sizzles, add the birds. Fry them on all sides for 5 minutes, or until they are a mid-brown colour.

Place some shallot, a sprig of thyme and a small knob of butter into the body cavity of each bird and arrange them in a roomy roasting tin. Season with salt and black pepper and pour ½ tbsp brandy into the cavity of each bird.

Place in the oven. After 12 minutes remove the tin from the oven and transfer the birds to a serving dish. Set it in a warm place, cover with foil and leave for 10 minutes. After this time a temperature probe pushed into the thickest part of the breast should read 55°C for medium rare.

Meanwhile add the stock to the roasting tin and mix to combine with the cooking juices. Simmer to reduce for a quick gravy. Toast the slices of bread and spread with salted butter. Place each woodcock on a piece of toast and serve with the gravy on the side.

Note: Woodcock are traditionally cooked with their innards intact. If you cook the woodcock intact, you will need to remove the innards with a teaspoon after cooking. Discard the small, hard, round gizzard and the tiny, dark green gall bladder which is attached to the liver. Melt 10g butter in a small saucepan with a little garlic, fry for a minute or two and then add the innards and 1 tbsp brandy. Flame and mash the mixture with a fork as it cooks. Spread onto the toast and top with the woodcock.

....

BRAISED HARE LEGS & SHOULDERS

✳ **Serves 4** ✳ **Preparation time 20 minutes** ✳ **Cooking time 3 hours**

Mrs Beeton cooked young hares, called leverets, in butter and stewed older animals in a ragout or braise. Here, the traditional vegetable accompaniments of onions, carrot and celery have been added to the braise to give a fully flavoured sauce. Only use the legs and shoulders, which in any case will easily feed four. The saddle is best cooked separately and saved for a special dinner when there are just two of you (see page 109).

40g unsalted butter

legs and shoulders from a 2kg hare, weighing about 900g

350ml light red wine

100g streaky dry-cure bacon, diced

1 onion, peeled and finely chopped

1 small carrot, peeled and cut into small chunks

1 stick celery, finely chopped

1 garlic clove, peeled and halved

1 small rosemary sprig

small bunch thyme

2 bay leaves

400ml dark chicken stock (see page 22)

salt and freshly ground black pepper

special equipment

a roasting dish

Preheat the oven to 140°C/gas mark 1.

Place a heavy-bottomed pan over a medium to high heat, and add 20g of the butter until hot and foaming. Season the legs with a large pinch of salt, add them to the pan and brown well all over. This should take about 10 minutes.

Transfer the meat into a snug-fitting roasting dish and discard any fat from the pan. Now pour a little of the red wine into the pan and stir to dissolve any sediment. Pour this over the hare, then wipe out the pan and add the bacon. Cook the bacon, stirring, over a medium heat until it is golden.

Add the onion, carrot and celery and cook until softened and lightly brown. Add the garlic, herbs and a grinding of pepper and cook for 2 minutes. Then add the rest of the wine and cook until completely reduced and beginning to caramelise. Add the stock, bring the mixture to a boil and pour it over the legs.

Cover the roasting dish closely with non-stick baking paper and then seal with a layer of foil. Place in the oven for 2½ hours, until the vegetables are tender and the meat is falling off the bone. Remove from the oven and strain the liquid into a small pan placed on a high heat. Boil to reduce by half and then taste for seasoning.

Meanwhile, pick the meat from the bones in large chunks. Return to the pan with the reduced sauce and reheat to serve. Serve with mashed potatoes (see page 182) and a seasonal vegetable.

CURRIED RABBIT

✳ **Serves 4** ✳ **Preparation time 45 minutes** ✳ **Cooking time 2 hours 30 minutes–3 hours**

Mrs Beeton gives extensive notes on rabbits, including a simple rabbit curry. Here, rather than a generic curry powder as she would have used, a combination of spices is specified, which produces a spicy sauce that balances beautifully with the rich, fruity flavour of a wild rabbit. A bird's-eye chilli is used here because its heat is predictable and punchy. Serve with aged (high-quality) basmati rice.

6 tbsp sunflower oil

3 onions, finely chopped

1 tsp cumin seeds

2 bay leaves

1 tsp salt

1 tbsp coriander seeds

1 tsp fenugreek seeds

1 tsp ground turmeric

4 garlic cloves, finely chopped

30g piece fresh root ginger, peeled and finely chopped

1 bird's-eye chilli, finely chopped

400g tin chopped tomatoes

1 tbsp tomato purée

1kg rabbit (1 large or 2 small animals), jointed

lemon juice, to taste

2 tbsp chopped coriander, to garnish

to finish

1 garlic clove, peeled

30g piece fresh root ginger, peeled and chopped

50ml double cream

1 tsp garam masala

Place a pan over a high heat and add the oil, chopped onion, cumin seeds, bay leaves and salt. Add enough water to cover the onion and cook until all the water has evaporated. Reduce the heat slightly and fry until golden brown, then add the coriander and fenugreek seeds and the turmeric and fry for 2–3 minutes. Add the chopped garlic, ginger and chilli and fry for another 2–3 minutes then add the tomatoes, tomato purée and rabbit legs. Add 250ml boiling water, cover and cook gently either on the hob or in a low oven at 140°C/gas mark 1 for 2½–3 hours.

Keeping back the legs, pour the sauce into a jug blender with the finishing ingredients and blend for 2–3 minutes. Pass through a sieve back into the pan with the legs, and add the loins. Place in a pan over a low heat. Simmer for 5 minutes, or until the loins are cooked and the legs are heated through. Season everything with salt and fresh lemon juice to adjust the sharpness. Sprinkle with chopped coriander before serving.

Note: To cook the rice, weigh out 100g basmati rice per person. Soak in a large bowl of cold water for 10 minutes, then rinse and drain. Place a large pan of water on a high heat and when it boils stir in the rice. Bring back to a boil then simmer gently until the rice is almost tender. Add a good pinch of salt. Cook for 2–3 minutes longer, until tender. Drain well and return to the pan with the lid on. Leave for 2 minutes and then fluff with a fork.

PAN-FRIED VENISON LOIN
WITH WHITE WINE, CREAM & MUSTARD

* Serves 4 * Preparation time 10 minutes * Cooking time 15 minutes including resting time

The loin of any animal (that section immediately between the top of the pelvis and the ribcage) is a prime cut. Though it is tender, in the case of venison it is best cooked medium to keep it juicy. Mrs Beeton tended to cook meat either as whole joints or to give recipes for leftovers cooked as fricassees, most probably because this suited the ovens, fires and spits, which were the cooking methods of her day. Today, we are used to cooking meat on the top of the stove, a technique this recipe illustrates perfectly.

4 x 160–200g pieces of red or roe venison loin

1 tbsp sunflower oil

½ tsp salt

1 tsp cracked black pepper

1 tsp crushed juniper berries

20g unsalted butter, plus an extra knob

2 shallots, peeled and finely chopped

1 bay leaf

75ml dry white wine

100ml dark chicken or jellied game stock (see page 22 or 17)

150ml single cream

2 tsp Dijon mustard

Preheat the oven to 120°C/gas mark ½ and place a large plate in the oven. Trim the venison pieces or loin of all skin and fat and cut into pieces about 12–15cm long. Place the pieces in a shallow bowl, add the sunflower oil and ½ tsp salt and toss to coat.

Place a large frying pan over high heat. Add the loins and sear on all sides for about 7–8 minutes, or until they are evenly dark brown all over. Start with a high heat and turn the heat down once the meat has begun to brown. Add the pepper and juniper berries and cook for 1–2 minutes, then transfer the loins to the warm plate in the oven and cover with foil. Leave for 5 minutes while you finish the sauce.

Drain any oil from the pan and set it over a medium heat. To the spices remaining in the pan add the butter, shallots and a small pinch of salt. Fry until the shallots brown at the edges, then add the bay leaf, white wine and stock.

Turn the heat to high and bring to a boil. Allow the liquid to reduce to a sticky glaze, then turn the heat down to low, add the cream and simmer, scraping all the sediment and juices from the bottom of the pan into the sauce. Stir in the Dijon mustard and a knob of unsalted butter, and then return the loins to the pan along with any juices from the plate. Once everything has warmed through, slice the loins on the diagonal into long slices and serve with the sauce.

BRAISED OXTAIL

✳ Serves 4 ✳ Preparation time 30 minutes ✳ Cooking time 4 hours–4 hours 30 minutes

This recipe tastes even better if you cook it a day ahead – which makes it ideal for serving to guests because all the work is done the day before, leaving you free to entertain. Mrs Beeton uses very traditional English seasonings in this dish, including mace, mushroom ketchup and cloves, to which I have added ale for a really meaty, savoury dish.

1 oxtail, weighing around 1.5kg, cut in slices

150g cured streaky bacon, diced

2 onions, peeled and chopped into chunks

500ml light beer

8 allspice berries

1 pinch ground mace

juice and zest of ½ lemon, plus extra juice to taste

30ml mushroom ketchup

2 cloves

350ml jellied beef or dark chicken stock (see page 19 or 22)

2 bay leaves

2 tbsp finely chopped parsley

salt and freshly ground black pepper

special equipment

a large roasting tin and a flameproof casserole with a lid

Ask your butcher to slice the oxtail for you if you are unsure about doing it yourself. Preheat the oven to 220°C/gas mark 7. Place the oxtail pieces in a large roasting tin, season with a pinch of salt and pepper, and scatter over the bacon. Roast for 30 minutes, until the meat is golden brown all over.

Pour off and discard most of the fat, then add the onions and return the tin to the oven. Cook, stirring occasionally, for 10–15 minutes, or until the onion begins to colour. Remove from the oven and reduce the heat to 160°C/gas mark 3.

Scrape the oxtail and onions from the roasting tin into the casserole. Pour half of the beer into the roasting tin and stir to dissolve any caramelised bits sticking to the bottom. Then pour this, along with all of the rest of the ingredients except the chopped parsley, into the casserole. Stir well, cover tightly with a lid or foil and place in the oven.

After 1 hour turn the meat to ensure it cooks evenly in the liquid. After 4 hours the meat should be very tender and sticky. If not, leave it in the oven for another 15–30 minutes.

Remove from the oven and pour the liquid into a large measuring jug, discarding the bay leaves and leaving everything else behind in the casserole dish. Let the liquid settle in the jug and then use a ladle or large spoon to skim off and discard any fat that rises to the top. Taste the liquid and add a little salt, pepper and lemon juice if needed, then pour the sauce back over the meat and turn the pieces in it to moisten them. Stir through the chopped parsley then serve with confit of parsnips (see page 169) and freshly boiled sweetheart or Savoy cabbage.

PAN-FRIED VENISON LOIN
WITH WHITE WINE, CREAM & MUSTARD

✳ **Serves 4** ✳ **Preparation time 10 minutes** ✳ **Cooking time 15 minutes including resting time**

The loin of any animal (that section immediately between the top of the pelvis and the ribcage) is a prime cut. Though it is tender, in the case of venison it is best cooked medium to keep it juicy. Mrs Beeton tended to cook meat either as whole joints or to give recipes for leftovers cooked as fricassees, most probably because this suited the ovens, fires and spits, which were the cooking methods of her day. Today, we are used to cooking meat on the top of the stove, a technique this recipe illustrates perfectly.

4 x 160–200g pieces of red or roe venison loin

1 tbsp sunflower oil

½ tsp salt

1 tsp cracked black pepper

1 tsp crushed juniper berries

20g unsalted butter, plus an extra knob

2 shallots, peeled and finely chopped

1 bay leaf

75ml dry white wine

100ml dark chicken or jellied game stock (see page 22 or 17)

150ml single cream

2 tsp Dijon mustard

Preheat the oven to 120°C/gas mark ½ and place a large plate in the oven. Trim the venison pieces or loin of all skin and fat and cut into pieces about 12–15cm long. Place the pieces in a shallow bowl, add the sunflower oil and ½ tsp salt and toss to coat.

Place a large frying pan over high heat. Add the loins and sear on all sides for about 7–8 minutes, or until they are evenly dark brown all over. Start with a high heat and turn the heat down once the meat has begun to brown. Add the pepper and juniper berries and cook for 1–2 minutes, then transfer the loins to the warm plate in the oven and cover with foil. Leave for 5 minutes while you finish the sauce.

Drain any oil from the pan and set it over a medium heat. To the spices remaining in the pan add the butter, shallots and a small pinch of salt. Fry until the shallots brown at the edges, then add the bay leaf, white wine and stock.

Turn the heat to high and bring to a boil. Allow the liquid to reduce to a sticky glaze, then turn the heat down to low, add the cream and simmer, scraping all the sediment and juices from the bottom of the pan into the sauce. Stir in the Dijon mustard and a knob of unsalted butter, and then return the loins to the pan along with any juices from the plate. Once everything has warmed through, slice the loins on the diagonal into long slices and serve with the sauce.

MEAT

Red meat has always been popular in the UK, and there is a long history of association between Englishmen and beef. Historically, however, the most economical animal to rear for meat, and therefore the most commonly consumed, was the pig, which provides a large quantity of versatile fat in addition to a variety of cuts of meat. It also produces large litters. Cows were valued for their milk and so would have been killed only when their milking days had passed, or when an event warranted it. Sheep, too, were often not butchered until they had aged, which partly explains why our collective memory of mutton is of a scraggy beast, because these were the only animals that would have been eaten by most people. Properly raised mutton gives a rich, aromatic meat without too much fat; lamb, by comparison, is tender and delicate.

THE DEVELOPMENT OF ANIMAL BREEDS

Different breeds are valued for their individual characteristics. For example, some breeds of cattle are prized for the flavour or tenderness of their meat, others for their high milk production. Still others, mountain cattle for example, are esteemed for their ability to produce meat on poor land where most other breeds would not thrive. Unfortunately, the majority of the beef and pork we eat today comes from breeds that are chosen for their ability to mature quickly, producing a large quantity of meat in a relatively short time. Pigs and sheep usually reach the market within their first year; beef animals can be up to 30 months old before they are killed, but even that is very young compared to the age at which animals would have been killed at the time Mrs Beeton was writing her book. However, an increasing number of farms are now reviving traditional breeds known for their characterful meat, and these are well worth tracking down at farm shops or farmers' markets.

Sheep are not usually farmed as intensively as cows and pigs, so breed distribution remains much more varied, even in the meat that reaches supermarket shelves.

MEAT PRODUCTION TODAY

The majority of the meat we buy comes from conventional (including free-range) and factory production, with organically reared animals making up a small, but increasing, proportion of total sales. Most livestock are fed on grass or cereal and soya-based foods milled to precise nutritional specifications. Free-range animals, particularly those reared on old pasture, benefit from a more varied diet, and this is reflected in the vastly superior flavour of the meat. Meat raised under strict free-range specifications will be labelled as such. Some meat also carries the RSPCA Freedom Food mark, indicating that the animals have been well cared for to certain recognised standards.

Ageing meat

Beef, lamb and mutton benefit from hanging, a process of slow drying that concentrates and enriches the flavour of the flesh. Pork is generally not hung because the animal's skin deteriorates in condition during the process. Lamb should be hung for at least ten days; beef for a minimum of three weeks and up to five weeks, at a low temperature just above freezing.

Curing meat

Salting or pickling, also called curing, is a centuries-old method of preserving meat to extend the length of time it can be stored. Although we now have the option of freezing meat to preserve it, curing adds flavour, texture and character, and you can do it at home: there is a simple recipe for curing bacon on page 143. Very little equipment is required: just a large, lidded container, and perhaps a meat slicer if you choose to make your own bacon. A supplier of the specialist ingredients needed for curing meat can be found at the back of the book.

Curing and hygiene

You must pay particular attention to hygiene when curing at home. In a properly cured piece of meat, the concentration of salt prohibits the growth of most microbes, but if the curing process is not thorough, or the level of salt is not high enough, the meat will spoil. For that reason, always ensure your hands are very clean or wear disposable gloves when handling the meat, and use a sterilising agent to clean plastic containers for storing brine. It is also a good idea to take advantage of modern technology and freeze the meat after curing it, until it is required. If at any time the meat smells bad, or mould begins to grow on the surface, it has been contaminated and should be discarded. Take no risks.

COOKING METHODS

Braising: This is the process of submerging meat in water, stock or a mixture of these, with alcohol, such as wine or beer, and some vegetables and herbs. The meat is then cooked slowly until it breaks down to a soft, sticky, melt-in-the-mouth consistency. Braising is good for using certain cuts of meat that, though flavourful, would be very tough if cooked any other way. Sometimes the meat is browned by frying it before braising to add flavour and colour. Cuts suitable for braising include shin, flank, oxtail, shortribs, pork belly, pork shoulder, beef cheeks, lamb and mutton breast and shoulder.

Frying: This is a quick method for browning the surface of meat by cooking it at a high temperature in fat. When frying it is important not to crowd too much meat into the pan all at once, otherwise it will not fry but stew and turn grey rather than browning properly. All cuts of steak, including skirt, along with cutlets, chops, fillets and loins are suitable for frying. They should then be left to rest before serving, to allow the temperature inside to equalise so that the juices remain in the meat and do not run out when it is sliced. In some cases, meat is fried first to add flavour and colour before being braised, roasted or pot roasted. This method is often called 'sealing'.

Oven roasting: Larger joints of meat are wonderful roasted in the oven. The meat is put into a hot oven initially to ensure that it browns and begins to cook quickly, then the heat is reduced until the joint cooks through. The lower the temperature at which this second cooking takes place, the more evenly the joint will cook, so temperatures between 120°C and 160°C are suitable for this second phase. Sirloin or rib of beef, legs, shoulder and loin of lamb, mutton or pork all make good roasts.

Pot roasting: In this method meat is usually browned well in hot fat then placed in a covered pot with aromatics, vegetables and a little stock or wine. This creates a humid environment to ensure that the meat doesn't dry out while it is cooking. It is a good method for cooking a joint that is to be eaten rare, such as a joint of top rump, or for a cut of meat that requires slower cooking, such as a rolled shoulder of lamb, or a whole tied shin.

Other meats that suit roasting in a pot are topside and silverside of beef, and griskin (the lean part of a pork loin) and shoulder of pork.

Grilling: You can grill meat under hot grill elements in an oven or over coals on a barbecue, though the meat first needs to be oiled a little in order for it to brown. Placing the meat on to a grill rack allows the fat to drip off while it is cooking, making it a healthy, as well as delicious, way to cook meat. Smaller cuts of meat such as steaks and cutlets, and kebabs are good for grilling.

COOKING TIMES FOR MEAT

M rs Beeton would not have had a temperature probe. Instead, she would have calculated cooking times according to the weight of the meat, and known her recipes and her equipment well. Today, however, we enjoy a greater variety of dishes, often use recipes or cuts of meat that we haven't tried before, and many of us are less at one with our cookers. We can still use the weight of the meat and the oven temperature as a good guide, but in order to get perfect results every time – especially with a new recipe or in an unfamiliar kitchen – it is well worth investing a few pounds in a temperature probe. Some thermometers even have alarms that sound when your meat reaches your chosen temperature.

It will take a bit of experimentation with cooking meat to different internal temperatures and resting joints for different amounts of time to thoroughly understand how the changes you make affect the final result, but you should find that even the first time you use a temperature probe the results will be more accurate than if you were using old-fashioned methods alone.

All of the recipes in this book are perfectly manageable without a temperature probe, but you might find yourself having to cut into a piece of meat to check that it's cooked through, rather than having the confidence to assume that it is. The table below is a quick guide to cooking times by weight (the old-fashioned way) as well as by internal temperature.

Before cooking, remove the meat from the fridge and allow it to come to room temperature (about 15°C) for a couple of hours, uncovered. Beef and lamb can both be eaten rare to well done, while pork is traditionally served well done as it can contain a harmful parasite, trichinosis, if not cooked through – though cases of the disease today are rare. Pork cooked to an internal temperature of 70°C or showing no signs of pinkness at its centre is safe to eat.

Internal temperatures and cooking times

In order to achieve the correct final internal temperature, weigh the meat first and calculate the cooking time. Start from an initial oven temperature of 200–220°C. After 30 minutes, lower the temperature to 140–160°C for the remainder of the cooking time. Use the table below to calculate the total cooking time for your meat.

	Cooking time per 500g	Internal temperature
Rare beef and lamb	10–12 minutes	50–55°C
Medium beef and lamb	15 minutes	55–60°C
Well done pork, beef and lamb	20 minutes	70°C

Resting

Meat cooks from the outside inwards, which means that when a joint is removed from the oven, the outer layers will be hotter than the core. For the best results, remove the meat from the oven when the internal temperature is still a little short of the temperature you are aiming for. Resting the meat, covered loosely in foil in a warm place, allows the heat to equalise (spread from the outside to the centre). In a large joint, the temperature at the centre can rise by as much as 10°C while it is resting.

Carving loin

To carve a piece of loin on the bone, first remove the meat from the bones. Place the meat on a board, resting on its edge with the ribs uppermost, as shown in the illustration. Make a cut along the ribs, keeping your knife as close to the bone as possible.

Cut down to the base of the ribs, then turn your knife and slice along the base of the loin to remove it from the backbone.

Once the bones have been removed, you can cut down through the loin, producing neat slices.

When carving a piece of rolled loin or sirloin, there are no bones to remove. You can simply cut through the piece, slicing it into even, thick slices.

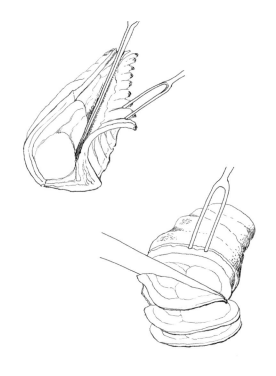

Carving fore rib

When you carve a piece of forerib, let the joint sit on its ribs – it will be more stable this way. First slice into the joint horizontally, between the meat and the rib bones. This can be done a little at a time – just enough to allow you to cut a few slices. If you cut too far, the meat will slide around while you are carving it.

Next, cut vertically into the meat, carving it into thick, even slices, which should come cleanly away from the bones.

Continue to cut horizontally and then vertically until you have cut the required amount of meat.

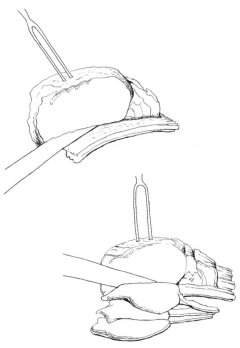

HUNTER'S SPICED BEEF

✳ Serves 8 ✳ Preparation time 30 minutes plus 5 days marinating and 2–3 days resting
✳ Cooking time 1 hour

This unusual recipe for a salted and spiced beef is truly excellent, but you do have to start it up to 10 days ahead of serving. Mrs Beeton used a round of beef, which is a huge cut, but this recipe uses a smaller joint known as the salmon cut of silverside. It is a very lean joint, containing hardly any fat, so it must only be cooked to medium to remain moist. To get nearer to the old-fashioned taste of beef, try to source an old-fashioned breed such as a Dexter, suppliers of which can be found at the back of the book.

50g soft brown sugar

20g Maldon sea salt
or other flaky sea salt

4 bay leaves

1 tsp allspice berries

1 tsp black peppercorns

1 tsp juniper berries

4 whole cloves

1kg piece salmon cut of silverside, ideally from a Dexter animal (a small silverside from a Dexter animal will be roughly 8cm in diameter. If it is from a conventional animal it will be much thicker, and will need cutting into 2 even, thinner pieces)

1 tbsp sunflower oil

special equipment

a ceramic baking dish or stainless steel bowl, a roasting tin and a temperature probe

Mix the sugar, salt, bay leaves and all the spices together in a ceramic baking dish or stainless steel bowl. Add the beef and turn it in the spices to ensure it is evenly coated, rubbing the seasoning in well. Cover with cling film and refrigerate for 5 days, turning the meat over once a day. By the end of this time the beef will be firm and cured.

Remove the beef from the fridge and leave it to sit for 1–2 hours to come up to room temperature. Rinse off the spices under cold water and dry with a piece of kitchen paper.

Preheat the oven to 160°C/gas mark 3.

Place a large frying pan over a medium to high heat. Add the oil and brown the beef all over until it is uniformly dark and richly coloured. If you have 2 pieces of beef, fry them one at a time.

Place the beef in the roasting tin and roast for 15 minutes per 500g. When a temperature probe inserted into the centre reads 55°C the meat is done. Remove the beef from the roasting tin, set it on a plate and leave it to cool.

Once the beef is cold wrap it very tightly with cling film, winding it around snugly to compress the meat. This will make it easier to slice.

Leave the beef to chill for 2–3 days. To serve, slice it as thinly as you can and enjoy it with a watercress salad (see page 175).

BRAISED SHORTRIBS OF BEEF

✳ Serves 4 ✳ Preparation time 45 minutes
✳ Cooking time 9–10 hours in a slow cooker or 5–6 hours in the oven

Shortribs, sometimes also called boiling beef ribs or rising rib, are a very inexpensive cut of meat. They are popular in Scotland, but often overlooked elsewhere – which is a shame as they have a delicious flavour and texture. Mrs Beeton cooked shortribs plainly with water, which makes for a good, gelatinous stew, but the addition of vegetables, herbs and ale gives a richer, more generous one-pot meal that is perfect for a winter weekend supper.

1.7kg shortribs, cut into 8 x 10cm pieces

2 onions, peeled and thickly sliced

2 carrots, peeled and cut into 2.5cm chunks

2 sticks celery, trimmed and cut into 2.5cm chunks

500ml medium-strength dark ale

250ml jellied beef stock (see page 19)

1 garlic clove, peeled and left whole

1 large thyme sprig

1 bay leaf

4 carrots, peeled and cut into 8cm lengths

special equipment

a large roasting tin and a flameproof casserole dish or 3-litre slow cooker

Preheat the oven to 220°C/gas mark 7. Arrange the shortribs in a large roasting tin, leaving plenty of space between them. Roast for 30 minutes, or until well browned.

Remove to the casserole dish or slow cooker. Add the onion, carrot chunks and celery to the roasting tin and toss them in the dripping that has come from the ribs. Roast for 10–15 minutes, or until browned. Pour off the excess fat and reserve it for another dish.

Add the cooked vegetables to the ribs along with the ale, stock, garlic, thyme and bay leaf. Either slow cook for 9–10 hours on a low heat or put in the oven at 140°C/gas mark 1 for 5–6 hours. An hour before serving, add the second quantity of carrots and cook until both they and the meat are tender.

POT-ROAST TOP RUMP

✳ Serves 6 ✳ Preparation time 20 minutes ✳ Cooking time 1 hour 30 minutes

This is a super way of maximising the flavour of a piece of beef. Ask your butcher to cut you a piece of top rump or the corner end of the silverside and tie it to keep its shape during cooking. Mrs Beeton tended to cook her stewed or braised beef for many hours, but a top rump can be pot roasted and eaten medium and it will be delicious.

1.5kg top rump, tied

5g Maldon or other flaky sea salt

1 stick celery, trimmed and cut into 3cm chunks

2 carrots, peeled and cut into 3cm chunks

2 onions, peeled and cut into large chunks

3 bay leaves

bunch fresh thyme

¼ tsp freshly ground black pepper

150ml jellied beef stock (see page 19)

300ml white wine

special equipment

a large flameproof casserole with a lid and a temperature probe

Preheat the oven to 160°C/gas mark 3.

Place a large frying pan over a low–medium heat. Put the rump fat-side down in the pan and allow the fat to render for 10 minutes, or until the meat is golden brown. Then turn the heat up high and brown the meat well on all sides, adding a little of the salt and turning frequently until it is a rich, dark brown all over. Remove from the pan and set aside to rest.

Place the vegetables and all the remaining ingredients into the large casserole and place over a medium to high heat. When the mixture is boiling, set the meat on top of the vegetables and cover with a lid. For medium-rare, cook the meat in the oven for 30 minutes or until a temperature probe inserted into the centre reads 50°C, then remove from the oven and set aside to rest with the lid slightly open. If you prefer your meat medium to well done, increase the cooking time to 45 minutes or until the temperature reads 60°C before resting as above.

After 20–30 minutes' resting time, carve the meat and arrange it on a large, warmed serving dish with the vegetables. Pour the pan juices into a serving jug and offer alongside the meat. Serve with a potato & cream gratin (see page 181) and a green salad.

Note: If you have any leftover beef, serve cold slices for lunch or in sandwiches, or use it to make potted beef (see page 134).

ROAST FORE RIB OF BEEF

* Serves 6–8 * Preparation time 5 minutes
* Cooking time 1 hour 30 minutes plus 30 minutes resting time

Mrs Beeton notes that 'the fore-rib is considered the primest roasting piece' and that 'a Yorkshire pudding … will be considered an agreeable addition'. As always with roast beef, she also recommends a garnish of horseradish. This joint is perfect for roasting as the fat from the rib bastes the meat as it cooks. Ask your butcher to cut through the base of the ribs to make the joint easier to carve once it has been cooked.

3.5kg joint beef fore
rib on the bone

2 onions, peeled and chopped

1 carrot, peeled and chopped

1 stick celery, trimmed
and chopped

200ml light red wine

1 large thyme sprig

500ml jellied beef stock
(see page 19)

10g unsalted butter

10g flour (optional)

salt and freshly ground
black pepper

special equipment

a roasting tin and a
temperature probe

Preheat the oven to 230°C/gas mark 8. Sprinkle the meat with 1 tsp salt and some freshly ground black pepper, rubbing it into the cut sides of the meat and the fat. Put the vegetables in a roasting tin, set the beef on top and place the tin in the hot oven. After 30 minutes turn the heat down to 140°C/gas mark 1.

For a rare joint, cook for a further 45 minutes to 1 hour at the lower temperature – it is ready when the internal temperature reaches 45°C. Remove the joint from the oven, wrap it well in foil and leave it in a warm place to rest for 30 minutes. The internal temperature should rise another 10°C during the resting time. For a medium joint, cook at the lower temperature for 1½ hours or until a temperature probe inserted into the meat reads 50–55°C, then remove from the oven and rest as above.

While the meat rests, make the gravy. Remove and discard the vegetables from the roasting tin and pour away the fat. Add the red wine and place the tin over a medium heat to reduce, stirring to scrape up any sediment from the bottom of the tin. Once the wine is reduced, add the thyme and stock, bring to a simmer and whisk in the butter. The jellied stock gives a light, syrupy gravy. If you prefer it thicker, mash 10g flour with the butter before adding it to the pan. Simmer for 3 minutes and then strain the gravy into a warmed sauceboat.

Serve thin slices of the meat with roast potatoes, steamed cabbage and Yorkshire puddings (see pages 179 and 190).

BRAISED OX CHEEKS

✳ Serves 4 ✳ Preparation time 30minutes ✳ Cooking time 3–4 hours

It is typical of Mrs Beeton to include a recipe for an extremely economical cut of beef and yet make something of it fit to grace any table. The ingredients have been adjusted here to substitute easily available ingredients as well as to refine the flavours for the modern palate, but the net result is true to the original. Try these beef cheeks for a family dinner. They have a distinctive, rich taste and offer great value for money. Ask your butcher to trim them for you to remove any sinew and fat.

2 tbsp light olive oil

2 boned beef cheeks, trimmed

1 onion, peeled and cut into large chunks

1 carrot, peeled and cut into large chunks

1 stick celery, trimmed and cut into large chunks

1 small leek, cut in half lengthways and then into chunks

6 cherry tomatoes or 1 tbsp tomato purée

500ml red wine

350ml jellied beef stock (see page 19)

2 bay leaves

few thyme sprigs

2 garlic cloves, peeled

8 allspice berries

2 cloves

salt and freshly ground black pepper

special equipment

a flameproof casserole dish with a lid

Preheat the oven to 140°C/gas mark 1.

Heat a large frying pan over a high heat and add half the olive oil. Season the cheeks with ½ tsp salt and add them to the pan. Brown the cheeks well on all sides then remove them to a plate. Lower the heat under the pan to medium, add the other half of the oil and fry the onion, carrot, celery and leek until well coloured, then add the tomatoes or tomato purée and cook until the mixture is thick and starting to catch.

Transfer the vegetables to the plate with the beef. Remove the pan from the heat and add the wine, stirring to dissolve all of the sediment. Then arrange the beef and vegetables snugly in the casserole, pour the wine over the top and then add the stock, bay leaves, thyme, garlic and spices. Place the lid on the casserole and bake in the oven for 3–4 hours, until the meat is very tender.

Pour the liquid from the casserole through a fine sieve into a pan over a medium heat. The meat and vegetables should be left in the casserole, and kept warm. Skim any fat from the surface of the liquid with a large spoon and then simmer the mixture to reduce until you have a lovely rich sauce. Season with salt and black pepper. Carve the cheeks into thick slices and serve with the vegetables alongside, pouring the sauce back over the top.

BRAISED OXTAIL

✳ Serves 4 ✳ Preparation time 30 minutes ✳ Cooking time 4 hours–4 hours 30 minutes

This recipe tastes even better if you cook it a day ahead – which makes it ideal for serving to guests because all the work is done the day before, leaving you free to entertain. Mrs Beeton uses very traditional English seasonings in this dish, including mace, mushroom ketchup and cloves, to which I have added ale for a really meaty, savoury dish.

1 oxtail, weighing around 1.5kg, cut in slices

150g cured streaky bacon, diced

2 onions, peeled and chopped into chunks

500ml light beer

8 allspice berries

1 pinch ground mace

juice and zest of ½ lemon, plus extra juice to taste

30ml mushroom ketchup

2 cloves

350ml jellied beef or dark chicken stock (see page 19 or 22)

2 bay leaves

2 tbsp finely chopped parsley

salt and freshly ground black pepper

special equipment

a large roasting tin and a flameproof casserole with a lid

Ask your butcher to slice the oxtail for you if you are unsure about doing it yourself. Preheat the oven to 220°C/gas mark 7. Place the oxtail pieces in a large roasting tin, season with a pinch of salt and pepper, and scatter over the bacon. Roast for 30 minutes, until the meat is golden brown all over.

Pour off and discard most of the fat, then add the onions and return the tin to the oven. Cook, stirring occasionally, for 10–15 minutes, or until the onion begins to colour. Remove from the oven and reduce the heat to 160°C/gas mark 3.

Scrape the oxtail and onions from the roasting tin into the casserole. Pour half of the beer into the roasting tin and stir to dissolve any caramelised bits sticking to the bottom. Then pour this, along with all of the rest of the ingredients except the chopped parsley, into the casserole. Stir well, cover tightly with a lid or foil and place in the oven.

After 1 hour turn the meat to ensure it cooks evenly in the liquid. After 4 hours the meat should be very tender and sticky. If not, leave it in the oven for another 15–30 minutes.

Remove from the oven and pour the liquid into a large measuring jug, discarding the bay leaves and leaving everything else behind in the casserole dish. Let the liquid settle in the jug and then use a ladle or large spoon to skim off and discard any fat that rises to the top. Taste the liquid and add a little salt, pepper and lemon juice if needed, then pour the sauce back over the meat and turn the pieces in it to moisten them. Stir through the chopped parsley then serve with confit of parsnips (see page 169) and freshly boiled sweetheart or Savoy cabbage.

RUMP STEAK

✳ Serves 4 ✳ Preparation time 5 minutes ✳ Cooking time 20–25 minutes

Bringing a large steak to the table for everyone to share always offers an element of drama. Rump steak is made up from several different muscles, each with a different texture – and the flavour is superb. Mrs Beeton comments that rump can be less tender than fillet or sirloin, but by cooking the steak in a large piece and resting it, you maximise the tenderness and get all of the super flavour that rump has to offer.

2 tbsp light olive oil

1kg rump steak, no more than 4cm thick, tied in one large piece

10g unsalted butter

1 large shallot, finely chopped

1 tsp fresh thyme leaves

50ml light red wine

100ml jellied beef or dark chicken stock (see page 19 or 22)

salt and freshly ground black pepper

special equipment

a roasting tin and a temperature probe

Preheat the oven to 200°C/gas mark 6.

Place a large frying pan over a medium to high heat. Add the oil, then the steak. Fry for 3 minutes then turn and fry the other side for a further 3 minutes, seasoning with a little salt and black pepper as it cooks. If the steak begins to lift up from the pan, press it down with a fish slice to ensure that it colours evenly. When it is done transfer the steak to the roasting tin. Pour off any excess fat from the pan and set it to one side for finishing the sauce later.

Place the roasting tin in the oven. For a rare steak, roast for 10–12 minutes, or until a temperature probe inserted in the meat reads 45–50°C. For a medium steak, roast for 15–18 minutes, or until a temperature probe inserted in the meat reads 50–55°C. Remove from the oven, wrap the steak in foil and leave to rest in a warm place for 10 minutes.

Meanwhile, melt the butter in the frying pan over a medium heat and add the shallot. Cook, stirring, for 2 minutes, or until the shallot is softening and beginning to brown at the edges. Add the thyme leaves and stir in the red wine. Simmer until the wine has reduced and then add the stock. Simmer and reduce again until the sauce has a syrupy consistency. Unwrap the steak and pour any juices left behind in the foil back into the pan with the sauce and stir them in. Pour the sauce into a jug or sauceboat. Place the steak on a large, warmed serving dish and take it to the table. Carve it on the bias, placing slices onto diners' plates and passing round the sauce. Serve it with potatoes à la maître d'hôtel (see page 178) and grilled mushroom flaps (see page 175).

POTTED BEEF

✳ Serves 4–6 as a starter ✳ Preparation time 30 minutes ✳ Cooking time 10 minutes

This smooth, buttery paste is flavoured with mace and cayenne pepper to give a bit of bite. Mrs Beeton recommends using the trimmed outer slices of roast beef for this recipe, which she then stores for some time. Today, we tend to make potted meats to eat within a few days, so I have added some shallot and ginger to lighten the mixture somewhat. If you intend to keep the meat for more than a week, it is best stored in the freezer. This recipe works equally well with the same quantity of venison or pork.

100g unsalted butter

500g cooked beef

½–1 tsp ground mace

½ tsp cayenne pepper

4 shallots, peeled and chopped

50g root ginger,
peeled and sliced

50g clarified butter
(see glossary)

salt and freshly ground
black pepper

special equipment

4–6 ramekins, one per diner

Trim the cooked meat, removing any sinews or blood vessels. Place the butter in a saucepan over a very low heat, add the vegetables and spices and let them stew for 10 minutes, or until soft and coloured but not browned.

Place the meat in a food processor and pour in the butter from the pan, keeping back all but 1 tbsp of the shallots. Blend the mixture thoroughly, season assertively with salt and black pepper, then press into ramekins. Seal the pots with clarified butter, cover with cling film and refrigerate.

Potted meat should be used within one week. It can be served as a starter with a sharp fruit jelly such as apple (see page 367) or redcurrant, and crusty bread.

STEAK & KIDNEY PUDDING

✳ Serves 4 ✳ Preparation time 45 minutes ✳ Cooking time 4 hours

The use of kidney in this steak pudding supplanted the traditional use of oysters as a filler in beef dishes. A 'Sussex lady' contributed the recipe to the *English Woman's Domestic Magazine*, which Mrs Beeton edited.

1 quantity (approx 600g) suet pastry (see page 217)

2 tbsp dripping or sunflower oil, plus extra for greasing

130g beef kidney, diced

600g chuck steak, cut into 2cm dice

1 onion, peeled and finely sliced

½ tbsp plain flour

1 heaped tsp thyme leaves

1 large bay leaf

2 tbsp Worcestershire sauce

2 tbsp mushroom ketchup

130ml stout

130ml jellied beef stock (see page 19)

salt and freshly ground black pepper

special equipment

a 1-litre pudding basin, a pastry cutter or muffin ring and a 4-litre saucepan

Make the pastry and leave it to rest for 10 minutes. Roll out two-thirds for lining the pudding basin, and the remainder to make the lid. Set these on a plate, cover with cling film and chill until needed. Grease the pudding basin and set aside.

Heat half the fat in a frying pan over a high heat and add the kidney. Brown it all over, then remove it from the pan and set aside. Add the remaining fat to the pan, then the steak and 1 tsp salt. Brown well, then add the onion, reduce the heat and cook for 10 minutes, or until the onion is soft. Sprinkle over the flour and add the thyme, bay leaf, Worcestershire sauce, mushroom ketchup and ½ tsp black pepper. Cook, stirring, for 5 minutes, ensuring the flour is well blended in. Return the kidney to the pan and add the stout and stock, then check the seasoning and remove from the heat.

Once the filling is cold, line the pudding basin with the suet pastry and pour the filling into the lined basin. If the filling is warm at this point it will melt the pastry and cause it to be tough. Dampen the edge of the pastry with a little water and place the pastry lid on top, crimping the edges well.

Pleat a large piece of greaseproof paper down the centre to allow room for expansion during steaming. Cover the top of the pudding with the pleated paper, then a pleated layer of foil, and secure with kitchen string around the edge of the basin, leaving some extra string to make a handle for lifting.

Set a pastry cutter or muffin ring in the base of a 4-litre saucepan and place the pudding basin on top. Pour boiling water around the pudding basin to a depth of 15cm. Cover with a lid and bring the water to a simmer, then reduce the heat and simmer for 4 hours, topping up with boiling water as necessary. Once cooked, invert the pudding onto a warmed seving dish and serve with steamed vegetables.

ROAST LEG OF MUTTON

❋ Serves 6–8 ❋ Preparation time 5 minutes
❋ Cooking time 1 hour 30 minutes plus 45 minutes resting time

The ingredients for this recipe haven't changed in 150 years – all that is really needed is a leg of mutton and a little salt to enhance the flavour of the meat. Mrs Beeton roasted the meat in front of the fire, basting it continually, but today it's a far less labour-intensive process. Use a leg of Herdwick or Manx Loaghtan mutton if you can, for its rich and nutty flavour. Two of the best producers in the UK are listed at the back of the book.

2.7kg leg of mutton, H-bone removed

salt and freshly ground black pepper

special equipment

a roasting tin and a temperature probe

If you are unsure about doing it yourself, ask your butcher to remove the H-bone to make carving easier. Preheat the oven to 220°C/gas mark 7.

Season the leg all over with 1 tsp salt and a few grindings of black pepper and place it in a roasting tin. Roast for 30 minutes then turn the heat down to 140°C/gas mark 1. For medium to medium-rare meat, cook for a further 45 minutes, or until a temperature probe inserted to the thickest part of the leg reads 50°C, before removing. If you prefer your meat medium to well done, cook for an additional 25 minutes, or until a temperature probe inserted to the thickest part of the leg reads 60°C.

Remove the meat from the oven, cover with foil and put in a warm place to rest for up to 45 minutes before slicing. Serve this dish with haricot beans (see page 165) and some spinach cooked with a little butter, garlic and nutmeg.

BRAISED MUTTON WITH BARLEY & MINT

✳ Serves 4　✳ Preparation time 10 minutes　✳ Cooking time 3–4 hours

In this recipe, pearl barley has been used in place of the haricot beans Mrs Beeton specified, but if you prefer the original combination, use the haricot beans recipe on page 165 and simply add the cooked beans to the roasting tin in place of the cooked barley, finishing the recipe in the same way. Save any leftovers for the leftover mutton broth on page 38.

2.7kg shoulder of mutton

2 onions, peeled and cut into large chunks

1 large carrot, peeled and cut into large chunks

2 sticks celery, trimmed and cut into large chunks

small bunch thyme

4 bay leaves

500ml dark chicken stock (see page 22)

200ml water

80g pearl barley

few mint sprigs, stems discarded and leaves chopped

salt and freshly ground black pepper

special equipment

a roasting tin

Preheat the oven to 220°C/gas mark 7.

Trim off and discard any excess fat from the shoulder, then place in a roasting tin and season with 1 teaspoon salt and a few grindings of black pepper.

Roast for 30 minutes, or until dark golden brown, then, remove from the oven and pour off any fat. Place the vegetables, thyme, 3 bay leaves, stock and water into the tin with the meat, cover tightly with greaseproof paper and foil and return to the oven at 140°C/gas mark 1 for 3½ hours, until the meat is very tender and falling off the bone.

When the mutton has gone back into the oven, cover the barley with water and leave it to soak. About 1 hour before the meat is ready, simmer the barley with the remaining bay leaf for about 30–40 minutes, or until cooked and tender. Strain it through a sieve, fish out and discard the bay leaf and set the barley aside until needed.

When the shoulder is ready, lift it out of the tin and place it on a warmed serving dish, cover loosely with foil and leave to rest. Meanwhile, pour the cooking liquid from the tin through a sieve into a large measuring jug. Skim and discard any fat that floats to the surface. Then return the liquid to the roasting tin with the vegetables. Add the strained barley and place over a medium heat. Warm through and check the seasoning. Fish out and discard the bay leaves then stir through the chopped mint and serve with steamed green vegetables.

BREAST OF LAMB EPIGRAMMES

✳ Serves 4 ✳ Preparation time 20 minutes ✳ Cooking time 3 hours

Mrs Beeton originally intended this recipe for oxtail but in the intervening years the technique has come to be used more commonly with lamb. Belly of lamb, like oxtail, needs long, slow cooking to make the best of its tasty, soft meat, and is usually served as a braise. The second cooking in breadcrumbs adds a pleasing crunch to the final dish and shows that this usually fatty cut is capable of surprising delicacy.

700g belly of lamb, including bones

1 small carrot, peeled and cut into chunks

1 small onion, peeled and cut into chunks

1 stick celery, trimmed and cut into chunks

small bunch thyme

1 bay leaf

500ml light chicken or lamb stock (see page 23)

plain flour, for dusting

1 medium egg

3 tsp Dijon mustard

80g breadcrumbs

50g clarified butter (see glossary)

salt and freshly ground black pepper

special equipment

an ovenproof dish, a 20 x 10cm baking tray and a weight

Preheat the oven to 140°C/gas mark 1. Season the lamb with salt and pepper and place it into the ovenproof dish with the vegetables, thyme and bay leaf. Heat the stock in a small saucepan over a medium heat and pour it over the lamb. Cover tightly with greaseproof paper and foil and braise in the oven for 3 hours, or until the meat is falling off the bones. Remove the lamb from the liquid using a slotted spoon or tongs and place it in a large bowl.

When it has cooled a little, strip the meat away from the bones and set it on a plate. You should have around 300g of meat. Discard the bones, skin and sinew, and season the meat with a large pinch of salt and a few grindings of black pepper. Drizzle over 2 tbsp of the cooking liquor.

Line the baking tray with cling film, leaving a long overhang on 2 sides, and press the meat into it to form a layer 1–1.5cm deep. Pull the cling film up and over the meat to make a tight parcel, press with a weight and chill until cold. The gelatine in the meat will cause it to set.

Meanwhile, preheat the oven to 200°C/gas mark 6. Put some flour on a plate and sprinkle over ½ tsp salt. Beat together the egg and mustard in a bowl and spread the breadcrumbs on another plate. When the meat is cold, cut it into 8 equal pieces. Dip each piece first into the seasoned flour, then into the egg mixture and finally into the breadcrumbs to coat.

Melt the butter in a frying pan over a high heat and fry the epigrammes on both sides until golden brown. Transfer onto a baking sheet and into the oven for 10 minutes. Serve with Dijon mustard and a watercress salad (see page 175).

LAMB CHOPS BRAISED WITH SPRING VEGETABLES

✳ Serves 4 ✳ Preparation time 15 minutes ✳ Cooking time 25 minutes

Mrs Beeton recommends peas and asparagus as the 'favourite accompaniments of lamb chops', and this recipe provides a method for combining the three elements together in a simple one-pot dish. The lamb cooks quickly so it's best to cook the fat first to add flavour, before seasoning and browning the meat itself. This simple springtime dish makes a quick and delicious midweek dinner.

8 lamb chops

150g podded baby broad beans

25g unsalted butter

4 spring onions, trimmed and cut into 10cm pieces

150g young peas,

20 asparagus tips, cut in half

200ml dark chicken stock (see page 22)

small bunch parsley, large stalks removed, leaves finely chopped

zest of ½ lemon, finely grated

salt and freshly ground black pepper

Heat a frying pan large enough to take all the chops in a single layer over a low to medium heat.

Stand the chops up on their skin edges, side by side, and cook to render and brown the fat for 15 minutes, or until the fat is a deep golden brown. Alternatively, place the chops skin-side up in a roasting tin under a low to medium grill so that the fat browns and renders without shrinking. Whichever way you decide to do this, keep an eye on the chops to ensure that they do not burn.

While the fat renders, bring a small pan of water to a boil over a high heat and add a large pinch of salt. Add the broad beans and bring the water back to boiling. Let them cook for 1 minute and then drain and plunge them into a bowl of iced water. Peel off the skins and save the tiny green beans.

When the fat has rendered and you are ready to cook the lamb, season the chops on both sides with a pinch of salt and pepper and turn the heat under the frying pan to high. Brown the chops well on both sides and then set aside on a plate and cover loosely with foil.

Discard any fat from the pan, reduce the heat to medium and add the unsalted butter and the spring onions. Cook for one minute, stirring, and then add all of the vegetables and the stock. Turn the heat to high and simmer for one minute. Return the chops to the pan to heat through for 5 minutes. Turn them occasionally and allow the sauce to reduce a little. Just before serving sprinkle over the chopped parsley and the lemon zest.

DEVILLED KIDNEYS

✳ Serves 4 ✳ Preparation time 15 minutes ✳ Cooking time 10 minutes

Mrs Beeton usually fried kidneys and served them simply on toast with lemon juice or gravy poured over. We still serve kidneys on toast today, but the accompanying sauce has been refined to a sharp, spicy mixture that provides an excellent foil to the richness of the kidneys. This devilled kidneys recipe is a modern classic. Ask your butcher to save you some fresh British lambs' kidneys. Avoid the vacuum-packed ones brought in from abroad as they are inferior.

1 tbsp sherry vinegar

1 tsp Worcestershire sauce

dash Tabasco sauce, to taste

2 tsp English mustard powder

8 lambs' kidneys

20g unsalted butter

60ml white wine

2 tbsp single cream

squeeze of lemon juice (optional)

small bunch parsley, stems discarded, leaves chopped

4 slices good bread, toasted and buttered, to serve

salt and freshly ground black pepper

In a bowl whisk together the vinegar, Worcestershire sauce, Tabasco and mustard powder (this is the devilling mixture) and set aside until needed. Now place the kidneys on their sides on a chopping board. Cut them in half horizontally and open them up to reveal a white core. Use a small knife to remove all of it, then cut each half kidney in half across to give 2 equal segments.

Place a frying pan over a high heat. When hot, add the butter, and then the kidneys. Fry for 4–5 minutes, or until they are browned on all sides. Remove the kidneys from the pan and set them aside. Reduce the heat to medium and stir the wine into the pan, scraping up the sediment to dissolve it.

When the wine has reduced by half, stir in the devilling mixture and cook for 1 minute, then add the cream and let it cook for another minute.

Remove from the heat, season with a good pinch of salt and a few grindings of black pepper. If you like, you can adjust the sharpness with a squeeze of fresh lemon juice. Sprinkle with chopped parsley and serve on hot buttered toast.

PIG CHEEK JELLY

✳ Serves 8 ✳ Preparation time 10 minutes ✳ Curing time 4 days ✳ Rinsing time 1 day
✳ Cooking time 4 hours plus chilling overnight

Pig cheeks have a delicious, strong, meaty flavour. They are easily obtained and much easier to handle at home than a whole head, which is what Mrs Beeton would have used. The cheeks are brined, cooked and shredded with aromatics to form a jellied meat.

2 litres cider or water

200g sea salt

50g brown sugar

4 blades mace

10 black peppercorns

4–5 pigs' cheeks, boned, skin on

1 stick celery, trimmed and cut into chunks

1 large onion, peeled and cut into chunks

1 medium carrot, peeled and cut into chunks

2 bay leaves

4 allspice berries

1 clove

2 sheets gelatine

small bunch parsley, chopped

1 garlic clove, crushed

1 tsp red wine vinegar

salt and freshly ground black pepper

To make the brine set a large pan over a high heat and add the cider or water, salt, brown sugar, mace and peppercorns. Bring to a boil then remove from the heat. Once cool, pour the brine into a large bowl and add the pigs' cheeks. Cover and chill. After 4 days, lift out the cheeks and discard the brine. Place the cheeks into a large bowl of water, cover and chill overnight.

The next day, remove the cheeks from the water and place in a large saucepan. Cover with fresh cold water and set over a high heat. Bring the pan to a simmer and taste the water. If it is very salty, discard it and boil the cheeks again with fresh water. When the water is boiling, add the celery, onion, carrot, bay leaves, allspice berries and the clove. Simmer over a very low heat for 1½ hours, or until the cheeks are tender and beginning to fall apart.

Remove from the heat and leave the cheeks in the liquid. When they are cool enough to handle, shred the meat into a serving bowl, discarding the fat and skin. You should end up with approximately 370–400g meat.

Pour just over 500ml of the cooking liquid into a large measuring jug and skim off and discard any fat that floats to the surface with a large spoon. Then pour the cooking liquid into a saucepan and place it over a low heat.

Soak the gelatine sheets in cold water for 10 minutes, or until soft. Squeeze them to get rid of any excess water and then add them to the warm cooking liquid, stirring to dissolve. Stir in the parsley, garlic and red wine vinegar. Season the liquid to taste, and then stir it thoroughly into the meat. Cover with cling film and chill. Once the jelly has set, serve it with good bread and piccalilli.

CHESTNUT FORCEMEAT

✳ Serves 8 ✳ Preparation time 15 minutes ✳ Cooking time 1 hour 15 minutes

Forcemeat is often a combination of cooked and raw meat, flavoured with herbs or lemon, and traditionally baked and used as a stuffing. It was very popular at the time Mrs Beeton was writing, and she included several recipes for it in her book. The addition of chestnuts and apples here gives the forcemeat both texture and a light acidity. Make it to accompany your roast goose or turkey.

500g fresh white breadcrumbs

500g chestnuts, boiled, skinned and roughly chopped

500g sausage meat or skinned sausages

2 large onions, peeled and roughly chopped

200g chopped ready-to-eat prunes

large bunch thyme, leaves only, stems discarded

6 sage leaves, finely chopped

100g suet, grated

½ tsp freshly ground black pepper

75ml white wine

75ml dark chicken stock (see page 22)

1 tsp salt

500g cooking apples, peeled, cored and chopped

50g softened butter

special equipment

a ceramic or metal roasting tin or a pie dish

Combine all the ingredients in a large bowl and squeeze them together with your hands to amalgamate. Now proceed one of two ways.

The first option is to preheat the oven to 180°C/gas mark 5, press everything into a ceramic or metal roasting tin and smooth the surface. Bake for 45 minutes, until lightly browned, then stir up the mixture to break it up, and press down again. Bake for another 30 minutes, or until browned well and crisp on top.

The second method is to preheat the oven to 200°C/gas mark 6. Form the forcemeat into golf ball-sized balls and place them snugly into a pie dish. Bake for 20 minutes.

Serve with roast goose or turkey.

LIVER & BACON

✳ Serves 4 ✳ Preparation time 10 minutes ✳ Cooking time 25 minutes

Recommended by Mrs Beeton for its flavour and economy, liver has fallen out of favour in recent years. If you haven't cooked it before, this is one of the best ways to enjoy it. Liver is often sliced and fried as Mrs Beeton recommends, but this can leave it dry. Here it is roasted as a complete lobe or chunk, and then sliced to pink perfection. Free-range or rare-breed liver is the best, if you can find it.

8 rashers back or streaky bacon

600g thick lobe of free-range pig's liver, trimmed of any large tubes

2–3 tbsp sunflower oil or dripping

2 large or 3 medium onions, peeled and cut into 3mm slices

100ml dark chicken or jellied beef stock (see page 22 or 19)

6 sage leaves, sliced finely

salt and freshly ground black pepper

special equipment

a roasting tin and a temperature probe

Preheat the oven to 200°C/gas mark 6. Lay the rashers of bacon in a roasting tin, ensuring they do not overlap, and set aside until needed.

Rub the liver with 1 tbsp of the fat and season with salt and black pepper. Place a large frying pan over a medium to high heat and, when the pan is hot, add the liver. Cook, turning occasionally, until the liver is firm and evenly browned. Turn the heat off but keep the pan for cooking the onions. Place the liver in the roasting tin with the bacon and transfer to the oven. Remove the bacon after 12–15 minutes, drain any excess fat and keep warm on a plate. Then pierce the thickest part of the liver with a temperature probe. When it reads 50–55°C, or when the liver begins to be resistant to the tip of your finger, remove it from the oven and wrap closely with foil. Cover with a tea towel and set it aside to rest, keeping the probe in place to check that the temperature has risen to 60-65°C before serving. The liver will be evenly pink and medium. If you like well-done liver, cook it initially until it reaches 65°C, then leave it to rest.

Heat the remaining fat in the frying pan over a medium heat and add a pinch of salt. Add the onions and cook, stirring occasionally, for about 10 minutes, or until they soften and begin to brown. Add the stock and the sage, turn the heat down and simmer until the liquid has reduced to a sticky glaze.

Slice the liver into large, thin pieces. Serve with the bacon and onions on the side and a salad of ripe, sliced tomatoes and finely chopped red onion.

ROAST LOIN OF PORK

✳ Serves 8 ✳ Preparation time 10 minutes
✳ Cooking time 1–2 hours plus 30 minutes resting time

A loin of pork is pure carnivore indulgence – moist and succulent inside and crispy outside. Ask your butcher to cut you a piece of loin on the bone, and then to cut through the backbone so that you can carve the loin into chops at home once it is cooked. Also ask to have the pork skin scored for crackling. When you get home, remove the pork from its wrapping and place, uncovered, on a tray in the fridge to allow the skin to dry well. This helps the crackling form.

2.5kg loin of free-range pork with 8 ribs

1 tbsp sunflower oil

fine salt and freshly ground black pepper

special equipment

a large roasting tin and a temperature probe

Preheat the oven to 220°C/gas mark 7.

Place the pork, skin-side up, in a large roasting tin. Ensure that the skin is completely dry, then brush with the oil and sprinkle all over with salt. Roast for 40 minutes to crackle the skin then reduce the heat to 140°C/gas mark 1 for a further hour. At this point a temperature probe inserted into the middle of the pork should read at least 60°C. If it does not, leave the meat in the oven for a further 20 minutes, then retest.

When it has cooked, remove the pork from the oven. Cover with foil and leave to rest in a warm place for at least 40 minutes. If the skin is not crackly all over, place it under a medium to hot grill until it crisps up, but be careful not to let it burn.

When you are ready to serve, transfer the pork to a chopping board and carve into thick slices, down through the line of the chops, giving a chop to each person. This is delicious served with apple sauce (see page 331) and potato & cream gratin (see page 181).

ROAST SHOULDER OF PORK

✳ Serves 6–8 ✳ Preparation time 15 minutes ✳ Cooking time 3 hours plus 30 minutes resting

Although Mrs Beeton featured several pork roasts, shoulder wasn't one of them. However, this is a good joint to try if you are new to the kitchen. It is very forgiving as it has a number of small muscles interwoven with a little fat, which helps keep it moist. It is also a very economical cut of meat. To keep the dish true to Mrs Beeton it is roasted with sage and served with a modern interpretation of her apple sauce: a cider gravy.

2.5kg rolled shoulder joint of free-range or rare-breed pork

2 sticks celery, trimmed and cut into chunks

2 onions, peeled and cut into chunks

1 carrot, peeled and cut into chunks

4 sage leaves

125ml medium dry cider

500ml light chicken or pork stock (see page 23)

10g unsalted butter (optional)

10g plain flour (optional)

salt and freshly ground black pepper

special equipment

a roasting tin

Preheat the oven to 220°C/gas mark 7.

Ensure that the pork skin is well dried so that it makes good crackling, then season lightly all over with salt and black pepper. Place the vegetables and sage into a roasting tin and set the pork on top. Roast for 30 minutes, or until the fat starts to render and the skin begins to crackle.

Reduce the heat to 140°C/gas mark 1 and cook for a further 2½ hours. After this time the pork will be fully cooked through. Remove the meat to a warmed serving dish, cover with foil and leave in a warm place for at least 30 minutes while you finish the sauce.

Pour any excess fat from the roasting tin (you can reserve this for another dish) and place the tin over a medium heat. Add the cider and, using a wooden spatula, scrape up any the caramelised bits, dissolving them in the liquid. Simmer until the cider has reduced by half. Add the stock and reduce a little more. Season the sauce to taste with a little salt and a grinding of black pepper.

If you like a thicker sauce, mash 10g unsalted butter with 10g plain flour and whisk it into the sauce until it dissolves then let it simmer for 3 minutes to thicken. Strain the sauce into a hot sauceboat.

If your pork skin has not crackled well, preheat the grill to high. Put the pork joint, skin-side up, under the grill until it is crisp and brown all over, turning it with a pair of tongs. Be careful not to burn the skin. Serve the pork sliced and accompanied by braised red cabbage (see page 161) and braised Puy lentils (see page 164).

VEGETABLES

THE VEGETABLE MARKET

The market gardens of inner London that Isabella Beeton knew have almost all disappeared. In fact, the move away from local producers was already underway by the time she published her book of household management in 1861. By the middle of the nineteenth century the railway network had already begun transporting garden produce at greater speed and from further away into London markets. While this brought increased choice, it also created more competition, causing the decline of the inner London market garden.

The majority of vegetables produced in Britain are now delivered directly to supermarket depots and into industrial food-processing units. However, many British cities are still ringed with farms that supply local wholesale vegetable markets on a daily basis. This ensures that the fresh produce found at local greengrocers in such cities is much more likely to be grown locally and brought in on a daily basis.

If you are looking for something unusual, small producers at farmers' markets are often the best source for specialist vegetables and salad crops. There are even some enterprising collectors of wild herbs and leaves, reviving the centuries-old practice of foraging, who will send goods to you by mail order.

YEAR-ROUND AVAILABILITY

The phrase 'permanent global summertime' has been recently coined to describe the more or less permanent availability of all types of fruit and vegetables in wealthier countries. Approximately 60 per cent of the fruits and vegetables on sale in Britain are imported, either by air or by sea, often from as far away as the southern hemisphere during their summer to see us through our winter. This raises many issues, but to bring it down to the most personal level, eating in season what is grown locally to you and days, rather than weeks, after it has been harvested makes most sense for your health and your pocket.

WHY FRESHNESS MATTERS

Maximum nutrient content

Vegetables are an excellent source of nutrients and dietary fibre, making them an essential component of a healthy diet. Eating a mixture of cooked and raw vegetables will ensure you receive a balanced intake of most vitamins and minerals. Once picked, however, the vitamin content of vegetables drops rapidly so, if possible, it is best only to buy what you will need for one or two days at a time.

Even though the nutritional value of vegetables has been understood for many centuries, vitamins were unheard of until the first half of the twentieth century. Cooking vegetables in order to retain their vitamin content was not a concept known to Mrs Beeton or her contemporaries. We now know that some methods of cooking are better than others for preserving the vitamins in vegetables. For example, green vegetables in particular contain water-soluble vitamins such as B and C, which can easily be lost through lengthy boiling. Therefore, some of the modernisation of the recipes in this book has revolved around preserving goodness that might have been lost using the method in the original recipes.

Superior flavour

When a vegetable is harvested it begins to either die or prepare itself for a period of inactive growth, and this alters the flavour. The fresher the vegetable the better the flavour is. In the case of vegetables where the edible part is a storage organ, such as potatoes and onions, the initial sweetness of the freshly picked vegetable immediately alters. Anyone who has ever harvested his or her own vegetables will have noticed how rapidly this change can occur. A freshly picked pea or asparagus spear will taste noticeably less sweet just hours after being picked. Once harvested from the parent plant, they begin to turn any sugars they contain to starch, which is the complex form of carbohydrate that most vegetables produce as they age. Starch can be split into smaller sugar molecules, as when vegetables are cooked at very high temperatures, causing them to brown and caramelise. Grill some asparagus over wood embers and you will experience this to delicious effect.

COOKING TECHNIQUES

When considering how to prepare a vegetable, the cook's first thought should be to maximise the flavour and retain the nutrient value.

Steaming: This is the best technique for cooking vegetables because none of the flavour and very few of the nutrients will be lost during the cooking process. During steaming, ensure that the water is boiling rapidly and turn the vegetables regularly to ensure they cook evenly. A little salt will ensure that green vegetables remain green and bright. Some varieties of potato are best steamed if they are to be mashed or roasted, as they break up less and are drier cooked this way.

Boiling: This technique is commonly used to cook vegetables, and is especially useful when cooking more than your steamer can hold. Salt added to vegetable cooking water will help to maintain the colour of green vegetables in particular. It is best only to boil vegetables briefly in order to retain the maximum flavour and nutrient content. If you are using a large quantity of green vegetables, cook them in small batches and cool them once cooked. Then, reheat in a little butter in a pan and stir over a medium heat to warm them through.

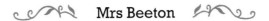
Frying: Frying vegetables in oil or butter is a very rapid way to cook them because the high heat used when frying makes the vegetables brown quickly and easily. Stir-frying in particular is good for retaining colour, flavour, texture and nutrient content.

Braising: This relatively slow method of cooking vegetables using moisture is excellent for roots such as carrots, and onions, red cabbage and dried beans. The flavour of the original vegetable softens and amalgamates more easily with that of the other ingredients, as in the recipe for braised red cabbage (see page 160).

Roasting: Most root and stem vegetables roast beautifully. In almost all cases, partly cooking the vegetables by boiling or steaming them first helps them roast evenly and prevents them going rubbery during the roasting process.

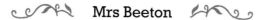

GLOBE ARTICHOKES

❋ **Serves 4** ❋ **Preparation time 15 minutes** ❋ **Cooking time approx 45 minutes**

This is an uncomplicated way of enjoying one of the most delicious vegetables it is possible to grow in our climate. Mrs Beeton recommended serving artichokes in several ways, but try this one first. Use mature artichokes, which are easy to find.

4 large globe artichokes

1 tbsp salt

1 lemon, sliced

50ml light olive oil

1 quantity hollandaise sauce (see page 338), to serve

special equipment

4 ramekins

Prepare the artichokes by trimming the stems just beneath the base of the globe. Using a pair of scissors, trim any spikes from the leaves. Wash well and check closely for dirt.

Choose a pan that will hold all of the artichokes at once. Fill it half full with water, add the salt, cover and bring to a boil over a high heat. When the water is boiling, add the lemon and olive oil and drop in the artichokes.

Cover the pan and bring to a simmer. Cook over a low heat for 35–45 minutes, depending on the size and age of the artichokes. Meanwhile, make the Hollandaise sauce and keep it warm in a bowl suspended over a pan of hot water until ready to use.

The artichokes are done when you can pierce the base easily with a thin knife and a lower leaf pulls off easily. Drain the artichokes upside down on a wire rack placed over a bowl for 10 minutes.

To serve, place each artichoke upright on a plate and provide each person with a ramekin of hollandaise sauce.

To eat, pull the leaves from the artichokes individually, dip each one into the sauce and then scrape the fleshy part of the leaf onto your tongue using your front teeth. Discard the leaf. Pull all of the leaves off in this way. When you get to the centre, discard the choke (the fibrous part) and eat the solid base of the artichoke.

JERUSALEM ARTICHOKES
WITH BACON & CREAM

* Serves 4 as a starter or 6 as a side dish * Preparation time 15 minutes
* Cooking time 25–30 minutes

Mrs Beeton serves this richly flavoured, sweet-tasting vegetable with a white sauce. The additional touch of bacon here marries perfectly with the sweet vegetables.

25g unsalted butter

150g dry cured bacon, cut into small strips

150g shallots, peeled and finely sliced

2 bay leaves

1 large sprig thyme, leaves only

700g peeled Jerusalem artichokes

250ml double cream

salt and freshly ground black pepper

Melt the butter in a saucepan over a medium heat, then add the bacon and fry gently until it renders its fat and begins to brown a little at the edges. Add the shallots, bay leaves and thyme and cook, stirring, for 3–4 minutes, until the vegetables begin to release their juices, then stir in the artichokes. Add 200ml water to the pan and bring to a simmer, then cover with a lid, turn the heat down low and cook for 10 minutes, stirring occasionally. Poke the artichokes with a skewer to test them for tenderness. When they are just beginning to soften, add the cream, turn the heat up and cook uncovered until the artichokes are soft and the cream is reduced to a coating sauce. Season with a little salt and black pepper and serve.

BOILED CORN ON THE COB

* Serves 4 * Preparation time 5 minutes * Cooking time 8 minutes

Mrs Beeton admired this vegetable, though she noted that it was rarely seen in Britain. How things change. Corn is now commonplace, and modern varieties exist that can ripen easily in our climate as well as taking much less time to cook.

4 fresh cobs of corn weighing 200g each

30g unsalted butter

salt and freshly ground black pepper

Bring a large pan containing about 3 litres of water to a rapid boil over a high heat. Add 2–3 tsp salt, then drop in the cobs and cover with a lid. When the pan returns to the boil, set the timer for 8 minutes, removing the lid if necessary. Once cooked, use long-handled tongs to lift the cobs out. Let the water drain off, then put each cob onto a warmed plate and serve with butter and salt and pepper.

BRAISED CELERY

✳ Serves 4 ✳ Preparation time 10 minutes ✳ Cooking time 1 hour

This makes a first-rate accompaniment for winter roast chicken or game. Mrs Beeton used traditional white celery and cooked it with milk or cream, but our modern green varieties have a stronger flavour, which calls for a more flavoursome cooking liquor.

6 sticks celery weighing approx 400g in total

350ml light chicken stock (see page 23)

1 bay leaf

¼ tsp salt

special equipment

a shallow ovenproof dish

Preheat the oven to 160°C/gas mark 3. Cut each celery stick into 3 even pieces and arrange them in a single layer in a shallow ovenproof dish. Bring the stock to a gentle simmer in a small saucepan over a medium heat. Add the bay leaf and salt, then pour the mixture over the celery. Cover the dish with greaseproof paper, then tightly wrap with foil and place in the oven for 1 hour. It is cooked when the celery can be easily pierced with the tip of a knife. Serve immediately.

BRAISED BEETROOT

✳ Serves 4 ✳ Preparation time 10 minutes ✳ Cooking time 1 hour 15 minutes

Deeply aromatic, braised beetroot accompanies pork, game or fish dishes superbly. Mrs Beeton suggested stewing some onions with the beetroot. If you like, add 100g peeled shallots or small onions to the pan with the beetroot in the second stage of their cooking.

500g young beetroot, topped and tailed

large pinch Maldon sea salt or other flaky salt

1 garlic clove, peeled and finely chopped

40g unsalted butter

100ml dark chicken stock (see page 22)

salt and freshly ground black pepper

Preheat the oven to 180°C/gas mark 4. Place the beetroot on a large sheet of foil and sprinkle over the salt and garlic. Shape the foil into a parcel around the ingredients and seal it well. Place on a baking tray and bake in the oven for 1 hour. Remove from the oven, open the parcel and allow the beetroot to cool. When they are cool enough to handle, peel and cut each one into 8 evenly sized pieces.

To finish the dish, melt the butter in a saucepan over a medium heat. Add the beetroot and stir to coat with the butter. Raise the heat and add the stock, simmering to reduce it to a syrupy glaze. Season with salt and black pepper and serve.

BRAISED RED CABBAGE

✳ **Serves 6–8** ✳ **Preparation time 30 minutes** ✳ **Cooking time 2 hours**

Mrs Beeton's recipe for red cabbage calls for a mixture of vinegar and sugar to give piquancy to this wonderful vegetable. I have added spice and a little fresh apple to lighten it. This can be used as a dish in its own right, served with good bread and butter, but it also makes a beautiful accompaniment to pork and poultry dishes.

25g salted butter

1 onion, peeled and finely chopped

250g peeled and cored cooking apples, diced small

1 x 500g red cabbage, quartered, cored and finely shredded

1 cinnamon stick

2 cloves

seeds from 4 cardamom pods

2 tsp English honey

1 tsp red wine vinegar

100ml red wine

salt and freshly ground black pepper

special equipment

an ovenproof dish

Preheat the oven to 160°C/gas mark 3.

Place the butter in a large pan over a low heat. Add the chopped onion together with a large pinch of salt and cook, stirring, for 5 minutes, until the onion is soft and beginning to colour a little at the edges. Turn the heat to medium, add all the remaining ingredients and combine well.

Place the mixture in an ovenproof dish and press down to an even thickness. Cover the dish with a sheet of greaseproof paper and then seal with a layer of foil. Transfer the dish to the oven and cook for about 2 hours, or until the cabbage is tender, stirring occasionally. Season to taste with salt and black pepper before serving.

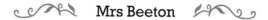

CARROT & SWEDE MASH

✳ **Serves 4** ✳ **Preparation time 10 minutes** ✳ **Cooking time 20–25 minutes**

Carrots and turnips (the family to which the swede belongs) were popular 150 years ago and remain so today. Mrs Beeton offered several options for each; this recipe goes further and combines the two, seasoning with nutmeg, which often featured in her carrot dishes.

350g swede, peeled and cut into 2cm dice

350g carrots, peeled and cut into 2cm dice

30g unsalted butter

salt and freshly ground black pepper

large pinch grated nutmeg

Put 1 litre water in a saucepan over a high heat. Add 1 tsp salt and bring to a boil. Add the swede and simmer for 10 minutes, then add the carrot and continue to simmer for a further 10 minutes, or until both vegetables are tender.

Drain off as much water as you can and then add the butter, along with plenty of freshly ground black pepper and a large pinch of freshly grated nutmeg. Mash well with a potato masher, transfer to a serving dish and serve.

BRAISED PUY LENTILS

* Serves 4 * Preparation time 20 minutes * Cooking time 45 minutes

Mrs Beeton notes how useful lentils and beans are for meat-free times, Lent especially. Many people now choose not to eat meat, but even meat-eaters will enjoy this lovely recipe. These lentils are used as the base for the goat cheese with lentils recipe on page 208, but they are also ideal for serving with roast goose or any game dish.

200g Puy lentils

3 tbsp olive oil

½ onion, peeled and finely chopped

1 small carrot, peeled and finely chopped

½ stick celery, trimmed and finely chopped

1 bay leaf

1 thyme sprig

2 garlic cloves, finely chopped

small bunch flat-leaf parsley, stems discarded, leaves finely chopped

3 tbsp extra virgin olive oil

salt and freshly ground black pepper

Place the lentils in a medium-sized pan over a high heat and add 1.5 litres of water. Bring to a boil then turn down and simmer for 10 minutes, or until just tender. Drain and set aside.

Put the olive oil in a large frying pan over a low heat and add the onion, carrot, celery, bay leaf, thyme and half the chopped garlic. Cook for 10 minutes, or until the vegetables begin to soften. Then add the lentils and enough fresh water to cover everything.

Let the mixture simmer very gently for 20–25 minutes. Then remove the pan from the heat and drain the mixture into a sieve, discarding the liquid and the bay leaf. Place the lentil mixture into a serving dish and stir in the remaining chopped garlic and the parsley. Drizzle over the extra virgin olive oil, season to taste with salt and black pepper and serve.

HARICOT BEANS

✳ Serves 4 ✳ Preparation time 5 minutes plus 12 hours soaking time
✳ Cooking time approx 1 hour 15 minutes

Mrs Beeton's method for white haricot beans has been adapted here to work with
any dried bean. The key to using dried beans is to buy them from a shop with a high
turnover so that they are as fresh as possible. This means they will plump up and
become tender without having to be cooked for an enormous length of time.

150g dried haricot beans

1 carrot, peeled and
cut into tiny dice

1 onion, peeled and
finely chopped

1 stick celery, trimmed
and finely chopped

3 garlic cloves, peeled
and left whole

1 bay leaf

1 large thyme sprig

100ml extra virgin olive oil,
plus 3 tbsp extra to finish

small bunch flat-leaf parsley,
leaves and fine stalks only

salt and freshly ground
black pepper

Place the beans in a large bowl, cover them with cold
water and leave to soak overnight. The next day, drain and
pick over the beans, discarding any that have not swollen,
any that are discoloured and any foreign objects. Place
the beans in a large pan over a medium heat, cover with
cold water and bring to a simmer. Skim off any foam from
the surface then add half the carrot, half the onion, half the
celery, 2 garlic cloves, the bay leaf and the thyme. Simmer
gently for up to 1 hour, or until almost tender. The time
this takes will depend on the age of the beans. Add more
boiling water as necessary to ensure that they are always
covered. Once cooked, drain and discard the liquid.

Place 100ml olive oil in a large saucepan over a low heat
and add the remaining vegetables. Fry gently, stirring
occasionally, for 7–8 minutes, or until they are soft but
not coloured. Add the beans and enough water to cover.
Simmer gently until the beans are very tender, topping the
pan up with boiling water as necessary so that they always
remain covered. Remove the pan from the heat, add a
pinch of salt and leave the beans to absorb their seasoning
for 5 minutes. Taste and adjust the seasoning if necessary,
then fish out and discard the bay leaf and thyme sprig.

If you are not using the beans immediately, they will keep
for 3–4 days in their liquid, stored in an airtight container
in the fridge.

To serve, drain the beans from the liquid and place in a
serving dish. Drizzle over 3 tbsp olive oil. Finely chop the
parsley and the remaining garlic clove together, stir this
mixture through the beans and serve.

CAULIFLOWER PARMESAN

* Serves 4 * Preparation time 15 minutes * Cooking time 50 minutes

Mrs Beeton used Parmesan cheese to flavour her cauliflower gratin, but you can substitute any strongly flavoured, dry cheese you like, such as Isle of Mull Cheddar. Avoid Cheddar coated in wax, though, which tends to be too soft.

1 quantity béchamel sauce (see page 329)

600g cauliflower, tough leaves discarded

½ tsp English mustard powder

100g finely grated Parmesan cheese

salt and freshly ground black pepper

special equipment

a large ovenproof dish

Make the béchamel sauce according to the recipe and keep it warm until you need it.

Trim the ends off the pale inner leaves of the cauliflower, and cut them into 3cm lengths. Cut the cauliflower florets into 2–3cm chunks. Place 1 litre of water in a saucepan over a high heat and add a large pinch of salt. When the water boils, add the cauliflower florets and trimmed leaves and simmer for about 5 minutes, or until tender to the tip of a sharp knife. Drain well, transfer to an ovenproof dish and arrange in a layer 5–6cm thick.

Preheat the grill to medium-high. Add the mustard and two-thirds of the Parmesan to the béchamel sauce and mix well until smooth, then season with salt and black pepper.

Pour the sauce over the cauliflower, ensuring all the cauliflower is covered. Sprinkle the top with the remaining cheese and place under the grill. Cook for 4–5 minutes, or until the top is well browned and bubbling, and serve.

CONFIT OF PARSNIPS

* **Serves 4** * **Preparation time 10 minutes** * **Cooking time 1 hour**

Mrs Beeton herself was not particularly adventurous with parsnips, although she did report that they had been used successfully to make both bread and wine. As a vegetable, they did not come into their own until the years of World War II, when their sweetness was suddenly craved by a nation starved of sugar. This recipe is based on a method suggested for carrots or turnips, but uses ingredients that heighten the natural sweetness of the parsnips.

800g parsnips
75g softened unsalted butter
250ml fresh orange juice
1 tbsp English honey
1 tsp chopped fresh thyme
salt and freshly ground
black pepper

special equipment
a roasting tin

Preheat the oven to 200°C/gas mark 6. Cut the parsnips in half crossways, then halve the thinner root end lengthways, and quarter the thicker top end lengthways. This will give you 6 roughly equal-sized pieces per parsnip.

Place 1 litre of water into a saucepan over a high heat. Add ½ tsp fine salt and bring to a boil. Add the parsnips and boil for 15–20 minutes, or until tender and the point of a knife will easily slip through the pieces.

Remove from the heat and drain. When they are cool enough to handle take a sharp knife and remove and discard the core from the quartered pieces of parsnip.

Place the parsnip pieces in a single layer on the roasting tin, add the remaining ingredients and stir everything around to coat. Bake, turning regularly for 45 minutes, or until all of the liquid has evaporated and the parsnips are plump and lightly browned. Remove from oven as soon as the parsnips are ready, so that the honey does not burn and taste bitter, and serve.

GLAZED TURNIPS

✳ Serves 4 ✳ Preparation time 15 minutes ✳ Cooking time 20 minutes

This is a version of Mrs Beeton's so-called German method of cooking turnips and is a super way with this underrated vegetable. Turnips, as opposed to swede, can be grown at any time of the year, but in the late spring, harvested when they are still at the 'baby' stage, they are at their most juicy and tender.

300g small purple- or white-topped turnips

2 tbsp light olive oil

300ml light chicken stock (see page 23)

25g unsalted butter

salt and freshly ground black pepper

Peel and top and tail the turnips and trim off any dark or bruised parts. Cut into small wedges about 1.5cm thick and set aside.

Place the oil in a large frying pan over a high heat. Add the turnip wedges and a pinch of salt and fry, stirring, until they are lightly browned. Add the stock, reduce the heat to low and cover. Simmer gently for about 10 minutes, or until the turnips are almost tender, then remove the lid and add the butter. Turn the heat up a little and cook until the liquid is reduced to a nice glaze. Season to taste with salt and black pepper and serve.

ROAST CHICORY WITH PEARS

✳ **Serves 4** ✳ **Preparation time 10 minutes** ✳ **Cooking time 1 hour 20 minutes**

Mrs Beeton recommends that any seasoning used with endive (or chicory) should be delicate: this pale, white vegetable is almost more texture than flavour, though you can detect a lovely hint of bitterness when it is roasted. The original recipe calls for a mixture of stock, lemon juice and sugar, but the addition of soft, fruity pears, which appear in our shops at the same time of year as the first home-grown chicory, balance the light bitterness beautifully. This is an excellent accompaniment to game or pork dishes.

40g unsalted butter, plus extra for greasing

2 heads white chicory, cut in half lengthways

50ml dark chicken or jellied game stock (see page 22 or 17)

pinch of salt

10g caster sugar

1 tsp lemon juice

2 large semi-ripe pears, peeled and quartered

1 tsp chopped thyme leaves

special equipment

a gratin dish

Preheat the oven to 200°C/gas mark 6 and butter the gratin dish. Place the chicory halves into the dish in a single layer, cut-side down, and bake for 30 minutes, or until the chicory has begun to release its juice. Turn them a couple of times during cooking to help them brown a little on all sides.

Remove from the oven and add the chicken stock, salt, sugar and lemon juice. Cook for a further 30 minutes, until the stock reduces, still turning the chicory occasionally. Remove from the oven and add the pears, tossing everything together to coat the pears with the buttery juices. Sprinkle over the chopped thyme and cook for 20 minutes or until the pears are tender. Serve immediately.

YELLOW SPLIT PEAS WITH SMOKED BACON

Serves 4 ✳ Preparation time 5 minutes ✳ Cooking time 1 hour 30 minutes

Mrs Beeton uses split peas in her pease pudding, which she comments 'should always be sent to table with boiled leg of pork'. Here, the pork (in the form of bacon) is combined with the peas to make a modern take on pease pudding, which also has the advantage of being far quicker to cook than the original. It is an inspired accompaniment for a roast.

350g yellow split peas

1 bay leaf

25g melted butter

100g smoked bacon, cut into small pieces

small bunch parsley, thick stems discarded, leaves finely chopped

salt and freshly ground black pepper

Put the peas and bay leaf in a saucepan over a medium to high heat, cover with water and bring to a boil, stirring. Reduce the heat and simmer for 1 hour, or until the peas are tender. Drain through a sieve, fish out and discard the bay leaf and set the peas aside.

Place the butter in another saucepan over a medium heat. Add the bacon and fry until it begins to render its fat and colours a little at the edges. Then reduce the heat, add the peas and toss everything together. Season to taste with a little salt, if needed, and some black pepper. Stir the parsley through, transfer to a dish and serve.

WATERCRESS SALAD

✳ Serves 4 ✳ Preparation time 10 minutes

Watercress and many other wild plants were so commonly collected and used historically that we rarely see recipes for them – they are simply taken for granted. Hampshire watercress came to prominence when the railways brought crops into the London markets at around the time Mrs Beeton's book was published, and it is still the best. This flavourful strong leaf is an ideal accompaniment to any game or meat dish.

4 large handfuls fresh watercress

3 tbsp extra virgin olive oil

juice of ¼ lemon

pinch sea salt

Place the watercress in a large bowl of iced water, and then pick the pieces out, discarding any tough stems as you go. Transfer the leaves to a salad spinner. Just before you are ready to serve, give the leaves a spin to dry them then place them in a salad bowl. Drizzle over the olive oil, a good squeeze of lemon and a little salt. Toss gently to coat and serve.

GRILLED MUSHROOM FLAPS

✳ Serves 4 ✳ Preparation time 5 minutes ✳ Cooking time 8–10 minutes

Mrs Beeton noted that large mushroom flaps (or tops) are best for this recipe, while she reserved button mushrooms for stews. Of course, you can use whichever you prefer, but the larger, mature mushrooms do have a more intense, almost animal flavour. You can grill them simply with butter and perhaps a sprinkle of lemon juice, as in the original recipe, but the addition of garlic gives a rich, savoury flavour.

8 large, flat field mushrooms, each about 8–10cm in diameter

2 tbsp olive oil, for brushing

½ quantity parsley & garlic butter (see page 336)

salt and freshly ground black pepper

Preheat the grill to high. Peel the mushrooms and remove their stalks. Place them on a baking tray in a single layer, gill-side down. Brush the caps with the olive oil, season with a light sprinkling of salt and place under the grill at a distance of no less than 10cm from the element. Cook until the mushrooms start to collapse and turn golden brown. Flip them over, divide the parsley and garlic butter between the mushrooms, then place them back under the grill and cook for 2 minutes, or until the butter is foaming and beginning to colour. Serve immediately.

MUSHROOM RAGOUT

✳ **Serves 4 as a starter** ✳ **Preparation time 5 minutes** ✳ **Cooking time 25 minutes**

This is a light dish that serves four as a snack or starter or as an accompaniment to grilled meat or poultry. If you have access to seasonal wild mushrooms from a reliable source then replace the chestnut mushrooms with a selection of whatever is available. Mrs Beeton used lemon in her mushrooms, so she also added flour to prevent the sauce curdling. A similar result is achieved here using cream and a little sherry, which allows the fine taste of the mushrooms to come through.

50g unsalted butter

2 shallots, peeled and finely chopped

250g chestnut mushrooms, wiped and cut into quarters

1 garlic clove, finely chopped

1 thyme sprig

20ml sherry

50ml white wine

300ml dark chicken stock (see page 22)

100ml double cream

bunch flat-leaf parsley, stems discarded, leaves finely chopped

salt and freshly ground black pepper

Place the butter in a large frying pan over a low heat, add the shallots and fry gently, stirring, for 3–4 minutes until they soften. Add the mushrooms, garlic, thyme, sherry and white wine and simmer for 5 minutes until the liquid has reduced to nothing. Pour in the stock and cook for 10 minutes, or until it has reduced by two-thirds. Add the double cream and simmer gently until reduced by half and thickened to a creamy consistency. Season with salt and black pepper to taste then stir the parsley through the mushrooms and serve.

POTATOES A LA MAITRE D'HOTEL

✳ Serves 4 ✳ Preparation time 10 minutes ✳ Cooking time 25 minutes

Charlotte potatoes or small new potatoes, both of which have less starch than other varieties, are just right for making this special recipe. The 'maître d'hôtel' combination of butter, lemon and parsley is one of Mrs Beeton's most commonly used flavourings.

400g small Charlotte or new potatoes

3 tbsp light olive oil

50g butter

1 banana shallot, peeled and chopped

100ml light chicken stock (see page 23)

finely grated zest of ½ lemon

large handful flat-leaf parsley, stems discarded, leaves finely chopped

salt and freshly ground black pepper

Place the potatoes in a large pan over a high heat. Cover them with water and add a large pinch of salt. Bring to a boil and cook for 10 minutes, or until the potatoes are tender, then drain well. Place the oil in a large frying pan over a medium to heat and fry the potatoes for 5–7 minutes, or until they lightly browned on all sides. Stir them occasionally to prevent them burning.

Season the potatoes with salt and black pepper then reduce the heat and add the butter and shallot to the pan. Toss gently together for 2 minutes to cook the shallot then add the stock. Continue cooking until the liquid is reduced to a glaze.

Remove the pan from the heat and transfer the potatoes to a serving dish. Add the lemon zest and parsley and toss everything together gently to combine. Serve immediately.

ROAST POTATOES

✳ **Serves 4** ✳ **Preparation time 30 minutes** ✳ **Cooking time 1 hour 30 minutes**

Mrs Beeton only mentioned roast potatoes in passing: she cooked them in front of the fire, and noted that they should be sent to the table with additional cold butter. Of course, it is now more convenient to roast potatoes inside the oven according to the instructions in this recipe.

800g peeled potatoes cut into 3–4cm cubes

100g goose fat or dripping

salt

special equipment

a large roasting tin

Preheat the oven to 220°C/gas mark 7.

Place the potatoes in a large saucepan over a medium to high heat and cover them with water. Add 1 tsp salt and bring to a light boil. After 15 minutes remove from the heat and drain well. Shake the colander a few times to ruffle the edges of the potatoes, which will give them a crisper skin after roasting.

When you are ready to roast the potatoes, put the goose fat or dripping in the roasting tin and place in the oven just until the fat melts, then arrange the potatoes in the melted fat and return the tin to the oven. Turn the potatoes every 20 minutes. After 60 minutes, reduce the heat to 180°C/ gas mark 4 and cook for a further 30 minutes, or until the potatoes are crisp and brown. Meanwhile, line a baking tray with kitchen paper and keep it handy near the oven. When the potatoes have finished roasting, remove them from the oven and switch the oven off. Using a pair of tongs, lift the potatoes out of the fat and onto the prepared baking tray. Place them back in the oven for 5 minutes to finish draining and serve.

POTATO & CREAM GRATIN

✳ **Serves 4** ✳ **Preparation time 20 minutes** ✳ **Cooking time 1 hour**

Mrs Beeton used gravy rather than cream in her 'German method of cooking potatoes', adding a bay leaf to improve the flavour. Here, cream makes the dish more luxurious, and avoids any conflict of flavours if you are serving the gratin with another dish.

20g unsalted butter,
for greasing

600g peeled and thinly sliced
King Edward potatoes

400ml single cream

2 large pinches ground mace

2 bay leaves

2 garlic cloves, sliced

salt and freshly ground
black pepper

special equipment

a shallow 1.5-litre ovenproof
dish

Preheat the oven to 200°C/gas mark 6 and butter the ovenproof dish. Wash the potato slices in several changes of water, drain and set aside.

Pour the cream into a large, shallow pan over a medium heat and add the mace, bay leaves, garlic, ½ tsp salt and freshly ground black pepper to taste. Bring to a gentle simmer, and then add the potatoes. Cook, stirring, until the cream begins to simmer and thicken. Taste for seasoning and add a little more salt, mace and freshly ground black pepper, if necessary. As the potatoes begin to cook they will absorb the salt from the cream so season it assertively.

Pour the contents of the pan into the prepared dish, pressing the potatoes into an even layer. Bake in the centre of the oven. After 45 minutes remove the dish from the oven and leave to rest in a warm place for 5 minutes before serving.

MASHED POTATOES

✳ **Serves 4** ✳ **Preparation time 10 minutes** ✳ **Cooking time 35 minutes**

Mrs Beeton gave several recipes for different methods of making mashed potato, reflecting perhaps that we all seem to have our favourite method. Make them as soft and buttery as you like, using this recipe as a starting point.

650–700g peeled Maris piper or King Edward potatoes, cut into 3cm cubes

10g salt

130g butter

1 tbsp milk

salt and freshly ground black pepper

Place the potatoes in a large saucepan, add enough water to cover and the salt. Bring to a boil over a high heat, then reduce the heat and simmer very gently for about 20 minutes, checking them regularly with a sharp knife. As soon as they are tender, remove from the heat.

Drain through a large colander. To ensure any excess water is driven off, leave the potatoes to sit, uncovered, until quite dry and still warm, then return them to the pan.

Melt the butter in a small pan over a medium heat. When it is hot and foaming add the milk and stir, then pour the mixture over the potatoes. Turn the heat under the potatoes to medium and mash them with a potato masher to break them up, then beat them with a wooden spoon until light and fluffy. Alternatively, melt the butter in a larger pan and then press the potatoes through a ricer onto the hot butter and milk, beating after that with a wooden spoon. Adjust the seasoning to taste, and serve piping hot.

STOVED POTATOES

✳ **Serves 4** ✳ **Preparation time 5 minutes** ✳ **Cooking time 25–35 minutes, depending on size**

Really fresh new potatoes are still a seasonal treat, and Jersey Mids, which appear in March, command a high price. This recipe concentrates their delicious flavour.

600g small new potatoes or Jersey Mids, as fresh as possible

50g unsalted butter

1 tsp snipped chives, to serve

salt and freshly ground black pepper

Place the potatoes in a saucepan. Add the butter, a large pinch of salt and enough water to cover and bring to a boil over a high heat, then turn down and leave to simmer gently for 15–20 minutes. Shake the pan occasionally to ensure the potatoes cook evenly.

When they are almost tender, raise the heat to reduce the liquid to a glaze. Transfer to a serving dish, sprinkle with the chives, season and serve.

EGGS & CHEESE

EGGS

Eggs vary a good deal in size and quality. They are graded by size, and those used for most of the recipes in this book, unless specified otherwise, are medium hen's eggs, weighing on average 60g each (comprising 10g shell, 20g yolk and 30g white). All eggs have the same properties, so you can substitute an equal weight of egg from any other bird, such as duck, turkey or goose, for example. Aside from the lovely flavour they impart, eggs are valued in the kitchen for their proteins, contained in both yolk and whites. These coagulate when heated, which is why eggs harden as they cook, and can be used to bind other ingredients. Additionally, egg yolks contain compounds that help emulsify fats and liquids together, making them indispensable in many sauces.

Storing and using eggs

Eggs can be stored at room temperature but keep fresh for longer if stored in the fridge, ideally in a plastic box to prevent them drying out. If you have an excess of eggs for any reason, they can be cracked and beaten and then frozen. Freeze them in multiples of four or six in small plastic containers or freezer bags. In this form, once defrosted, they will be suitable for scrambling or for use in baking – use 60g of the mixture for every egg required in your recipe. Whether refrigerated or frozen, eggs should be brought up to room temperature before cooking, especially when making cakes and soufflés.

When separating eggs for beating or for making meringues, it is important that no yolk is mixed with the whites, and that all utensils are absolutely clean and fat-free. This is because even a minute amount of grease will prevent the eggs forming foam. Stainless steel, glass or ceramic bowls are the best for whisking egg whites because they are easier to clean than plastic ones.

CHEESE

When milk curdles it splits into a solid portion (the curd), and a liquid portion (the whey). Curd contains a mixture of milk protein (casein), fats and other components. Whey also contains some soluble nutrients, and a small amount of fat and whey proteins (from which whey cheeses such as ricotta are made). Traditionally, whey left over from the cheese-making process was either served as a drink or given to livestock.

Milk will sour naturally if left for long enough, but in order to obtain a consistent result, cheese-makers curdle milk using either rennet, which is derived from the stomach of calves, or a vegetarian alternative. The way in which this initial curd is made, and the bacteria and moulds that it is inoculated with, determine the characteristics of the finished cheese.

Pasteurised and unpasteurised cheeses

Pasteurisation is a heat treatment that is used to kill off most of the bacteria that spoils dairy products and can cause food-borne illnesses. However, it also alters the structure of some of the enzymes present in the milk, which affects the flavour and condition of the resulting cheese. Pregnant women are advised not to eat unpasteurised cheeses due to the risk of contracting food-borne illnesses.

Storing cheese

Cheese is a perishable product, and the higher the water content, the quicker it will deteriorate. Some hard cheeses can be safely matured for 2–3 years without spoiling because they are dry and have a relatively high salt content and acidity. Cheese that comes from an artisan producer may very well be matured at temperatures slightly higher than the temperature of most fridges – sometimes as high as 12–15°C. Once cheese leaves the dairy, however, it is transported and held at or below 4°C, which slows down its maturation considerably, making it keep for longer.

Cheese should not be kept in plastic or cling film, because this will cause it to sweat and will encourage the growth of mould. A good cheesemonger will usually wrap their cheese in greaseproof paper, which will allow it to breathe. It is best to only buy what you will use in a few days and check it regularly for mould or signs of deterioration. If the surface of a cheese has dried, developed small mould spots or is sweating, scrape the surface clean with a sharp knife.

The ideal temperature for eating cheese, to gain the benefit of its full flavour, is about 15°C: any warmer and it will begin to sweat. Cheese stored in the fridge will keep longer, and can be brought up to room temperature for serving. Alternatively, you could keep it in a cool larder at a temperature of 10–15°C, where it will continue to mature gradually over the course of a few days. This way the cheese will ripen (and then deteriorate) more quickly than if stored in the fridge, but will mean you can enjoy the cheese as the maker intended. Pregnant women are advised not to eat cheeses stored above 4°C due to the risk of contracting a food-borne illness.

Eating and serving cheese

If you buy good cheese, eat it as nature intended to enjoy its true flavour. When serving a cheese course as part of a meal, put together a cheeseboard of no more than perhaps two or three perfectly ripe cheeses. These can be served with a combination of oatcakes or other cheese biscuits, bread (nut or fruit versions work well), nuts, fruit and celery – whatever harmonises with the flavour and texture of the cheese. In the chapter on Jams, Jellies & Pickles you will find three recipes for fruit preserves, known as cheeses (see pages 362–364). Fruit cheese is an excellent foil to the richness of milk cheeses.

Cooking cheese alters the flavour, reducing its strength. This is why it is advisable to use strong Cheddar or Parmesan for cooking.

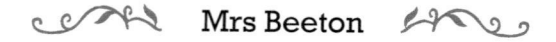

BRITISH AND IRISH CHEESES

There are more excellent cheeses made in the British Isles now than probably at any point in our history – and they rightly take their place among the best in the world, thanks to a new generation of farmers and cheese-makers who have revolutionised the industry in recent years.

In Mrs Beeton's time, many large Victorian houses were built with their own dairy and cheese rooms. These were lined with marble and slate, and people made their own dairy products there. Those who did buy dairy products did so mostly from small, farm-based dairies. The majority of cheeses were consumed locally and so few cheeses – Stilton and Cheddar being two notable exceptions – were known beyond their local markets. At a time when refrigeration was only just being developed, the quality of the finished product can only have been variable.

A combination of the nineteenth-century decline in the real value of agricultural wages, rural depression and two World Wars, along with the industrialisation of food production, very nearly killed off any remnants of cheese production as a business. Still, makers of fine cheese persisted and continued to thrive, thanks to the demand for good food.

Significant in the development of modern British cheeses are people such as the cheese-maker and teacher James Aldridge, who was active in the 1980s and 90s, and cheesemonger Randolph Hodgson, who is still chairman of Neal's Yard Dairy today. These two men, along with the authors who publicised the renaissance in the making and appreciation of cheese, have done more than anyone to encourage new cheese-makers to strive for perfection.

It is impossible to describe all of the new cheeses that have appeared on the market in recent years, let alone the land they spring from and the people who produce them. A selection of a few popular national favourites is listed below. You can find contact details of cheese suppliers at the back of the book.

Hard cheeses

Isle of Mull Cheddar – unpasteurised cows'-milk cheese, Isle of Mull, Scotland.
The grandest of strong Cheddars with a smooth, almost fudgy, texture and a lovely fruity, farmyard tang

Keen's Cheddar – unpasteurised cows'-milk cheese, Wincanton, Somerset.
A firm, nutty Cheddar with a long flavour and good bite at the end

Gorwydd Caerphilly – unpasteurised cows'-milk cheese, Llandewi Brefi, Wales.
A cheese of contrasting flavours and textures – citric, lactic and earthy – all balanced together

Cornish Yarg – pasteurised cows'-milk cheese, Pengreep, Cornwall.
A crumbly but moist cheese with delicate, sweet dairy notes

St Gall – unpasteurised cows'-milk cheese, Fermoy, County Cork.
A very smooth-textured cheese with long, creamy and nutty flavours

Ticklemore – pasteurised goats'-milk cheese, Sharpham Estate, Devon.
Lovely fresh, lactic flavours and a light, crumbly texture

Soft cheeses

Childwickbury – pasteurised goats'-milk cheese, St Albans, Hertfordshire.
Delicate, fresh, young cheese with a light, smooth texture and sharp milky flavour

St Tola – unpasteurised goats'-milk cheese, Inagh, County Clare.
A luxurious cheese with a light texture and a rich, creamy, sometimes floral, flavour

Tymsboro – unpasteurised goats'-milk cheese, Timsbury, Somerset.
Full-flavoured, creamy goat cheese

Clava – pasteurised cows'-milk cheese, Ardersier, Inverness.
A creamy, brie-like cheese with a flavour that is full and deep, but lacking the bite of French brie

Ardrahan – pasteurised cows'-milk cheese, Kanturk, County Cork.
A semi-soft cheese with a buttery texture. The washed rind has a delightfully pungent aroma, which provides the perfect contrast to the delicate, nutty flavour of the cheese

Elmhirst – unpasteurised cows'-milk cheese from the 60-year-old Sharpham Jersey herd, Sharpham Estate, Devon.
A rich, triple-cream cheese with a surprisingly light texture and flavour that develops as the cheese matures

Blue cheeses

Colston Bassett Stilton – pasteurised cows'-milk cheese, Colston Bassett, Nottinghamshire.
A rich, buttery-textured cheese with a balanced fruity and savoury mineral flavour

Beenleigh Blue – pasteurised ewes'-milk cheese, Ashprington, Devon.
A beautiful, rich, clean-tasting blue

Strathdon Blue – pasteurised cows'-milk cheese, Tain, Ross-shire
A smooth, pale-blue cheese with a salty yet well-balanced milky flavour

Cornish Blue – Liskeard, Cornwall.
A young blue cows'-milk cheese with a sweet, mild and creamy flavour and a soft, giving texture

Stichelton – unpasteurised organic cows'-milk cheese, Welbeck Estate, Nottinghamshire.
A firm but silky texture with long, complex flavours of spice and sugar

Yorkshire Blue – pasteurised cows'-milk cheese, Newsham, North Yorkshire.
A soft, creamy, blue-veined cheese with a sweet, buttery flavour but lacking the bite of traditional blue cheeses

YORKSHIRE PUDDINGS

* Makes 24 small Yorkshire puddings
* Preparation time 10 minutes plus 10 minutes resting time * Cooking time 20–25 minutes

Mrs Beeton made her Yorkshire pudding in a large shallow tin and then cut it into squares before serving. Her choice of cooking fat was beef dripping, and she also liked to stand the Yorkshire pudding tin under the meat as it cooked to collect the juices. To speed up the cooking time and for ease of portioning, this recipe is for small individual puddings, made in muffin trays, and they are best served piping hot with lots of gravy.

225g plain flour

600ml milk

3 medium eggs

large pinch salt

25g butter, melted

50g lard or dripping,
to cook

special equipment

2 x 12-hole muffin trays

Preheat the oven to 220°C/gas mark 7. Mix the flour, milk and eggs together with the salt in a bowl. Whisk until the batter is free of lumps. Leave to stand in a cool place for 10 minutes or until required. Strain the batter through a fine sieve into a jug and stir in the melted butter along with 3 tbsp cold water.

Set out two 12-hole muffin trays and place a small knob of lard or dripping into each hole, then place in the oven until the fat has melted and is hot but not smoking.

Remove the trays from the oven and carefully divide the batter between the holes. Bake the puddings for 10–15 minutes, or until they are well-risen and golden brown. Serve immediately.

SCRAMBLED EGGS

✳ **Serves 4** ✳ **Preparation time 5 minutes** ✳ **Cooking time 5 minutes**

Mrs Beeton called these mumbled eggs, and included the curious instruction to stir them in one direction with a silver spoon. A wooden spoon will do perfectly well, but constant stirring is vital, as is correctly judging when to remove them from the heat..

8 medium eggs

2 tbsp double cream

25g unsalted butter

salt and freshly ground black pepper

Preheat the oven to low and place 4 plates inside to warm. Whisk the eggs, cream and some freshly ground black pepper together. Melt the butter in a saucepan over a medium-high heat. When it is foaming add the egg mixture, stirring continuously with a spatula or wooden spoon and scraping the egg off the base and sides of the pan as it sets. After 2–3 minutes add the salt. When the eggs are still slightly loose, remove them from the heat and serve them on the warm plates, where they will continue to cook.

FRIED EGGS

✳ **Serves 4** ✳ **Preparation time 5 minutes** ✳ **Cooking time 3 minutes**

Mrs Beeton suggested presenting fried eggs on slices of fried bacon or ham. Today, they are served in a multitude of different dishes. Whatever accompaniment you choose, cook them quickly in hot fat to ensure crisp edges and a runny yolk.

2 tbsp clarified butter (see glossary) or dripping

4 medium eggs

Place 4 plates in a low oven to warm. Heat a large non-stick frying pan over a medium-high heat and add the butter. When that is hot crack the eggs into the pan, ensuring that they do not touch one another. Using a heatproof spatula, scrape the edges of the eggs in towards the yolk to tidy up and even the edges. When the whites are set, spoon the hot fat over the egg yolks to cook them thoroughly. They are ready when the whites are set, the edges crispy and the yolks beginning to grow pale on top. Remove the eggs with a fish slice and transfer to the warmed plates. Serve immediately.

POACHED EGGS

✳ Serves 4 ✳ Preparation time 10 minutes
✳ Cooking time 5 minutes for soft yolks, 7 minutes for hard

Only use very fresh eggs for this simple recipe – they will hold their shape perfectly.

30ml white wine vinegar

4 very fresh, medium eggs

Place 1 litre of water and the vinegar in a large, wide 2-litre saucepan over a medium heat, and bring to simmering. Line a plate with a layer of kitchen paper.

Crack an egg into a teacup or small bowl and gently slip it into the simmering water. Repeat with other eggs but ensure the eggs do not touch one another in the water.

Cook the eggs in the gently simmering water for 3–5 minutes for a softly poached egg, or 6–7 minutes for a firmly poached egg.

When the eggs are finished, lift them one at a time from the pan using a slotted spoon and set on the lined plate to drain.

Serve immediately.

Note: It is possible to poach eggs before they are needed, which is useful if they are being served as part of a more complicated dish. You will need to chill them immediately in a bowl of cold water to stop them cooking any further, and then reheat for 1 minute in a shallow pan of simmering water when you are ready to serve. A poached egg will keep in a sealed container for 1 day.

EGGS FLORENTINE

✴ **Serves 4** ✴ **Preparation time 30 minutes** ✴ **Cooking time 5 minutes**

One of Mrs Beeton's suggestions for poached eggs is to serve them on a bed of spinach. She also gives a recipe for poached eggs with cream, and from there it is only a small leap to the dish that we now know as eggs Florentine, which was probably created towards the end of the nineteenth century in New York. For eggs Benedict replace the spinach with four slices of ham, and for eggs royal, with four slices of smoked salmon. If you'd like to try the Mrs Beeton original, heat 70ml cream to boiling point, add 25g unsalted butter and stir until melted, season with salt, pepper and sugar to taste, and spoon over the eggs in place of the hollandaise sauce.

2 English muffins (see page 310), split open and toasted

1 quantity hollandaise sauce (see page 338)

1 tsp unsalted butter

200g baby spinach

4 medium eggs, poached (see opposite)

salt and freshly ground black pepper

Bake a batch of English muffins and keep 2 aside for this recipe. (The preparation time above does not include the time taken to prepare the muffins.) Prepare the hollandaise sauce and keep it warm in a bowl placed over a pan of hot water.

Place the butter in a large pan over a medium heat. When foaming, add the spinach along with a pinch of salt and a few grindings of black pepper. As soon as the spinach begins to wilt, begin poaching the eggs and place the muffins under the grill to toast.

By the time the spinach is wilting but not completely broken down the eggs should be finished poaching and muffins toasted. Drain the spinach, squeezing to remove as much liquid as possible.

Place a toasted muffin half on each plate, split-side up, and place one-quarter of the spinach on each muffin half. Top with a poached egg, then spoon over hollandaise sauce as desired. Finish with a grinding of black pepper to taste.

EGGS BAKED WITH CREAM & TARRAGON

* Serves 4 * Preparation time 10 minutes
* Cooking time 15–20 minutes

This is another variation on Mrs Beeton's poached eggs with cream. Here, rather than being poached, the eggs are baked with the cream and a little tarragon for added flavour.

butter, for greasing

1 French tarragon sprig

4 medium eggs

4 tbsp double cream

salt and freshly ground black pepper

special equipment

4 x 120ml ramekins and a roasting tin

Preheat the oven to 160°C/gas mark 3. Fill the kettle and bring it to boiling.

Butter the ramekins. Strip the leaves from the tarragon sprig and distribute them between the ramekins. Crack 1 egg into each ramekin and add a pinch of salt and a grinding of black pepper. Then pour 1 tbsp double cream into each ramekin.

Stand the ramekins in the roasting tin and carefully pour the boiling water into the tin around the ramekins to a depth of 2–3cm. Cover loosely with foil and bake for 15 minutes for a soft egg or 20 minutes for a firm egg. Serve immediately.

SCOTCH EGGS

✳ **Makes 4** ✳ **Preparation time 20–30 minutes** ✳ **Cooking time 10–12 minutes**

When Mrs Beeton was writing her book, Scotch eggs were usually eaten hot and served with gravy. Though today they are more usually eaten cold as a picnic or snack food, freshly made Scotch eggs are deliciously crisp and savoury, and worth a try. If you are using a large pan rather than a deep-fryer to make these, only fill the pan one-third full with oil and do not leave it unattended for even a minute.

5 medium eggs

400g sausage meat

30g flour

4 tbsp milk

80g fine breadcrumbs from a stale loaf

vegetable oil, for frying

salt and freshly ground black pepper

special equipment

a deep-fryer and a temperature probe

Fill a pan with water and place over a medium heat. When it is simmering steadily add the 4 eggs. Cook them for 7 minutes, then drain and place in a bowl of iced water for 5 minutes. Cool completely and peel carefully under cold water. Then set the eggs aside.

Season the sausage meat well with salt and black pepper and divide it into 4 equal portions. Using wet hands, flatten each piece then shape into a cup big enough to hold an egg. Place an egg into each cup and then pinch the meat around the egg to seal it inside. Set aside on a plate.

Line a plate with non-stick baking paper and set aside. Prepare the coating for the eggs by placing the flour on a flat dish and seasoning it with salt and black pepper. Then, in a wide, shallow bowl beat the remaining egg with the milk and, finally, spread the breadcrumbs on a plate.

Take a meat-wrapped egg and roll it in the seasoned flour to coat, shaking off the excess. Now dip it in the beaten egg mixture, and then roll it in the breadcrumbs. Set aside on the plate lined with non-stick paper and repeat with the remaining eggs.

Preheat the oil in a deep-fryer to 160°C and when it is ready fry 2 eggs at a time for 6 minutes. Using long-handled tongs, turn the eggs 3–4 times to ensure they brown evenly. Once they are cooked, drain the first 2 eggs on a plate lined with kitchen paper while you make the other 2. Cool a little before serving. If you are not serving them right away, chill the Scotch eggs in an airtight container and eat within 2 days.

CHEESE SOUFFLE

* **Serves 4** * **Preparation time 40 minutes** * **Cooking time 8–10 minutes**

Mrs Beeton served her cheese soufflé with the cheese course. This is a delightful idea but getting the timing right can be stressful for the cook if it is served after dinner. An alternative is to use the soufflé as a course in itself, but make sure your guests are in place at the table and ready to eat as soon as the soufflé emerges from the oven.

25g unsalted butter, plus extra for greasing

85g strong cheese such as Isle of Mull Cheddar or Parmesan, finely grated, plus extra for dusting

120ml milk

½ small onion, peeled and sliced

½ tsp black peppercorns

½ bay leaf

very small carrot, peeled and chopped

25g plain flour

1 tsp Dijon mustard

2 large eggs, separated, plus 1 egg white

special equipment

4 x 120ml ramekins and a roasting tin

Butter the ramekins, ensuring the butter covers the rim as well, dust with a little finely grated cheese and set aside.

Place the milk, onion, peppercorns, bay leaf and carrot in a medium saucepan and bring to boiling over a medium heat. As soon as the mixture boils remove from the heat and leave for the flavour to infuse for 30 minutes.

Meanwhile, melt the butter in a small pan over a medium heat. When it foams add the flour and cook, stirring gently, for 3–4 minutes. Do not let the flour burn – if it begins to turn brown at the edges, dip the base of the pan in cold water to halt the cooking process.

Strain the infused milk into a pan, discarding the vegetables and herbs, and bring to a simmer over a medium heat. Place the pan with the flour mixture back on a low heat and whisk in the hot milk mixture a little at a time, allowing it to simmer after each addition. Once all the milk has been added, simmer the sauce for 3–5 minutes, then add the cheese and mustard and continue to whisk over a low heat until the cheese is melted and the mixture is glossy. Remove from the heat and add the egg yolks, stirring quickly.

Preheat the oven to 200°C/gas mark 6 and boil the kettle.

Place the egg whites into a clean, stainless steel bowl and whisk until they form soft peaks. Fold one-third of the egg whites into the cheese mixture, then gently fold all of the cheese mixture back into the remaining egg whites.

Place the ramekins in the roasting tin and divide the mixture between them. Pour the boiling water into the tin to a depth of 2cm. Bake the soufflés for 8–10 minutes until they are well risen and golden. Serve immediately.

CHEESY PUFFS

＊ **Serves 8–10 as a snack** ＊ **Preparation time 20 minutes** ＊ **Cooking time 20 minutes**

Something of a leap from Mrs Beeton's traditional cheese straws in their texture and presentation, and yet retaining that moreish, tangy, cheesy flavour, these are wonderful party nibbles.

200g plain flour

salt

450ml milk

150g unsalted butter

6 large eggs, lightly beaten

200g strong Cheddar, such as Isle of Mull, coarsely grated

50g Parmesan cheese, finely grated

vegetable oil, for frying

special equipment

a deep-fryer

Sift the flour and a generous pinch of salt together into a large bowl. Place the milk and butter into a saucepan over a medium heat. Bring to boiling and then pour in all of the flour, stirring well until the mixture comes away from the sides of the pan and forms a ball in the centre. Transfer this mixture back into the large bowl and leave to cool for 5 minutes.

Add the eggs to the flour paste a little bit at a time, beating well with each addition until all the eggs have been added and the mixture is shiny. Add the Cheddar and half the Parmesan and stir well to amalgamate.

Preheat the oven to low and preheat the deep-fryer to 170°C. Line a baking sheet with a double layer of kitchen paper and place it in the oven. Drop teaspoonfuls of the mixture into the hot oil, cooking no more than 8 at a time. They are cooked when the balls are a deep dark brown all over. Lift them from the oil using a slotted spoon and place them on the lined baking sheet in the oven to drain well. Repeat until all of the mixture is used up, then place the puffs onto a serving dish and sprinkle with the remaining Parmesan cheese and serve hot.

WELSH RAREBIT

✳ **Serves 4** ✳ **Preparation time 10 minutes** ✳ **Cooking time 10 minutes**

A simple, tasty way to serve hot cheese. Mrs Beeton recommends the use of little heated dishes to help keep the cheese warm – in a modern kitchen we have the advantage of a grill under which we can heat the mixture to bubbling perfection.

200g Isle of Mull Cheddar, or other strong cheese, grated

1 medium egg

50ml milk or beer

½ tsp English mustard powder

1 tbsp Worcestershire sauce, plus extra to serve

freshly ground black pepper

4 large slices bread

Place the grated cheese into a large bowl. Add the egg, milk or beer, mustard powder and Worcestershire sauce. Grind over some black pepper and mix well together.

Turn the grill on to high and toast each slice of bread on one side. Spread the cheese mixture onto the untoasted side of the bread and place the slices back under the grill, cheese-side up, not less than 10cm from the grill element. Let it cook until golden and bubbling. Remove from the heat and sprinkle with extra Worcestershire sauce, to taste. This is lovely served with tomato chutney. (See page 374 if you'd like to make your own.)

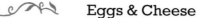

FRESH CREAM CHEESE

✳ **Serves 4** ✳ **Preparation time 10 minutes** ✳ **Cooking time 10 minutes**

This simple, delicately flavoured cheese is easy to make, and luscious served on its own with summer berries. Alternatively it can be used in place of bought cream cheese in sweet and savoury recipes, for example to make the lemon cremet on page 256. .

325ml single cream

325ml milk

¾ tsp rennet or vegetable rennet

caster sugar, for sprinkling

Put the cream and milk in a large pan and warm gently until hand-hot (around 32–35°C). Remove from the heat, add the rennet and leave in a warm place until set.

Line a sieve with some buttered muslin and place over a large bowl. Spoon the mixture into the sieve, cover and chill for 4–5 hours or overnight. During this time the whey will drain from the cheese and can be discarded.

Transfer the curds to a dish and serve sprinkled with caster sugar and accompanied by Jersey cream and fresh fruit compote or bottled fruit (see page 361) on the side.

GOAT CHEESE, RADISH & BROAD BEAN SALAD

✳ **Serves 4** ✳ **Preparation time 25 minutes** ✳ **Cooking time 2 minutes**

Fresh cheeses, such as a soft, unrinded goat cheese, are just one step up from the curds and whey Mrs Beeton made. Goat cheese is the simplest type of cheese, and it is made all over the world. This superb, light salad shows how versatile fresh goat cheese can be.

for the dressing

1½ tbsp cider vinegar or good white wine vinegar

1 small shallot, peeled and finely chopped

pinch salt

6 tbsp extra virgin olive oil

1 tbsp finely chopped mint leaves

for the salad

100g baby broad beans, podded weight

75g radishes, trimmed and quartered

2 small handfuls picked watercress leaves

for the goat cheese mousse

200g fresh, unripened goat cheese

zest of ½ lemon

1 tbsp olive oil

1 tbsp milk

Start the dressing off by placing the vinegar in a small bowl and adding the shallot and a pinch of salt. Leave, covered, for 10 minutes while you prepare the salad ingredients.

Bring a small pan of salted water to boiling over a high heat. Add the broad beans and cook for 2 minutes, then drain and plunge into a bowl of iced water. Once cool, peel off the pale outer skins and place the beans into a large bowl. Add the radishes and watercress, toss to combine, cover and set aside.

Now prepare the mousse. Place the goat cheese, lemon zest, olive oil and milk in a bowl and beat well with a fork until light and fluffy enough to just hold its shape.

Finish the dressing by whisking the olive oil into the shallot and vinegar mixture. Stir in the mint, then pour over the salad ingredients and toss well.

Divide the goat cheese mousse between 4 plates and pile a portion of salad alongside the cheese, drizzling over any excess dressing. Serve with crusty bread.

GOAT CHEESE WITH LENTILS

✻ Serves 4 ✻ Preparation time 30 minutes ✻ Cooking time 45 minutes

Mrs Beeton noted how useful lentils are to those avoiding meat in their diet, though she also commented on their decline in British cooking. Lentils have since found favour again and here, combined with radicchio, they provide a lovely bed for a winter goat cheese salad.

1 quantity of braised Puy lentils (see page 164)

2 tsp sherry vinegar

2 tsp Dijon mustard

½ garlic clove, crushed

3 tbsp olive oil

small bunch flat-leaf parsley, leaves only, finely chopped

80g radicchio leaves, chopped into 2cm strips

160g ripened goat cheese, such as Tymsboro or Kidderton Ash, broken into 1cm pieces

lemon juice, to taste

salt and freshly ground black pepper

Make the braised Puy lentils, complete with the vegetables. Drain and set aside.

In a large bowl, whisk together the vinegar, mustard and garlic with a pinch of salt to taste. Add the oil in a thin trickle, whisking all the while until the mixture is emulsified.

Season the lentils with ¼ tsp salt and stir them into the oil mixture then add the parsley and radicchio. Fold all the ingredients together gently until evenly combined. Gently fold in the goat cheese pieces. Add a squeeze of lemon, season to taste and divide among the plates to serve.

PASTRY

WHY BOTHER TO MAKE YOUR OWN PASTRY?

It is almost impossible to buy good pastry, so if you want to eat the best, you must learn to make your own. Shop-bought pastry contains additives to make the pastry last longer on the supermarket shelf. It also has any number of colour and flavour compounds to improve its appearance and taste, all of which would be unnecessary if the best ingredients were used in the first place.

Essentially, pastry is a mixture of flour, fat and water. The proportions of these ingredients can be altered to give different results, as can the type of fat and flour used. You can, at a push, make pastry with almost any flour and fat, but all of your ingredients need to be looked after.

Flour

Freshness in flour is just as important as it is in fat. Flour that has been recently ground and well stored has a delightful, fresh smell and runs easily through the fingers. It should feel dry and not 'cake' in the hand when squeezed tightly. Old flour discolours and will smell rancid, like old fat, and should be avoided.

Butter

Most of the butter we buy in the UK today is salted. Unsalted butter is easily available, but will not keep for as long. Pastry has a delicate flavour, so if you use salted butter in a recipe that calls for unsalted, remember to reduce the amount of salt added to the recipe to compensate.

Note: Lemon juice is often added to pastry to make it crisper.

WORKING AND COOKING TEMPERATURES

Because fat softens when warm, it is essential to make pastry in cool conditions, using cool ingredients, unless a recipe says otherwise. Generally, if pastry becomes too warm when it is mixed (and becomes sticky or oily), it should be chilled until the mixture is dry again before adding any liquid, so that the balance can be maintained.

If the pastry is made with too little water (which is likely if it is too warm) it is said to be 'short' and will crumble. If too much water is added, the pastry will be sticky to handle and tough when baked.

Cooking temperature is also important. For perfect pastry, the oven temperature needs to be sufficiently high to cause the starch in the flour to expand and to set as the fat melts, so that the two can combine. If the temperature is too low when the pastry goes into the oven, the fat will melt and run from the pastry before the starch cooks, resulting in tough pastry.

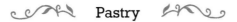

When baking pastry blind, for example, for a tart case, the pastry must be allowed to dry once set, otherwise the bottom of the tart will be soft and flabby. To ensure that the pastry is properly cooked remove the baking beans and finish cooking the pastry at a lower temperature to ensure it cooks thoroughly and evenly before any filling is added.

TYPES OF PASTRY

Shortcrust: This is the simplest pastry of all. It is usually made with two parts flour to one part fat, plus water to mix. It can be made using butter, lard, dripping or suet, or any combination of these. Shortcrust pastry is used for all pies, tarts and small pastries, both sweet and savoury.

Flaky shortcrust: This enriched pastry has a larger portion of fat, which is added in very small lumps. As a result, it flakes wonderfully when baked, and so is used to top pies and to line tarts. Flaky pastry can be made with the same type of fats as shortcrust pastry.

Rich shortcrust: This is a French variation of shortcrust pastry, and is often referred to by its French name, pâte brisée. Rich shortcrust pastry usually has a slightly higher proportion of fat to flour than plain shortcrust pastry, and egg is added to enrich it. It is commonly used for wrapping meat or fish and for lining raised pies such as game terrine (see pages 104–105). Rich shortcrust is usually made with butter.

Sweet pastry: Creaming together (see page 282) a large proportion of fat with flour and adding sugar and egg makes sweet pastry. This method produces a rich, light, delicate pastry. It is probably the most difficult to handle for novices. Sweet pastry is only made with butter.

Puff pastry: This pastry is made by a method that may appear complicated but, in fact, is more time-consuming than difficult. For this reason, it is best made in a large batch and frozen in portions for later use. Puff pastry contains equal quantities of fat and strong white flour. It is usually made with butter but, for puff pastry to be used in a savoury dish, a mixture of half butter and lard is used.

Suet pastry: As its name implies, the fat used in suet pastry is suet. This is an animal fat, but vegetarian versions are widely available. Suet pastry is traditionally used for steamed puddings, and contains a smaller proportion of fat than, for example, shortcrust pastry. Self-raising flour is commonly used when making this pastry, in order to lighten it. It is best eaten hot.

PASTRY TIPS

✳ Read the recipe through and make sure you have all the materials to hand and at the correct temperature.

✳ If the flour and fat get warm and sticky when you are mixing them, chill the pastry for 30 minutes to firm the mixture and then proceed as before.

✳ Always use cold or iced water for mixing.

✳ Handle pastry gently, using your fingertips to bring the mixture together – remember that you are making pastry not kneading bread dough.

✳ Work with the pastry in as cool a place as possible, to help keep the ingredients at the optimum temperature.

MACHINE-MADE OR HANDMADE?

The quickest, and probably best, way of mixing the fat and flour together when making almost all pastries is to use a food processor. It keeps the ingredients cool while they are amalgamated and, once the fat and flour are incorporated, the water can be mixed in quickly and easily by hand. The more quickly and delicately you work the better because working, kneading or handling pastry dough too much results in tough pastry.

If you do not have a food processor, you will need to rub the fat into the flour by hand. Start by grating the chilled fat into the flour. You can start with larger pieces of butter, but this method enables you to work more quickly and keep the mixture cooler. Now, rub the fat and flour between your fingertips. Lifting it up as you do so will mean that more air gets to the mixture, keeping it cooler. Shake the bowl gently occasionally to bring the larger lumps to the surface, and continue rubbing in until you have a mixture that resembles evenly sized breadcrumbs. If the mixture does get warm while you work, simply chill it before adding the water.

SHORTCRUST PASTRY

* **Makes enough for 1 x 22–25cm pie**
* **Preparation time 10 minutes plus 1 hour chilling time**

Mrs Beeton gives several recipes for short or everyday pastry, varying the proportion of fat to flour depending on the purpose. However, this simple half-fat-to-flour recipe is really all you need ever use. A little lemon juice added to the mix gives a crisper result.

250g plain flour

pinch salt

125g cold unsalted butter, cubed or grated

½ tsp lemon juice

100ml iced water

If you have a food processor, sift the flour and salt into the bowl and mix. Add the cubed butter and pulse until the mixture resembles fine breadcrumbs. Pour the mixture into a bowl.

If you are working by hand, sift the flour and salt into a bowl and add the cubed or grated butter. Rub the butter and flour between your fingertips until it resembles fine breadcrumbs, working quickly to keep the mixture as cool as possible. If it starts to feel sticky, chill the mixture for 30 minutes before moving on to the next step.

Add the lemon juice to the water and pour two-thirds of this into the flour mixture. Blend well with a fork, stirring quickly but gently. Using your fingertips, bring the dough together. Add more water as necessary (you may need to use all of it) until everything is evenly mixed and there are no dry lumps of flour. Bring the mixture together into a smooth, supple lump. Carefully form the pastry into a flattened ball, wrap in cling film and chill for at least 1 hour before using.

FLAKY SHORTCRUST PASTRY

* **Makes enough for 1 x 22–25cm pie**
* **Preparation time 10 minutes plus 1 hour chilling time**

Mrs Beeton gives a recipe for a 'medium puff paste' that is a halfway house between shortcrust and puff pastry, but made in the same way as puff pastry. The recipe here achieves the same result with far less fuss. A portion of the fat is blended with the flour mixture while the remainder is added in small lumps. These melt as it bakes, giving the resulting pastry a delicious, yielding flakiness. This pastry is excellent for using in fruit or other pies.

250g plain flour

pinch salt

150g cold unsalted butter

½ tsp lemon juice

100ml iced water

If you have a food processor, sift the flour and salt into the bowl and mix. Cut 100g of the butter into rough cubes and add them to the flour mixture. Pulse until it resembles fine breadcrumbs. Cut the rest of the butter into small cubes, add them the blender and pulse briefly to combine. Small lumps of butter should still be obvious in the mixture.

If you are working by hand, sift the flour and salt into a large bowl. Coarsely grate 100g of the butter into the flour mixture. Rub the butter and flour between your fingertips working quickly to keep the mixture as cool as possible. If it starts to feel sticky, chill the mixture for 30 minutes. Then coarsely grate the remaining butter into the mixture and stir. Small lumps or strands of butter should be clearly visible.

Chill the mixture for 30 minutes. Just before you are ready to proceed, stir the lemon juice into the water and pour two-thirds of this into the flour mixture. Blend well with a fork, stirring quickly but gently. Using your fingertips, bring the dough together, adding more water as necessary (you may need to use all of it) until everything is evenly mixed and there are no dry lumps of flour. Bring the mixture together into a smooth, supple lump, carefully form it into a flattened ball, wrap in cling film and chill for at least 1 hour before using.

RICH SHORTCRUST PASTRY

✳ **Makes approx 600g** ✳ **Preparation time 15 minutes plus 30 minutes chilling time**

The addition of an egg makes this pastry slightly less flaky than the other shortcrust pastries in this book. It is ideal for use in the game terrine recipe on pages 104–105.

300g plain flour

large pinch salt

200g cold salted butter, cubed

1 medium egg

1 tsp lemon juice

4 tbsp cold water

If you have a food processor, sift the flour and salt into the bowl and add the cubed butter. Pulse until the mixture resembles fine breadcrumbs then transfer it to a large bowl. If you are working by hand, sift the flour and salt into a bowl. Cut the butter into very small cubes, or grate it finely. Add it to the bowl and, working quickly, rub the butter into the flour using your fingertips. If it starts to feel sticky, chill the mixture for 30 minutes before continuing.

Combine the egg, lemon juice and water and stir two-thirds of this mixture into the flour and butter using a large fork. Now bring the mixture together with your fingertips into a supple, but not sticky, dough, adding more liquid as necessary. Gently form the dough into a ball, cover with cling film and chill for 30 minutes before using.

SUET PASTRY

✳ **Makes approx 600g** ✳ **Preparation time 10 minutes plus 30 minutes chilling time**

This pastry uses self-raising flour, which was not available to Mrs Beeton, but it lightens the resulting pastry considerably and also makes it more absorbent, which is excellent for puddings (such as the steak and kidney pudding on page 132) and dumplings.

375 g self-raising flour

scant 1 tsp salt

130g suet, grated

250ml cold water

Sift the flour and salt into a large bowl and mix in the suet. Add half of the water. Stir well with a fork, working quickly but gently. Using your fingertips, bring the dough together. Add more water as necessary until everything is evenly mixed and there are no dry lumps of flour.

Bring the mixture together into a smooth, supple lump. Carefully form it into a ball, wrap in cling film and chill for 30 minutes before using.

PUFF PASTRY

✳ Makes 2kg ✳ Preparation time 15 minutes plus 20 minutes of rolling over 3 hours

Mrs Beeton gives more than one recipe for 'puff paste' – this classic method is standard and based on the recipe written by Monsieur Ude, one of the foremost French chefs working in London at the beginning of the nineteenth century.

1kg strong plain flour, plus extra for dusting

2 tsp salt

1kg cold unsalted butter

1 tsp lemon juice

500ml cold water

Using a food processor, place all the flour with the salt and 250g of the butter, cut into cubes, into the bowl and pulse until the mixture resembles fine breadcrumbs. Pour this into a large bowl.

Add the lemon juice to the water and add two-thirds of the liquid to the bowl. Blend well with a fork, stirring quickly but gently. Using your fingertips, bring the dough together. Add more water as necessary (you may need all of it) until everything is evenly mixed and there are no dry lumps of flour. Bring the mixture together into a smooth, supple lump. Carefully form it into a flattened ball, wrap in cling film and chill for at least 1 hour before using.

Roll the remaining butter between 2 sheets of non-stick baking paper into an 18cm square that is 2.5cm thick. Lightly flour your work surface, then remove the dough from the fridge and unwrap. Place on the lightly floured surface and cut a deep cross in the dough, cutting about two-thirds of the way through to the work surface. Dust the ball with flour and fold the four segments out into a rough square shape. Dust this lightly with flour and roll it into a square about 28cm across, or large enough to take the block of butter set at a 45° angle.

Using a clean pastry brush, dust the pastry free of flour, place the butter in the centre at a 45° angle to the pastry and fold each corner of the pastry over the butter, pinching the dough together to seal any holes. Turn the dough over, dusting the work surface again with a little flour, and roll the pastry out into a 20 x 60cm rectangle. If the pastry sticks to the work surface dust it with a little more flour as required.

Once you have a rectangle of the right size, brush the pastry to remove any excess flour. Fold the third of the pastry nearest to you over the middle third, then fold in the top third on top of that so that you have a 20 x 20cm square and press, keeping the dough as square and even as you can. Place it on a plate in a cool place or the fridge to rest.

After 15 minutes remove the dough from the fridge and turn it 90° to the right from its original position, so that the top open fold is on your left. Roll out again to 20 x 60cm and repeat the action above. Do this a total of 6 times, allowing the dough to rest in between each fold. After resting it for the last time, roll the pastry into a 30 x 20cm rectangle. Cut this evenly into 4 parts. If you are not using any of the puff pastry straight away, wrap each portion tightly in cling film, then seal in foil and freeze.

HOT WATER PASTRY

✳ **Makes approx 1.5kg** ✳ **Preparation time 15 minutes**

This pastry is made in a completely different way to the other forms of pastry because the fat and water are heated together before being added to the flour. The end result is a pastry that is malleable and sets firm when cooked. This means it is ideal for raised pies, for example, which require a longer time in the oven. This recipe gives you enough pastry to make the two pork pies on pages 232–233.

850g plain flour

15g salt

430ml water

240g lard

Sift the flour and salt together in a large bowl and set aside. Place the water and lard into a pan over a medium heat and bring to a gentle simmer. Remove from the heat and stir the liquid into the flour mixture using a large fork to blend thoroughly. Pour the mixture onto a work surface and mix with your hands to bring it together into a smooth ball, working carefully as the mixture will be hot. Cover the pastry with an inverted bowl and leave it to cool further for 5 minutes before using.

SWEET PASTRY

✳ **Makes approx 700g** ✳ **Preparation time 10 minutes plus 1–2 hours chilling time**

This pastry is a combination of two of Mrs Beeton's recipes. The key is to blend the butter well with the flour and, to make this easier, in this recipe you start off with butter that is at room temperature, not chilled, and then beat it until it is light, as you would if you were making a cake. The pastry is then chilled before use, and kneaded lightly to make it supple before rolling it out. This pastry recipe makes enough for a 30cm tart case.

200g unsalted butter, at room temperature

125g icing sugar

1 medium egg, lightly beaten

285g plain flour, plus extra for dusting

In a large bowl, cream the softened butter with a wooden spoon until light. Sift in the icing sugar and combine gently until the two are well mixed.

Add the beaten egg to the bowl, mixing well, then sift in the flour and combine well. When you have obtained a soft dough scrape it into a ball and then flatten it onto a piece of cling film. Cover the dough with the cling film and chill.

After 1–2 hours the dough will be easier to handle. When you are ready to roll out the pastry, remove it from the cling film and knead it lightly to make it supple enough for rolling. Place a sheet of non-stick baking paper on your work surface and scatter it with a little flour. Place the dough on the baking paper and cover with another sheet of baking paper, then roll out between the 2 sheets. This will make it easier to transfer the dough to a pie dish once it has been rolled out.

CUSTARD TART

✳ Serves 8–10 ✳ Preparation time 40 minutes plus 1–2 hours chilling time
✳ Cooking time 1 hour 15 minutes

This recipe, based on Mrs Beeton's baked custard pudding, produces a crisp pastry case filled with silky, smooth custard. Brushing the pastry with egg white after blind baking seals the surface and keeps the pastry crisp while the filling cooks.

1 quantity sweet pastry (see opposite)

unsalted butter, for greasing

plain flour, for dusting

1 egg white, beaten

300ml double cream

300ml whole milk

50g caster sugar

6 large egg yolks

½ tsp nutmeg, finely grated

special equipment

a 20cm loose-based cake tin and some baking beans

Make the pastry, cover and chill for 1–2 hours. Towards the end of this time, grease the cake tin. When you are ready to start rolling, place a large sheet of non-stick baking paper on your work surface and dust it with a little flour. Knead the pastry lightly to make it supple enough to roll, then place it on the baking paper, dust again with flour and put another sheet of baking paper on top. Roll the pastry out between the sheets of paper to a diameter of 30cm. With floured fingers, place the pastry over the tin, pressing it carefully it into the bottom. Trim the edges, cover the lined tin with cling film and chill for 20 minutes.

Preheat the oven to 200°C/gas mark 6. Line the pastry case with non-stick baking paper, fill with baking beans and place in the oven. After 20 minutes turn the oven down to 160°C/gas mark 3 and bake for a further 15–20 minutes, or until the pastry is cooked through. Remove the pastry case from of the oven and take out the paper and beans. If there are any cracks, roll some of the off-cuts in your fingers and use them to fill the gaps, then brush the pastry case with the beaten egg white and return it to the oven for 5 minutes, or until it has browned evenly. Remove from the oven and reduce the temperature to 140°C/gas mark 1.

Place the cream, milk and half the sugar in a saucepan over a low heat and stir occasionally until the sugar dissolves. Meanwhile, in a bowl, whisk the egg yolks with the remaining sugar. Pour the egg yolk mixture into the cream mixture, stir until fully combined, then pass the custard through a sieve and into the pastry case. Sprinkle with the grated nutmeg. Make a loose tent of foil over the tart and bake for 35 minutes, or until the edges are set and the centre is still a little wobbly.

CORNISH PASTIES

❋ Makes 8 pasties ❋ Preparation time 35 minutes plus 1 hour chilling time
❋ Cooking time 40 minutes

A traditional Cornish pasty has a nice thick rim of pleated pastry, to be used as a handle for the hungry diner. You can crimp your pasties in the traditional way, as shown in the illustration, or simply press the two halves together firmly. Just make sure that none of the delicious filling escapes. Mrs Beeton gives an unusual recipe for a pasty using just meat and potato, but onions and swede have been added here to give the traditional and familiar Cornish pasty flavour. Use skirt steak: it is inexpensive and can easily be procured from a good butcher.

for the pastry

500g plain flour, plus
extra for dusting

1 tsp salt

125g suet

125g lard

for the filling

300g lean beef skirt,
finely chopped

150g potato, peeled and grated

150g onions, peeled and grated

150g swede, peeled and grated

1½ tsp freshly ground
black pepper

1½ tsp salt

1 egg, beaten, for brushing

special equipment

a 17cm round saucer to use
as a template

To make the pastry, place the flour, salt, and half the suet in the bowl of a food processor and blend until fine. Then add the lard and blitz again until it is fully incorporated. Place the mixture into a bowl and add the rest of the suet, stirring well.

Add 120–150ml cold water and mix with a large fork until the dough begins to come together, adding a little more water if required. Pinch the pastry together with your fingertips until it forms a dough, then roll into a ball, wrap in cling film and chill. Meanwhile, add the beef and vegetables to a bowl. Sprinkle over the black pepper and stir together until fully combined.

Preheat the oven to 200°C/gas mark 6.

After the dough has been chilling for 1 hour, dust your work surface with some flour. Uncover the dough and roll it approximately 3–5mm thick, then cut out eight 17cm discs. You may need to re-roll the trimmings to cut the last 2 discs. Roll each disc into a slightly oval shape.

Now sprinkle the salt over the meat mixture, combine thoroughly and divide into 8 equal balls, placing one in the middle of each pastry oval.

Wet the edge of the pastry on one side of each oval with water. Fold the dry side up over the meat and, ensuring that no air has been trapped inside, press the edges well together to seal the pastry snugly round the filling.

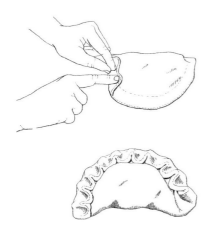

Crimp round the edge to perfect the seal, as shown in the illustrations (left). The finished pasty should have a D-shape.

Brush the beaten egg over the surface of the pasties, arrange them on a baking sheet lined with non-stick baking paper and place in the oven. After 10 minutes, turn the oven down to 160°C/gas mark 3 and bake for a further 30 minutes, or until the pasties are well browned and crisp. Remove from the oven and leave to cool on a wire rack for a few minutes before serving. These can be wrapped in foil and kept in the fridge for up to 4 days.

APPLE TURNOVERS

✳ Serves 1–2 ✳ Preparation time 5 minutes ✳ Cooking time 15–20 minutes

Here is a handy way of using up off-cuts of puff or flaky shortcrust pastry. You can adjust the quantities of the other ingredients depending on how much leftover pastry you have. Mrs Beeton suggested making fruit turnovers for a picnic. Hers were smaller – better for using up small amounts of leftover pastry, but they didn't leave much room for any filling. This larger size gives a better balance of flavours.

plain flour, for dusting

100g puff or flaky shortcrust pastry off-cuts

80g unsweetened apple purée

1 egg white

1 tsp granulated sugar, plus extra for sprinkling

Preheat the oven to 200°C/gas mark 6. Scatter some flour over your work surface. Place the pastry on the surface and roll it out to a 16cm square about 2mm thick.

Spoon the apple purée into the centre then dampen 2 sides of the pastry with a little water. Pull one corner over to form a triangle. Press the edges together firmly to seal. Now whisk the egg white with 1 tsp sugar and brush the mixture all over the surface of the pastry. Sprinkle with a little more granulated sugar, and then carefully lift the turnover onto a baking sheet lined with non-stick baking paper. Place in the oven for 15–20 minutes, or until the turnover is well browned and crisp.

Remove from the oven, leave to cool on a wire rack for a few minutes and serve with Jersey cream.

DEEP APPLE PIE

✳ Serves 8 ✳ Preparation time 25 minutes plus 30 minutes chilling time
✳ Cooking time 45 minutes plus 10 minutes cooling time

In the years since Mrs Beeton published her book the Bramley apple has arrived on the scene and has come to dominate to such an extent that other varieties of cooking apple are rarely seen for sale. Bramleys taste particularly sharp, so if you have access to a different variety you will need to adjust the quantity of sugar to taste.

1½ quantities flaky shortcrust pastry (see page 216)

1½ kg peeled and cored cooking apples

150g plus 1 tbsp caster sugar

1 tbsp lemon juice

1 egg white

2 tbsp granulated sugar, for dredging

special equipment

a deep 22–25cm pie dish and a temperature probe

Make the flaky shortcrust pastry, cover and chill for 30 minutes. Meanwhile, cut the prepared apples into 3mm thick slices and place them in a bowl. Sprinkle over 150g sugar and the lemon juice, stir well and leave to macerate for 5–10 minutes. Preheat the oven to 200°C/gas mark 6.

Roll the pastry into a circle 16cm larger than the diameter of your pie dish. Pile the apple and any juice into dish – it will come high above the rim. Moisten the rim of the pie dish with water. Now cut a 4mm strip from around the outside of the pastry circle and attach it to the rim of the pie dish. Moisten this with a little water and drape the circle of pastry over top to form a lid, sealing well by crimping the edges of the pastry together. Cut away any surplus pastry and reserve.

Cut a 4cm cross in the top of the pie and fold back the four parts to leave a hole for steam to escape. Use any pastry trimmings to make a few leaves as a decoration to surround the hole, but set them aside for the moment.

Beat the egg white with 1 tbsp caster sugar and brush this mixture onto the top of the pie. Now add the leaves as decoration and brush again. Dredge the surface of the pie with the granulated sugar. Place the pie on a baking sheet and set in the centre of the oven for 45 minutes. If the pie browns very quickly, reduce the heat to 160°C/gas mark 3.

At the end of the cooking time, insert a temperature probe into the pie. If it reads 85°C the pie is done. Remove the pie from oven and leave to cool for 10 minutes then serve it warm with Jersey cream.

ECCLES CAKES

✳ **Makes 6–8 large cakes** ✳ **Prep time 10 minutes** ✳ **Cooking time 35 minutes**

Mrs Beeton's mince pies were made with puff pastry rather than the shortcrust that is more often used today, giving a result that is strongly reminiscent of Eccles cakes. As there is already a faithfully rendered Mrs Beeton mince pie recipe on page 228, her mincemeat filling has been replaced here with a simple mixture of currants and lemon zest to give a true Eccles cake. Although Mrs Beeton may not have approved, these are delicious served with some good Cheshire or Lancashire cheese. If you've got some homemade puff pastry (see pages 218–219) in the freezer, thaw out 500g and use it here.

500g currants

125g unsalted butter

125g caster sugar, plus an extra pinch

zest of 2 lemons

plain flour, for dusting

500g puff pastry (see pages 218–219)

1 egg white, beaten

pinch caster sugar

granulated sugar, for dredging

special equipment

a 10–12cm round pastry cutter

Preheat the oven to 200°C/gas mark 6 and line a baking sheet with non-stick baking paper. Place the currants, butter, caster sugar and lemon zest in a small pan over a low heat. Cook, stirring, for 5 minutes then remove from the heat and leave to cool.

Scatter some flour onto your work surface and roll the puff pastry out to a 3–4mm thick sheet. Cut out 6–8 rounds using a cutter (or a small saucer). Re-roll any trimmings if you need to.

Divide the filling between the circles and dampen the edges of the pastry with a little water. Bring the edges together, making sure the filling is covered, and pinch hard, twisting off any excess. Turn the balls over, flattening them slightly, keeping their shape circular. Place on the prepared baking sheet.

Mix the beaten egg white with a pinch of caster sugar and brush the mixture over the cakes, then sprinkle them heavily with granulated sugar. Finally, cut a 2cm slit in the top of each.

Bake for 20 minutes, or until the cakes are brown and crispy then turn the heat down to 140°C/gas mark 1 for a further 15 minutes. The cakes are ready when the undersides are browned and firm. Remove to a cooling rack. Once the cakes are completely cold, they can be stored in an airtight tin for up to 3 days.

SAUSAGE ROLLS

✳ **Makes approx 20 mini sausage rolls or 10 larger ones** ✳ **Preparation time 15–30 minutes**
✳ **Cooking time 15–20 minutes**

A Mrs Beeton classic, this recipe is unchanged from the original except for the addition of a little cream to the egg yolk, giving the finished rolls a pleasing shine. Sausage rolls make a great lunch served with good English ale.

plain flour, for dusting

500g puff pastry (see pages 218–219)

500g sausage meat

1 tbsp chopped herbs of your choice (optional)

large pinch salt

1 egg yolk

1 tsp single cream

Preheat the oven to 200°C/gas mark 6 and line a baking tray with non-stick baking parchment. Dust your work surface with a little flour. Divide the puff pastry in half and roll each piece out into a 14 x 44cm rectangle.

Mix the sausage meat with the herbs, if using, and salt, then divide the mixture in half and roll each piece into a sausage shape 44cm long. Place the sausage meat on the rolled-out pastry, leaving 2cm bare along one long edge where the pastry will join. Fold the pastry over the meat to make a long roll, ensuring that no air is trapped inside. Whisk the egg yolk and cream together and brush the mixture over the inside edges, then pinch together to form a good seal, pressing down with a fork, and trim off any surplus, leaving a neat 1cm join to one side of the roll.

Brush all over the surface with the egg wash, then, using a sharp knife, divide the sausage roll crossways into either 10 large sausage rolls or 20 smaller ones. Arrange the sausage rolls on the prepared baking tray and place in the oven. If you are making mini sausage rolls, bake them for 15–20 minutes. The larger sausage rolls need 20 minutes in the oven, and then a further 10 minutes at 180°C/gas mark 4 to ensure the pastry is cooked through.

MINCE PIES

❋ Makes 12 deep pies ❋ Preparation time 20 minutes plus 1 hour chilling time
❋ Cooking time 35 minutes

The best thing about these mince pies is that they are made in good-sized tins – muffin tins are just right for the job. The result is that you get more filling than usual. The pastry is midway between the 'puff paste' specified by Mrs Beeton and the more usual shortcrust; the glaze, containing just egg white and sugar, is unusual too. The original recipe doesn't specify how much sugar to use, but here there is lots, to give a really crisp, light crust to the top of the pies.

2 quantities flaky shortcrust pastry (see page 216)

plain flour, for dusting

600g lemon mincemeat (see page 369), made 2–3 months ahead

1 egg white

2 tbsp caster sugar

granulated sugar, for dredging

special equipment

10cm and 5cm round pastry cutters and a deep 12-hole muffin tin

Make the flaky shortcrust pastry and chill it for 30 minutes. Just before the chilling time is over preheat the oven to 200°C/gas mark 6.

Dust your work surface with flour and roll out the pastry on it to a thickness of 3mm. Stamp out 12 rounds 10cm in size and 12 rounds 5cm in size.

Gently press each of the larger disks into one of the 12 holes of the muffin tin, making sure that the edge of the pastry sits slightly proud of the top edge. Divide the mincemeat evenly among the lined muffin-tin holes.

Moisten the edges of the small pastry discs and place each one on top of a pie. Crimp the edges of the pastry together to make a good seal to prevent the mincemeat boiling out. Whisk together the egg white and the caster sugar and brush this mixture over the tops of the pies. Dredge each pie with a little granulated sugar and pierce a hole in centre of each lid with sharp knife or a skewer.

Bake for 10 minutes, or until well browned on top, then reduce the heat to 160°C/gas mark 3. Bake for a further 25 minutes, or until the pies are deep golden brown. Remove the tin from the oven and leave to cool for a few minutes on a wire rack. Then carefully lift the pies from the muffin tin while they are still warm and place on a cooling rack. They are delicious eaten warm with clotted cream. They can be stored in an airtight tin for up to 3 days.

PLUM FRANGIPANE TART

✳ Serves 8 ✳ Preparation time 15 minutes plus 1 hour 30 minutes–2 hours 30 minutes chilling time ✳ Cooking time 1 hour 20 minutes

This elegant tart presents a perfect balance of fruit to almond frangipane. Mrs Beeton was a fan of filled pastry tarts, giving many recipes for all manner of nuts and grains that could be used in the filling. Following her lead, ground rice can be substituted for the almonds used here if you have a nut allergy – the resulting texture is pleasantly fine.

1 quantity sweet pastry
(see page 220)

150g softened unsalted butter

150g caster sugar

3 eggs

½ tsp almond extract

150g ground almonds

scant 2 tbsp plain flour, sifted,
plus extra for dusting

3 tbsp damson or plum jam

600g small purple plums,
stoned and quartered

2 tbsp flaked almonds

special equipment

a 22cm loose-bottomed
tart tin and some baking beans

Make the sweet pastry, cover and chill for 1–2 hours. When it has finished chilling, roll the pastry out to a 30cm circle. Flour your fingers and transfer it to the tart tin, pressing it carefully into the bottom and allowing any extra pastry to hang over the edge. This helps to prevent shrinkage during cooking. Cover the tin loosely with cling film and chill for 20 minutes. Preheat the oven to 200°C/gas mark 6.

Line the chilled pastry case with non-stick baking paper and fill it with baking beans. Bake for 20 minutes, then turn the oven down to 160°C/gas mark 3 for a further 15–20 minutes, or until the pastry is cooked through. Once the pastry case is cooked, remove the paper and beans from the tin carefully. If there are any cracks, roll some of the excess pastry trimmings between your fingers to make it pliable and use it to fill the gaps. Return the case to the oven and bake for a further 5 minutes, or until it is evenly brown, then remove it from the oven and set it on a wire rack to cool. Turn the oven up to 180°C/gas mark 4.

Cream the butter with the sugar until light and fluffy then mix in the eggs and almond extract. Fold in the ground almonds and sifted flour and set aside. Now spread the jam evenly over the bottom of the tart case. Pour in the almond mixture, spreading it to the edges to cover the jam, then arrange the quartered plums on top, pushing them lightly into the almond mixture. Sprinkle over the flaked almonds.

Bake for 35–40 minutes, or until the almond mixture is evenly browned and firm. Let stand for a few minutes, then trim any excess pastry from the edges, remove the tart from the tin and leave to cool a little. Serve with clotted cream.

PORK PIES

✳ Serves 12 ✳ Preparation time 1 hour ✳ Cooking time 1 hour 30 minutes

Mrs Beeton made raised pies using various different meats, but the humble pork pie is the one that has stood the test of time. You can make these in deep cake tins with thin walls if you cannot find proper pork pie tins. The jelly, added after the pies are cooked, was originally a thick jellied stock, but dark pork or chicken stock combined with gelatine ensures a firm set. The pies should be made 1–2 days before eating.

1 quantity hot water pastry (see page 219)

lard or butter, for greasing

1.75kg pork mince, ideally half shoulder and half belly from a free-range pig

250g dry-cure bacon, chopped small

6g ground white pepper

20g salt

8g ground mace

1 egg yolk

1 tbsp milk

500ml pork or light chicken stock (see page 23)

3 leaves gelatine

special equipment

2 x 17cm pork pie tins or cake tins and a temperature probe

Make the hot water pastry and while it is cooling for the final 5 minutes preheat the oven to 200°C/gas mark 6. Grease the tins with a little lard or butter and line the base of each with non-stick baking paper.

Line the tins while the pastry is still warm and malleable. You will need one-quarter of the pastry for the lids, rolled out into two 17cm circles. Roll the remainder, for the pie bases and sides, into two 35cm circles and then use these to line the tins, pressing the pastry right into the corners and making sure there are no gaps. Leave an overhang of 2cm for sealing the lids.

Place the pork mince, bacon, white pepper, salt and mace into a bowl and mix it well together. Then divide the mixture between the 2 pastry-lined tins.

Wet the edges of the lids with water and place on top of the meat, pushing the circles right to the edges of the meat. Fold the overhanging pastry over the lids and crimp these well together. Make a hole in centre of each lid and insert a rolled-up piece of foil to make a chimney for steam to escape through.

Whisk the egg yolk and milk together and brush the tops of the pies with the mixture, then place them in the oven. After 1 hour turn the heat down to 160°C/gas mark 3. Do not worry if the pies begin to weep, simply wipe the liquid away. After a further 30 minutes the pies should be a rich, golden-brown colour. Insert a temperature probe into the centre of one of the pies and if it reads 85°C the pies are cooked.

Transfer to a wire rack to cool and carefully remove the foil chimneys.

While the pies are cooling, soak the gelatine leaves in a small bowl of cold water for 10 minutes. Place the stock in a saucepan over medium heat. When the gelatine leaves are ready, squeeze them to get rid of any excess water and add them to the stock, stirring to dissolve.

Pour half the stock (about 250ml) slowly and gently through the hole in the lid of one of the pies, then repeat with the second pie. The liquid will find its way between the pastry and meat and set as the pie cools. Leave the pies in their tins until they are completely cold, then turn them out and store in a cool place wrapped in foil for 1–2 days before serving. They will keep like this for up to 1 week.

PUDDINGS & DESSERTS

PUDDINGS AND COLD DESSERTS

From the lightest lemon posset to a luscious trifle with its complex layering, puddings are a delicious way to end a meal. They should strike a balance between sheer decadence and perfect good taste, and each should fit its occasion. Choose a pudding well, and make it expertly, and your meals will be legendary among your friends and family.

Cold puddings

A chilled dessert is lovely at the end of a summer lunch or dinner, and because the British summer provides us with such lovely berries, one need look no further than a posset or cremet, or perhaps a custard to accompany macerated strawberries or raspberries (served at room temperature for the best flavour). Fruit jellies offer an excellent, light-handed way of making vibrantly fresh desserts to round off a rich meal. The two given here, for strawberry and raspberry jellies (see pages 261 and 262) will be a revelation to anyone who makes them.

Of course, cold puddings are not limited only to the months of summer. Poached autumn fruits such as pears, or winter fruit, such as rhubarb, make delicious accompaniments to a serving of homemade cream cheese (see page 205). Seville oranges are a truly seasonal fruit, and only available in the depths of winter. But don't just save them for marmalade. The zest is delicious and can be used to scent custards wonderfully.

For an added indulgence, cold puddings are delicious served with a homemade biscuit or two.

Hot puddings

On a cold day, the rich, seductive aroma of a chocolate soufflé (see page 250) or the nutmeg-scented fragrance of a rice pudding (see page 238) heralds the arrival of perfect comfort food.

Traditional hot puddings are usually mixtures of flour, suet and fruit that have been bound together in a cloth and then boiled or steamed. However, in this chapter there are other traditional hot puddings, such as Bakewell and lemon puddings (see pages 240 and 267), which are set in pastry cases and baked rather than steamed. Serve these hot puddings in warmed bowls, preferably with Jersey cream or custard (see pages 343 and 345).

Fruit puddings

Fruit is an incredibly versatile ingredient, and is widely used in puddings and desserts. In addition, many of the simple creams and custards in this chapter are delicious served with fresh or poached fruit alongside. Choose whatever is in season, and cook it lightly with a little sugar and lemon or orange juice.

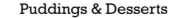
Chocolate

Plain chocolate with a high percentage of cocoa (usually more than 60%) is the best type of chocolate for cooking with. As the percentage of cocoa increases, the percentage of other ingredients, mostly sugar, decreases. Professional cooking chocolate or couverture is 'tempered', a process involving heating and cooling it under certain conditions. The result is a chocolate that breaks cleanly and melts sublimely. Milk chocolate contains a high proportion of milk solids and, consequently, has a lower cocoa content. White chocolate contains only cocoa butter from the cocoa beans, and has no cocoa mass at all.

Always melt chocolate slowly. All forms of chocolate should be kept in a cool dark environment, and it is best to only buy what you need, as chocolate stales quickly.

A NOTE ON GELATINE

Gelatine, which is derived from cartilage-rich animal tissues and bones, is the most commonly used setting agent in the kitchen today. Historically, other substances have been used as setting agents, including carageen moss (a seaweed), isinglass (derived from the swim bladders of fish) and agar agar (another seaweed derivative).

Gelatine can be bought in powdered form, but clear, brittle sheet gelatine has a finer flavour, gives a more accurate result and is easier to measure. In the course of testing the recipes for this book, we tested all of the different types of gelatine available. Platinum grade sheets weighing approximately 1.6g each are the best type, and are easy to obtain. Three sheets of this gelatine are sufficient to give a light set to 500ml of jelly served in a glass. If you want to use a mould and will need to turn the jelly out, use four sheets per 500ml.

To use leaf gelatine

Cover sheets of leaf gelatine in cold water for a minimum of 10 minutes to soften them. Give them a squeeze and then add them to the warm liquid that is specified in the particular recipe you are following, stirring to dissolve them. They will not dissolve if the water is cold.

Vegetarian gelatine can be bought, but will set while still quite warm, making it difficult to use with cold mousses (because it needs to be used warm, which tends to melt the cream when mixed). It is suitable for fruit jellies, however. Simply follow the manufacturer's instructions.

BAKED RICE PUDDING

✳ **Serves 4** ✳ **Preparation time 5 minutes** ✳ **Cooking time 3 hours including resting time**

Mrs Beeton wrote of rice that 'Baking it in puddings is the best mode of preparing it.' She had several recipes for rice puddings, most of which were boiled on the stove, but this baked version is fuss-free and can even cook alongside your roast if you have more than one oven. The key to making a good rice pudding is in allowing plenty of time for the rice to cook – and you will note that this dish can seem very liquid up until the final third of the cooking time, when the rice begins to swell.

500ml whole milk (Jersey for preference)

30g caster sugar

15g unsalted butter

50g pudding rice

1 bay leaf (optional)

nutmeg, freshly grated to taste

special equipment

a 17cm square baking dish, 3–4cm deep

Preheat the oven to 140°C/gas mark 1.

Place the milk and sugar in a saucepan over a medium heat. Add the butter and stir until the milk is hot and the butter has melted.

Put the rice into the baking dish. Pour over the heated milk mixture, add the bay leaf, if using, and stir well.

Bake for 2 ½ hours, giving the pudding a stir about every 30 minutes.

Remove from oven and grate a little nutmeg over top. Turn oven up to 160°C/gas mark 3, and return the pudding to the oven for 15 minutes.

Remove the bay leaf, if using, and leave the finished pudding to rest in a warm place for 10 minutes. Serve with warmed jam or bottled fruits (see page 361).

BAKEWELL PUDDING

✳ **Serves 6** ✳ **Preparation time 20 minutes plus 30 minutes resting time**
✳ **Cooking time 1 hour 25 minutes**

This lovely pudding is one of the treasures of this book. Mrs Beeton used puff pastry for her Bakewell pudding, but a well-baked shortcrust tart case is a better match, giving a crisp contrast to the rich, silky filling. Use homemade raspberry jam (see page 354) if you have it, or choose a sharp conserve to contrast with the sweet filling.

½ **quantity shortcrust pastry
(see page 215)**

for the filling

115g butter

160g caster sugar

30g ground almonds

5 egg yolks and 1 egg white

80g sharp, best-quality
raspberry jam

special equipment

a deep 22cm metal pie dish
and some baking beans

First make the pastry and leave it to rest in the fridge for 20 minutes. Then, roll the pastry out on a floured surface to a 27cm round. Place it in the pie dish, leaving the extra pastry hanging over the edge. Line the pastry with a large piece of non-stick baking paper and then fill with baking beans. Leave to rest in a cool place for 10 minutes.

Preheat the oven to 200°C/gas mark 6.

Place the pastry case on a baking tray and bake for 35 minutes until firm and golden brown. Remove the beans and paper and return the case to the oven for 5 minutes to bake further and dry slightly. Remove from the oven and set aside. Reduce the oven to 160°C/gas mark 3.

Make the filling by melting the butter in a medium pan over a low heat. Remove from the heat, and add the sugar, ground almonds and eggs, beating well to combine.

Spread the jam into the pastry case and carefully pour over the filling. Bake for 15 minutes, then turn the oven to 140°C/gas mark 1 for a further 30 minutes until the filling is just firm to the touch. Trim the pastry hanging over the rim with a sharp knife and cool to room temperature before serving.

BAKED BREAD PUDDING

* **Makes 12 servings** * **Preparation time 40 minutes including soaking time**
* **Cooking time 50 minutes**

Bread pudding is an enduring classic which, although it was clearly invented as a means of using up old bread, is delicious enough to hold its own among more extravagant, less thrifty desserts. Mrs Beeton's version has a nice mix of citrus and almond and is delicious hot or cold.

350g stale brown bread, crusts removed

40g caster sugar

40g soft brown sugar

70g candied peel

140g sultanas

¼ tsp ground cinnamon

¼ tsp freshly grated nutmeg

450ml milk

⅛ tsp almond essence

3 medium eggs

80g unsalted butter, plus extra for greasing

1 tbsp brandy

2 tbsp demerara sugar, for sprinkling

special equipment

a deep 22 x 17cm baking dish

Tear the stale bread into 2cm pieces and place in a large bowl. Add the sugars, candied peel, sultanas and spices and toss gently to mix.

In another bowl beat the milk, almond essence and eggs together and then pour into the bread mixture. Mix well and leave the ingredients to soak for 30 minutes.

Preheat the oven to 160°C/gas mark 3 and butter the baking dish.

Melt the butter in a small saucepan over a high heat until it is foaming, then beat into the bread mixture. Add the brandy and mix well until all the ingredients are combined.

Pour the mixture into the baking dish and sprinkle over the Demerara sugar.

Cook at 160°C/gas mark 3 for 20 minutes then turn the oven down to 150°C/gas mark 2 for 30 minutes until set and golden brown.

Just before the pudding is cooked, preheat the grill to hot. Place the finished pudding under the grill for about 2 minutes, or until the top has caramelised. Serve with plain yoghurt on the side.

PLUM CRUMBLE

✳ **Serves 4** ✳ **Preparation time 15 minutes** ✳ **Cooking time 45 minutes**

Although the fruit crumble as we know it today is most likely of twentieth-century origin, Mrs Beeton suggested scattering breadcrumbs over at least one of her fruit puddings as an economical alternative to pastry. The recipe below is for a modern crumble topping: light, crisp and perfect for plums – or other fruits such as gooseberries or apples. Just vary the amount of sugar you use, remembering that the fruit will taste slightly sweeter once it's hot.

700g ripe plums, stoned and quartered

50g caster sugar, to taste

for the crumble topping

125g self-raising flour

50g ground almonds

100g unsalted butter

80g caster sugar

special equipment

a 23 x 17cm baking dish

Preheat the oven to 180°C/gas mark 4.

Put the quartered plums into the baking dish, add the sugar and toss to coat. Taste a piece for sweetness and add a little more sugar if required.

Make the crumble topping by placing the flour, almonds, butter and sugar in the bowl of a food processor. Blend until the mixture resembles fine breadcrumbs then pulse the machine until the mixture begins to come together a little. Alternatively, grate the butter into the flour in a large bowl and rub in with your fingers, then add the almonds and sugar.

Spread the crumble evenly over the plums, then lightly smooth the surface. Place the dish on a baking tray to catch any drips and transfer to the oven.

Bake for 15 minutes, then reduce the heat to 160°C/gas mark 3, and continue cooking for another 30 minutes until the top is golden and the mixture is bubbling. Serve with custard (see pages 343 and 345) or Jersey cream.

STEAMED BLACKCURRANT PUDDING

✳ **Serves 6** ✳ **Preparation time 20 minutes plus 10 minutes resting time**
✳ **Cooking time 3 hours**

Mrs Beeton's recipe for a blackcurrant, or gooseberry, pudding steamed in a suet crust may sound formidable, but this is a splendid thing – steaming, vivid purple with the juice from the fruits, and with an intensity of flavour you will rarely find.

butter, for greasing

**1 ½ quantities suet pastry
(see page 217)**

for the filling

**400g fresh or frozen
blackcurrants, picked weight**

150g caster sugar

special equipment

**a 2-litre pudding basin and a
pastry cutter or muffin ring**

Grease the pudding basin and set aside. Make the suet pastry and leave it to rest for 10 minutes. Roll out two-thirds of the pastry and use it to line the pudding basin. Roll out the remainder to make the lid.

Thoroughly combine the fruit and sugar in a bowl. Transfer the mixture into the dough-lined pudding basin.

Wet the top edge of the pastry, and place the lid on. Gently seal the edges and trim off any excess pastry.

Take a large piece of greaseproof paper and pleat it down the centre to allow room for expansion during steaming. Cover the top of the pudding with this and then a pleated layer of foil and secure with kitchen string around the edge of the basin, leaving some extra string to make a handle for lifting the pudding basin.

Fill the kettle with water and bring to a boil. Place a pastry cutter or muffin ring in the bottom of a 4-litre pan and set it on the hob. Set the pudding basin on the ring in the bottom of the pan (this ensures that the basin does not crack) and add boiling water to a depth of 15cm. Turn the heat under the pan to medium and bring the water to a simmer. Continue simmering over low heat for 3 hours, topping up with boiling water as necessary.

After 3 hours, lift the pudding basin out of the pot and remove the paper and foil lid. Turn the pastry out of the basin onto a serving dish. Serve with custard (see pages 343 and 345) or Jersey cream.

CHRISTMAS PUDDING

* Makes 3 x 500g puddings * Preparation time 1 hour
* Cooking time 4 hours initial steaming, then 3 hours to reheat

Mrs Beeton gave several recipes for plum and other Christmas puddings; this recipe takes the best elements from each. Only a small amount of egg is used to bind the mixture, resulting in a lighter, fruitier pudding – but it is essential to use high-quality dried fruit.

butter, for greasing

170g extra-large Muscatel (Lexia) raisins

170g currants

170g sultanas

115g dark muscovado sugar

1 tbsp black treacle

225g white breadcrumbs

2 medium eggs

170g grated suet

50g chopped candied peel

zest of ½ lemon, finely grated

¼ tsp freshly grated nutmeg

¼ tsp ground cinnamon

100ml Jubilee Stout or milk, to mix

few drops almond extract

special equipment

3 x 500ml pudding basins and a pastry cutter or muffin ring

Butter the pudding basins well. Mix all of the rest of the ingredients together in a large bowl ensuring that everything is well blended. Divide the mixture between the 3 basins.

Take 3 pieces of greaseproof paper and make a pleat down the centre of each to allow room for expansion during steaming. Cover the top of each pudding with a pleated piece of greaseproof paper followed by a pleated piece of foil and secure by tying kitchen string around the edge of the basin, leaving some extra string to make a handle for lifting the pudding.

If you have a large steamer, steam all of the puddings at once, ensuring that the steamer does not boil dry. Alternatively, steam each pudding in turn, keeping them in the fridge until you are ready to cook them.

If you do not have a steamer, fill the kettle with water and bring to a boil. Place a pastry cutter or muffin ring in the base of a 4-litre pan and put it on the hob. Set 1 of the 3 pudding basins on the ring in the bottom of the pan (this ensures that the basin does not crack) and add boiling water to a depth of 15cm. Turn the heat under the pan to medium and bring the water to a simmer. Continue simmering over low heat for 4 hours, topping up with boiling water as necessary. Steam each pudding in turn.

When the puddings are cold, wrap them in foil and store in a cool dark place for up to 1 year.

BREAD & BUTTER PUDDING

✳ **Serves 6** ✳ **Preparation time 20 minutes plus 30 mintues soaking time**
✳ **Cooking time 50 minutes plus 5 minutes resting time**

Mrs Beeton recommends grated citrus peel for her bread and butter pudding, but a spoonful or two of marmalade gives a sweeter zing that sets this dish off perfectly. You can vary the richness of the pudding by altering the ratio of cream to milk.

800ml mixed cream and milk, half of each

120g caster sugar

4 medium eggs

4 yolks

75g softened unsalted butter

300g stale sliced bread

75g marmalade (or the grated zest of 1 orange)

25g granulated sugar

special equipment

a 20cm square ovenproof dish and a large roasting tin

Place the mixed milk and cream in a saucepan over a medium heat, add half the sugar and stir. Meanwhile, in a large bowl, beat the eggs and yolks with the remaining sugar until light and fluffy. When the milk mixture reaches simmering, pour it into the egg mixture and beat to amalgamate. Quickly strain it through a sieve into a large, cold bowl and set aside.

Butter the sliced bread and then spread with marmalade. Cut the slices in half and then arrange them overlapping in the ovenproof dish with the crusts uppermost.

Carefully pour the custard over the bread. Leave to stand for 30 minutes, or until all the liquid has been absorbed. Sprinkle over the granulated sugar.

Preheat the oven to 140°C/gas mark 1. Fill the kettle and bring to a boil. Place the ovenproof dish in a large roasting tin. Pour in enough boiling water to come halfway up sides of the dish. Bake for 50 minutes, or until lightly set and golden brown.

Remove from the oven and let the pudding sit for 5 minutes to rest before serving.

PANCAKES

* **Makes 12–15** * **Preparation time 10 minutes plus 10 minutes resting time**
* **Cooking time 30–45 minutes**

Mrs Beeton's basic pancake recipe is accompanied by the note that 'pancakes are almost never good unless eaten almost immediately they come from the frying pan' – advice worth heeding. She served them with 'sifted sugar and a cut lemon', much as we do in Britain today.

225g plain flour

600ml milk

3 medium eggs

small pinch salt

large pinch caster sugar

25g butter, melted

50ml clarified butter, to cook (see glossary)

to serve

caster sugar or honey

lemon wedges

special equipment

a 17–20cm frying pan or crêpe pan

Preheat oven to 220°C/gas mark 7. Mix the flour, milk and eggs together with the salt and sugar in a bowl. Whisk until the batter is free of lumps, then leave to stand in a cool place for at least 10 minutes, or until required. Strain the batter through a fine sieve into a jug and stir in the melted butter.

Line the frying pan with ½ tsp clarified butter and set it over a medium to high heat. When it is hot, pour in a little batter, swirling the pan to encourage the batter to cover the entire base. Cook the pancake for 1–2 minutes on each side, or until it is golden brown and firm. Remove to a plate. If you are not serving the pancakes immediately, layer them with non-stick baking paper and keep them warm on a plate in a low oven. Continue making pancakes until all of the batter has been used up.

To reheat, simply drop each pancake back into a hot pan and cook for 30 seconds on each side.

Serve with a sprinkling of sugar or honey and a squeeze of lemon.

CHOCOLATE SOUFFLE

※ **Serves 4 people** ※ **Preparation time 20 minutes** ※ **Cooking time 10 minutes**

This lovely soufflé is a perfect dinner-party dessert. The flour has been removed from Mrs Beeton's recipe because it is not really necessary; without it, this dish has the advantage of being gluten free. It is delicious served with vanilla ice cream.

to line the ramekins

softened butter, for greasing

1 tsp cocoa powder

1 tsp caster sugar

for the soufflé

80g plain chocolate (65–72% minimum cocoa solids)

3 medium eggs

1 ½ tbsp caster sugar

1 tbsp brandy (optional)

special equipment

4 x 120ml ramekins, a large heatproof bowl and a roasting tin

Preheat the oven to 200°C/gas mark 6.

Butter the ramekins well, taking care to ensure the top edge is buttered to allow the soufflé to rise without sticking. Combine the cocoa powder and sugar together and sprinkle a little of the mixture into each ramekin, rolling it around until the insides are coated. Set the ramekins aside until needed.

Break up the chocolate and place it in a large heatproof bowl set over a pan of barely simmering water, making sure that the bottom of the bowl does not touch the water. Do not stir vigorously, but stir occasionally to make sure that the chocolate does not seize on the bottom of the bowl and go stiff.

Place the eggs and sugar in the bowl of an electric mixer and beat until the mixture is mousse-like and very pale and thick. Alternatively, whisk with an electric handwhisk.

When the chocolate has fully melted, remove it from the heat and fold in one-third of the egg mixture. Then, working quickly and carefully, fold in the remaining egg mixture, along with the brandy, if liked.

Divide the mixture between the ramekins, wiping off any spills. Place them in a roasting tin and add enough boiling water to reach halfway up the sides of the ramekins.

Place in the oven for 10 minutes until risen but still a little soft in the middle and serve immediately.

BAKED APPLE DUMPLINGS

* Makes 4 dumplings * Preparation time 30 minutes * Cooking time 35 minutes

This dessert is simple and splendid. The original recipe doesn't include the spices, but who would serve baked apples without a touch of cinnamon and nutmeg today?

1 quantity suet pastry
(see page 217)

for the filling

4 cooking apples,
peeled and cored

80g unsalted butter, melted

4 tbsp caster sugar

½ tsp nutmeg, freshly grated

2 tsp ground cinnamon

for the glaze

1 egg white, beaten with
1 tbsp granulated sugar

granulated sugar, for dredging

Preheat the oven to 200°C/gas mark 6. Line a baking tray with non-stick baking paper.

Make the suet pastry, divide it into four pieces and leave in a cool place to rest while you peel and core the apples. Roll the apples in the melted butter to coat each one.

Mix the sugar, nutmeg and cinnamon in a large basin. Add the prepared apples and gently toss them to coat inside and out with the spice mixture.

Roll each piece of pastry into a round about 3mm thick, and big enough to cover an apple.

Place an apple in centre of each round, dampen the edges of the pastry with cold water and pull together over the apple. Crimp the edges securely. Place each pastry-wrapped apple on the baking tray.

Brush the egg white and sugar glaze all over the pastry, then dredge each apple with additional granulated sugar.

Bake for 10 minutes then reduce the heat to 140°C/gas mark 1 for 25 minutes, until the apples are cooked. Serve with Jersey cream.

CURRANT DUMPLINGS

✳ **Serves 4** ✳ **Preparation time 15 minutes** ✳ **Cooking time 1 hour 30 minutes**

This recipe is classic Mrs Beeton – simple, economical and delicious. The currants add a note of sweetness while the salted butter and lemon work together beautifully. A wedge of lemon and some salted butter are all you need to serve it with.

225g self-raising flour

110g currants

85g suet

140ml milk

to serve

1 lemon, quartered

cold salted butter

special equipment

4 x 20cm square pieces of butter muslin

Mix all the ingredients together in a bowl and bring together with your hands to form a soft dough. Divide the dough into 4 equal pieces, shaping each one into a dumpling.

Tie each piece loosely in a sheet of butter muslin and secure it with kitchen string. Place a large saucepan of water over a medium heat and bring to simmering point. Carefully place the dumplings into the water, making sure they are submerged and leave them to simmer for 1½ hours. Simmer the pan with the lid on, topping up with boiling water if necessary.

Remove the dumplings from the water using long-handled tongs and carefully unwrap them. Set the dumplings on a plate lined with kitchen paper to dry for 2–3 minutes, and then serve with a wedge of lemon and a knob of butter. Or, if you are making these ahead, leave them in their muslin wrapping and allow them to cool. Just before you are ready to serve the puddings, reheat them in a pan of boiling water for 20 minutes, unwrap, dry and serve as above.

GOOSEBERRY FOOL

✳ **Serves 4** ✳ **Preparation time 10 minutes** ✳ **Cooking time 10 minutes**

We commonly make gooseberry fool with cream these days as opposed to the more liquid form that Mrs Beeton gives with milk. This recipe gives a light fool that will just hold its shape, and which is perfect when eaten with shortbread. Red varieties of gooseberry can be used in place of the green, but you will need to reduce the quantity of sugar to taste.

400g freshly picked green gooseberries, topped and tailed

50g caster sugar, to taste

200ml double cream

shortbread (see page 303), to serve

Place the gooseberries and sugar into a saucepan over a medium heat and simmer gently for about 10 minutes, until the gooseberries break down. Remove from heat and beat with a whisk to break them up further.

Add 1 tsp sugar to the cream and lightly whip. Fold the whipped cream into the mashed gooseberries with a large metal spoon, until just combined.

Spoon the fool into 4 glasses and chill until ready to serve. Offer the gooseberry fool with a piece of shortbread on the side.

LEMON CREMET

✳ **Serves 4** ✳ **Preparation time 20 minutes spread over 2 days**

Cooks of Mrs Beeton's era were used to making their own curds and light cheeses – they had to. This recipe demonstrates just how easy it is to turn curds into a delightful summer dessert. Try it with homemade shortbread (see page 303).

1 quantity homemade cream cheese (see page 205)

finely grated zest of 1 lemon

100ml Jersey pouring cream

caster sugar, to sprinkle

350g poached rhubarb, raspberries or bottled plums (seep page 277 or 361), to serve

Make the cream cheese.

Beat the lemon zest into the cream cheese and then shape it into a mound on a pretty serving dish. Pour over the Jersey cream. Sprinkle with a little caster sugar and serve accompanied by the prepared fruit of your choice.

ICED VANILLA PARFAIT

❋ Serves 6–8 ❋ Preparation time 30 minutes ❋ Freezing time 4 hours

Mrs Beeton gives lots of recipes for frozen fruit purées, which are made into ice creams with double cream. These are delicious, but fiddly to make at home without an ice cream machine. An alternative recipe is this one for a parfait, which is easier to make and does not require constant stirring once it has been moved to the freezer.

4 egg yolks

seeds scraped from 3 vanilla pods

120g caster sugar

400ml double cream

special equipment

a small loaf tin and a balloon whisk

Line the loaf tin with cling film, leaving some overhanging to cover the parfait when made, and place on a level surface in the freezer.

Place the egg yolks and vanilla seeds into the bowl of an electric mixer fitted with the whisk attachment and whisk at high speed until the yolks are very light and pale and have tripled in volume. Meanwhile, place the sugar and 30ml water into a small pan over a high heat to dissolve the sugar. Let it simmer for 2 minutes to make a syrup, but be sure not to let it caramelise. With the electric mixer still running, steadily pour the hot syrup into the yolks and leave the mixer running until the mixture cools.

Place the cream into a bowl and whisk until it reaches a loose but whipped consistency, just before the soft peak stage. If it is too stiff it will be difficult to incorporate into the egg mixture and you will risk over-mixing it.

When the egg mixture has cooled and is very light and fluffy fold in one-third of the whipped cream, taking care not to lose any air. Then add this mixture back into the bowl with the rest of the cream. Combine thoroughly, using a balloon whisk but mixing as little as possible.

Pour the mixture into the lined loaf tin and cover with the overhanging cling film. Leave to freeze for a minimum of 4 hours, and preferably overnight.

Once it has frozen, turn the parfait out of the loaf tin and wrap it well in plenty of cling film as it will easily take on the flavour of other products in the freezer. Use within 1 month. To serve, unwrap and slice using a knife dipped in hot water.

VANILLA CREAM

✳ Serves 6 ✳ Preparation time 45 minutes ✳ Setting time 4 hours in the fridge

Mrs Beeton gives several recipes for creams and custards in her book, and often these sublimely smooth and delicate little sweets are all you need after a meal. The cream can also be infused with other flavours – bay, angelica or lavender, for example. Experiment and see what you like.

550ml whole milk

60g caster sugar

seeds scraped from
2 vanilla pods

8 egg yolks

3 leaves gelatine

special equipment

a temperature probe and
6 small serving glasses

Place the milk and half the sugar in a small saucepan over a medium heat until warm. Add the vanilla seeds and remove from the heat. Leave for 10 minutes to allow the vanilla to infuse the milk.

Meanwhile, in a large bowl, whisk the egg yolks with the remaining sugar until the mixture is light and creamy and set aside. Now place the gelatine leaves into a bowl of cold water for 10 minutes.

Place the vanilla-infused milk mixture back on the hob over a medium heat and bring it to a simmer. Then pour it, whisking all the while, onto the yolk mixture. Return the entire mixture to the pan and place over a low heat. Stir with a flat wooden spoon or heatproof spatula, ensuring that the mixture cooks but does not curdle. The time it takes to thicken will vary from 5–10 minutes. If you have a temperature probe, use it to monitor the temperature of the mixture until it registers 83°C. At this point quickly strain the mixture through a fine sieve into a cold jug or bowl.

Remove the gelatine sheets from the water and give them a squeeze. Stir them into the warm vanilla mixture until dissolved. Allow the mixture to cool, stirring from time, then pour into 6 small serving glasses. Cover each with cling film and chill for 4 hours, or overnight, before serving.

RASPBERRY JELLY

✳ **Serves 4–6** ✳ **Preparation time 20 minutes plus dripping overnight** ✳ **Chilling time 4 hours**

Gelatine, as we know it now, was not available to Mrs Beeton, who instead used isinglass, derived from fish. The development of setting agents fuelled a huge increase in the popularity of jellies and set creams, which were popular with adults and children alike. The by-product of this recipe is a good quantity of raspberry pulp, which can be used to make the raspberry vinegar on page 375.

2kg ripe raspberries, hulled

110g caster sugar plus extra to taste

1 tsp lemon juice

approx 3 leaves gelatine

special equipment

a square of muslin and 4–6 serving glasses

Place the raspberries in a large stainless steel or ceramic bowl, add 110g caster sugar and mix together. Crush with a potato masher to form a fairly smooth mass.

Leave the berries and sugar to steep for 1 hour then transfer to a jelly bag (or a piece of butter muslin placed in a sieve or colander) set over a large bowl. Do not press on the raspberries or the jelly will not be clear. Cover with a clean cloth and leave in a cool place overnight to allow the raspberry juice to drip through the fabric into the bowl.

This amount of raspberries should yield approximately 500ml juice. If it does not make enough, make up to 500ml with clear apple juice. If you have more than 500ml, you may need to use more gelatine (see page 237).

To complete the jelly, taste the juice in the bowl. Stir in a little more sugar if you like, and add the lemon juice.

Place half of the liquid in a small saucepan over a medium heat. When the juice it is hand hot remove it from the heat.

Soak the gelatine leaves in cold water for 10 minutes until soft. (If you prefer to set the jelly in a mould you will need to use an extra leaf of gelatine for a firmer set.) Drain, and add to the warm raspberry juice liquid, stirring to dissolve. Pour back into the bowl with the other half of the juice and stir to mix. Now pour the raspberry mixture into 4–6 pretty glasses and chill for 4 hours or overnight to set before serving.

STRAWBERRY JELLY

✳ **Serves 4** ✳ **Preparation time 20 minutes plus dripping overnight**
✳ **Chilling time overnight**

This delightful jelly has a beautiful colour and flavour. Do not be put off by the quantity of strawberries needed, because the pulp can be used in the strawberry water ice recipe on page 264. The two recipes make a winning combination and would make a highly refreshing dessert to follow a summer lunch.

2kg ripe strawberries, hulled

110g plus 1–2 tsp caster sugar

1 tsp lemon juice

clear apple juice

approx 4 leaves gelatine

special equipment

a square of muslin and a 500ml jelly mould

Place the strawberries in a large stainless steel or ceramic bowl, add 110g caster sugar and mix together. Crush with a potato masher to form a fairly smooth mass.

Leave the berries and sugar to steep for 1 hour then transfer to a jelly bag (or a piece of muslin placed in a sieve) set over a large bowl. Do not press on the fruit or the juice will not be clear. Cover with a clean cloth, and leave in a cool place overnight to allow the strawberry juice to drip through the fabric into the bowl.

This amount of strawberries should yield approximately 500ml juice. If it does not make enough, make up to 500ml with clear apple juice. If you have more than 500ml, you may need to use more gelatine (see page 237). Stir the lemon juice into the strawberry juice and then add 1–2 tsp caster sugar to taste, stirring to dissolve.

Place the sheets of gelatine into a bowl of cold water and leave to soak for 10 minutes. (If you prefer to serve the jelly in individual glasses, and do not intend to turn it out, you can use just 3 leaves of gelatine per 500ml juice instead of 4.) Pour half of the strawberry juice into a small pan over a low heat. When the juice is hand hot remove it from the heat. Squeeze the gelatine sheets to remove excess water and add them to the warm juice, stirring to dissolve. Pour the juice and gelatine mixture into the bowl with the rest of the strawberry juice and stir to mix well.

Strain the mixture through a fine sieve into the mould and chill overnight to set. Turn the jelly out by dipping the mould in boiling water for a few seconds to loosen the edges, and serve with the strawberry water ice.

STRAWBERRY WATER ICE

✳ Serves 4–8 ✳ Preparation time 15 minutes ✳ Freezing time 3–4 hours

This richly flavoured and coloured ice is best made with leftover pulp from the jelly recipe, because the pulp has less water content and is consequently thicker and more jellied as a result. If you have some lovely ripe strawberries and want to make it from scratch, use 800g prepared fruit.

pulp of 2kg strawberries used in jelly recipe (see page 262)

75g sifted icing sugar, to taste

juice of 1 lemon

Purée the pulp in a jug blender or food processor and pass it through a fine sieve, discarding the seeds left behind. You should be left with approximately 800g smooth pulp.

Place one-third of the pulp in a bowl and add the icing sugar, whisking until all the sugar has dissolved.

Whisk this mixture back into the remaining pulp with half of the lemon juice. Taste and adjust with more lemon juice or icing sugar if necessary. The flavour should be slightly sweeter than you like, because when it is cold it will taste less sweet.

Pour the liquid into a shallow plastic container and place in the freezer. Stir with a fork or flat whisk every half hour, until the mixture starts to freeze. Then, beat every 15 minutes until it holds a soft shape. Pile into small glasses and serve with strawberry jelly if you like.

If you decide to keep the water ice to eat another day, simply cover the plastic container and leave in the freezer for up to 1 month. When ready to use, place in the fridge for 30 minutes to soften, then beat well to loosen it just before serving.

LEMON TART

❋ **Serves 8** ❋ **Preparation time 30 minutes plus 30 minutes resting time**
❋ **Cooking time 1 hour 15 minutes**

Lemons have always been a popular dessert ingredient, providing a refreshing counterbalance to a rich meal. This classic tart is a perfect example, with the almonds adding a pleasant texture to the zesty filling. The original recipe uses a puff pastry case, but the shortcrust gives a weightier, more refined edge.

½ **quantity shortcrust pastry**

150g caster sugar

90ml double cream

6 egg yolks

150g butter, melted

40g ground almonds

zest and juice of 2 large lemons

special equipment

a 22cm metal pie or baking dish and some baking beans

First make the pastry and leave it to rest in the fridge for 20 minutes. Then, roll it out on a floured surface to a 27cm round. Place it in the pie dish, leaving the extra pastry hanging over the edge. This technique may seem wasteful, but it will help prevent the pastry shrinking back into the case.

Line the pastry case with a large piece of non-stick baking paper and then fill with baking beans. Leave to rest in a cool place for 10 minutes.

Preheat the oven to 200°C/gas mark 6. Place the pastry case on a baking tray and bake for 35 minutes until the pastry is firm and golden brown. Remove the beans and paper and return the case to the oven for five minutes to bake further and dry slightly.

Remove from the oven and set aside. Reduce the oven to 120°C/gas mark ½.

Now make the filling by beating together the sugar and cream. Then beat in the egg yolks. Beat the melted butter into the mixture, adding it a little at a time.

Fold in the ground almonds along with the lemon juice and zest. Pour the mixture into the pastry case and bake for 40 minutes, or until just set.

Trim the pastry hanging over the rim with a sharp knife and cool to room temperature before serving.

CHERRY CLAFOUTIS

✳ **Serves 4** ✳ **Preparation time 15 minutes plus 30 minutes resting time**
✳ **Cooking time 20–25 minutes plus 10 minutes cooling time**

A clafoutis, or batter pudding, can be made with any tart fruit, but cherries are the classic. Mrs Beeton used currants in winter, but recommended damsons, plums, apricots or gooseberries in season – showing just how flexible this dish can be. The stones of the cherries are left in here because they impart a subtle almond flavour to the finished clafoutis. Warn your guests to go gently, though, because they will encounter stones in the pudding.

400g ripe cherries, stems removed

80g caster sugar

2 large eggs

200ml milk

100g plain flour

pinch salt

5g unsalted butter

icing sugar, for dusting

special equipment

a 25cm ovenproof frying pan

Place the cherries in a bowl with 40g of the sugar, stir to mix and set aside.

Place the eggs in another bowl and whisk for a minute or two until frothy. Add the milk and whisk again to combine. Sift the flour, salt and remaining 40g sugar into a third bowl and make a well in the centre. Pour in the egg and milk mixture and whisk to combine into a smooth batter. Set aside to rest for half an hour.

Preheat the oven to 180°C/gas mark 4.

Heat a 25cm ovenproof frying pan over a medium heat and add the butter. When it begins to foam, add the cherries and any juice to the pan.

Give the batter a stir to fold any foam that has settled on top back into the mixture and pour carefully into the pan. Place into the oven for 20–25 minutes, or until set and golden on top. Allow the clafoutis to cool for 10 minutes before dusting with icing sugar and serving.

QUEEN'S PUDDING

✳ Serves 4–6 ✳ Preparation time 50 minutes ✳ Cooking time 45–55 minutes

Of all the flavoured milk and breadcrumb puddings that crop up in the British repertoire, this one is the best and originates long before Mrs Beeton wrote her book. It is very similar to her Manchester pudding but requires no pastry, so is quicker to make for the time-pressured cook. The lemon-scented base contrasts perfectly with the raspberry jam and light meringue topping.

650ml milk

25g unsalted butter, plus extra for greasing

25g caster sugar

seeds scraped from one vanilla pod

110g stale white bread or cake crumbs

finely grated zest of ½ lemon

pinch freshly grated nutmeg

4 egg yolks

200g sharp raspberry jam

for the meringue topping

6 egg whites

300g caster sugar

special equipment

a deep, 22cm pie dish and a roasting tin

Place the milk, butter, sugar and vanilla seeds in a saucepan over a medium heat and bring almost to simmering. Remove from the heat and leave for the flavour to infuse for 30 minutes.

Preheat the oven to 160°C/gas mark 3. Butter the pie dish.

Place the bread or cake crumbs, lemon zest and nutmeg into a large bowl and combine. Pour in the infused milk and mix together.

Fill the kettle and bring it to a boil.

Lightly beat the egg yolks and add them a little at a time to the bread mixture until fully incorporated. Then pour the mixture into a buttered baking dish and place in a roasting tin.

Pour boiling water into the roasting tin to a depth of 2cm and bake for 35–45 minutes, or until set. Remove from oven and spread the raspberry jam over the base.

Turn the oven up to 200°C/gas mark 6.

Make the meringue topping by placing the egg whites into the bowl of a mixer and beating them quickly for 2 minutes. Add the sugar and beat to make a stiff meringue. Pile this over the layer of jam, spreading the meringue carefully right to the edges of the dish. Bake for 10 minutes, or until the pudding turns golden brown on top. Allow the pudding to cool a little before serving.

TRIFLE

✻ Serves 6–8 ✻ Preparation time 1 hour 45 minutes split over 3 days

If one dessert sums up the British kitchen, it would probably be the trifle. This recipe is a combination of elements from several of Mrs Beeton's trifle recipes. At a pinch, you can use puréed fresh raspberries to make up the jelly quantities – just sweeten to taste.

lemon sponge (see page 293)

600ml raspberry jelly
(see page 261)

3 tbsp homemade or sharp
raspberry jam (see page 354)

100ml sweet sherry, or more,
to taste

1 quantity everyday custard
(see page 343)

for the topping

600ml double cream

15g caster sugar

finely grated zest of 1 lemon

45ml Amontillado sherry

special equipment

a large, attractive glass
serving bowl

Make the sponge and begin the jelly on the first day, leaving the jelly to drip overnight.

Cut the lemon sponge in half and spread the bottom half with the raspberry jam. Replace the top half and cut the sponge into small rectangles. Take a large glass serving bowl and line it with the sponge rectangles.

Sprinkle the sponge all over with the sherry, then finish the raspberry jelly and pour it over the sponge. Cover with cling film and chill overnight.

On the third day make the custard and set it aside to cool. Remove the trifle bowl from the fridge and peel back the cling film. Pour the custard over the raspberry jelly and smooth the surface with a palette knife. Re-cover with the cling film and store in a cool place until needed.

When you are ready to serve the trifle, remove the cling film and top with the topping. Whip the cream with the sugar, lemon zest and sherry until it forms soft peaks, then pile it on top of the custard, spreading it carefully to the edges of the dish.

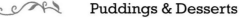
LEMON POSSET

✳ **Serves 6** ✳ **Preparation time 5 minutes** ✳ **Chilling time 1 hour**

This is probably the simplest dessert you can make – a flavoured cream that sets with the acidity of the lemon juice. The gelatine helps to stabilize the mixture, which is useful if you want to make it a day ahead, but a light set can be achieved without.

425ml double cream

125g caster sugar

juice and finely grated zest of 2 large or 3 small lemons

1 leaf gelatine (optional)

special equipment

6 x 120ml ramekins

Place the cream, sugar and lemon zest in a small pan over a low heat. Allow the mixture to simmer for 2 minutes, then remove from the heat.

If you are making the posset a day ahead, soak 1 leaf of gelatine in cold water for at least 10 minutes, squeeze dry and stir into the warm cream mixture at this stage.

Once the cream has cooled to tepid, stir in the lemon juice. Strain into 6 glasses, cover with cling film and put straight into the fridge to chill for at least 1 hour before serving.

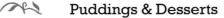

PEARS IN PORT

❋ **Serves 4** ❋ **Preparation time 5 minutes**
❋ **Cooking time 35–45 minutes plus 2 hours chilling time**

We rarely come across cooking pears today – historically they were grown because they stored well through the winter, while eating pears were more commonly bottled because they do not keep. The combination with port is a classic one, and you can reduce the syrup to the thickness you prefer.

140g caster sugar

6 cloves

6 allspice berries

300ml port

juice of 1 lemon

4 large pears, peeled, halved and cored

Place the sugar, cloves, allspice, port and 600ml water in a saucepan over medium heat and bring to a simmer.

Meanwhile place the lemon juice in a bowl and add the pear halves. Toss the pears in the juice to coat and to stop them going brown.

Transfer the peeled pears and lemon juice into the hot poaching liquid, cover with a lid and simmer very gently for 25–35 minutes until the pears are tender.

Gently transfer the pears from the liquid into a shallow dish large enough to hold them in a single layer. Strain the whole spices from the liquid, return the liquid to the heat and bring to a rapid simmer. Allow the mixture to reduce until you have about 150ml of a syrupy glaze. Pour over the pears, cover with cling film and chill thoroughly, overnight if you like, before serving. This is lovely served with whipped cream and gingernut biscuits.

POACHED RHUBARB

* Serves 4 * Preparation time 10 minutes
* Cooking time 25 minutes plus 2 hours chilling time

Rhubarb, as Mrs Beeton noted, comes into season just as apples go out, making it the first new crop of spring. This sharp-sweet poached fruit is a welcome change after the heavy desserts of winter. The original book had it encased in a puff pastry tart, but it is just as good served simply with Jersey cream or custard (see pages 343 and 345).

400g fresh rhubarb, trimmed and cut into 2cm pieces

zest and juice of 1 orange

200ml clear apple juice

50–80g caster sugar

special equipment

a ceramic ovenproof dish

Preheat the oven to 150°C/gas mark 2.

Place the rhubarb pieces into a ceramic ovenproof dish that will take the fruit more or less in a single layer.

Place the orange zest and juice and 50g caster sugar in a small saucepan over a high heat and bring to a boil, then pour over the rhubarb in the dish.

Cover with a layer of greaseproof paper and then wrap the dish with foil.

Bake for 10–15 minutes until the rhubarb is tender to the point of a knife. Remove from the oven and carefully pour off the liquid into a small saucepan. Place over a high heat and reduce the liquid to a syrupy glaze, then pour over the fruit. Allow the rhubarb to cool a little, then taste the fruit. If it tastes unduly tart, add more sugar to taste, then place in the fridge until thoroughly chilled before serving.

SEVILLE ORANGE CREAMS

❊ **Serves 6** ❊ **Preparation time 5 minutes** ❊ **Cooking time 1 hour plus chilling overnight**

This light custard is Mrs Beeton's beautiful way of using Seville oranges, as opposed to just using them for marmalade. Their taste is unique and available for only a couple of months, so make this while you can, in January or February.

2 Seville oranges

1 tbsp orange liqueur or brandy

4 egg yolks

80g caster sugar

600ml double cream

special equipment

6 x 120ml ramekins and a roasting tin

Preheat the oven to 140°C/gas mark 1.

Using a potato peeler, pare a thin layer of rind from the oranges. Place the rind in a pan of water over a high heat and bring to a boil for 15 minutes to soften. Remove from the heat and strain away the water and set the rind aside.

Place the orange liqueur or brandy, egg yolks, half the sugar, all the softened rind and the juice of 1 of the oranges into a jug blender and blend well until you have a fine purée. Transfer to a 1-litre bowl.

Place the cream in a small saucepan over a medium heat, add the remaining sugar and bring to simmering. Pour the hot cream mixture over the blended purée, stirring not whisking. Strain the mixture through a fine sieve into a jug and set aside.

Fill the kettle and bring to a boil. Meanwhile, divide the orange mixture between the ramekins and set them into a roasting tin. Slowly pour the boiling water into the roasting tin to a depth of 3cm. Cover the tin loosely with a sheet of foil and bake for 30 minutes. Lower the oven temperature to 120°C/gas mark ½ and bake for a further 5 minutes, or until the creams are set around the edges of ramekins but still wobble in the centre.

Remove the creams from the roasting tin and leave to cool for a few minutes before chilling, preferably overnight. Serve with shortbread biscuits.

TOFFEE APPLES

✳ **Makes 8** ✳ **Preparation time 10 minutes**
✳ **Cooking time 30 minutes plus 10 minutes cooling time**

Mrs Beeton gives a recipe for Everton toffee which, with its addition of lemon juice, is crisp and delicious. This recipe can be made into toffee, like hers, or used to wrap around dessert apples – which are great for fun children on bonfire night, or indeed at any other time of year.

8 medium Cox's Orange Pippin apples

40g salted butter, plus extra for greasing

350g soft brown sugar

125ml water

1 tsp lemon juice

170g golden syrup

special equipment

8 x 15cm long lolly sticks or pieces of dowel, some clear cellophane and a temperature probe

Wash the apples in very hot water to remove any wax and dry well.

Spear the stalk end of each apple with a lolly stick or a piece of dowel. Grease a baking tray and prepare a jug of very cold water large enough to dip an apple into. Set both aside.

Place the rest of the ingredients in a large pan over a medium heat and allow them to melt together and dissolve, then turn the heat to high and bring the mixture to a boil. Stir constantly and use a temperature probe to monitor the temperature. It is ready when it reaches approximately 148°C. If you don't have a temperature probe, test the set by dropping a small spoonful of the mixture into the jug of cold water. When it forms a crisp string of toffee, remove the pan from the heat.

Working quickly before the toffee sets, hold an apple by the stick and dip it into the toffee, swirling it to ensure it is completely covered. Lift it out of the mixture, allow it to drip for a few seconds and then plunge it into the jug of cold water. Leave it there for a minute while you dip the next apple. Remove the first apple from the jug and set it, with the stick pointing upwards, on the buttered baking tray. Repeat the process with the remaining apples. Leave them to cool for 10 minutes then wrap each apple in cellophane or non-stick baking paper.

CAKES, BISCUITS & BREADS

There is no denying that, as a nation, we have a sweet tooth. Walk down any high street today and bakeries still display a range of treats designed to tempt us inside.

The smell of butter, sugar and flour drifts on the wind in our cities – pumped into supermarket car parks – because nothing is so comforting or seductive as the smell of freshly baked bread. And yet we seem to have been persuaded to abandon our baking heritage in recent decades.

Some British classics persist – the Eccles cake (see page 226) is still found widely in various forms, but others, such as the pound cake, bara brith, and Sally Lunn (see pages 288, 286 and 322) have all but disappeared. Travel widely with a keen eye, and you will find them tucked away in small high-street bakeries, holding out against competition from supermarkets churning out American muffins and cupcakes in astonishing variety.

We have a vast heritage of fabulous cake, biscuit and bread recipes to draw on. Mrs Beeton was not an expressive or indulgent baker, whatever her reputation might suggest. Her cakes contained rather more flour and less sugar and butter than ours today, but it isn't difficult to work out why. She was a young woman running a household on limited resources. Clearly, money was not in plentiful supply. Nonetheless, she was keen to name butter as her fat of choice for baking – expensive as it was – and this sets a good example for us today.

Whatever you bake, your results will only be as good as the cheapest ingredient you use, so always aim high and buy the best ingredients you can afford. If you only allow yourself one piece of cake a week, you will want to make absolutely sure it is a very good piece of cake. And the best way to ensure that it is the best piece of cake ever is to have made it yourself.

TECHNIQUES

Creaming

The butter in cakes, such as the Victoria sandwich cake, is creamed. Here, softened, room-temperature butter is beaten with a wooden spoon or large whisk to add air. This lightens the butter's texture and colour. Once the butter has been beaten, sugar is added and the mixture beaten again, further lightening the mixture. Finally, egg is gradually beaten in resulting in a mixture that is shiny and glossy.

The main aim in creaming a mixture is to add the egg gradually and to beat the mixture thoroughly between each addition. This allows the egg and butter to be emulsified together properly, resulting in a mixture that holds air. If this emulsified mixture is broken, or curdled, a portion of the air is lost and the mixture will be heavier.

Whisking

This is the action of adding air to a mixture to lighten it in colour and texture. A metal balloon whisk is the best tool – either hand held or machine driven. Ingredients that are commonly whisked include eggs and cream. Properly whisked egg whites go through a dramatic transformation, first becoming frothy, and then turning pure white with a light and fluffy texture rather like shaving foam. The mixture should be able to hold its shape rather than running back into the bowl. In some recipes egg whites are whisked on their own before being folded into the other ingredients; in others (for example when making meringues), they are whisked with sugar, which gives them a glossier appearance and a firmer set. A meringue mixture is often said to be able to hold 'stiff peaks'. Egg yolks, when whisked, will pale significantly in colour and increase in volume, but they will never hold their shape as firmly as egg whites.

Folding

The aim when folding two or more ingredients together is to limit the loss of air from the mixture, and this is a method used commonly in baking and dessert cookery. The best tool to use is a large metal spoon or spatula, using a gentle motion of folding one ingredient into the other to blend them – as opposed to beating them – together.

Kneading

The technique of mixing and working dough, usually made of flour, yeast and water, in order to make it into a cohesive, supple mass, is known as kneading. This can be done either by hand or using a machine. However, once you have brought the ingredients together with your hands to make the dough, you should leave it to rest for 20 minutes before kneading.

Kneading plain, white bread-flour dough

Place the rested dough on a lightly floured work surface, and flour your hands. Using one hand to anchor the dough in front of you, push the heel of your other hand into the dough, stretching it as you push it away from you. Use your fingertips to pull the leading edge of the dough back over the middle portion, forming a ball, and repeat this action.

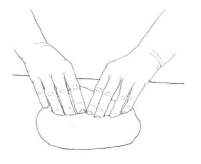
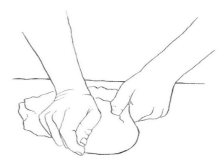

As you knead, occasionally take a piece of dough the size of a golf ball and stretch it between the first and second fingers of both hands. The aim is to make a thin window-like sheet of dough that stretches without tearing until it is thin enough to see light through. You will notice that as you knead this becomes increasingly possible, and this is a sign that the dough is developing. If the dough tears when stretched, keep kneading.

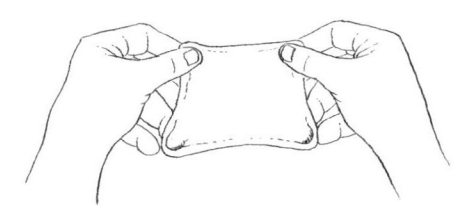

Kneading wholemeal bread-flour dough

Because wholemeal flour contains small pieces of wheat bran, it requires slightly different handling from white flour. It is even more important to leave the freshly mixed dough to rest before kneading for it to be able to develop properly. Knead the dough in stages, allowing it to rest for a couple of minutes occasionally before kneading it again. Do this over a period of 10–15 minutes.

When the dough (either plain white or wholemeal) is shiny and resistant but still very slightly sticky, it is fully developed. Now it can be left to rise in a large bowl in a warm place, covered with either a damp tea towel or oiled cling film.

Making yeast sponges for richer doughs

Bakers occasionally start a batch of yeasted dough using what is known as a 'sponge'. This is a loose batter made from a portion of the liquid, yeast and flour to be used in a recipe which will both give a deeper flavour and, especially when using spices, eggs or fat, a lighter texture because these ingredients tend to inhibit the action of the yeast.

COOKING TECHNIQUES

Temperature and timing

The high sugar content of baked goods means that they are prone to overcooking if the oven heat is too fierce. Fan ovens (also called convection ovens) circulate hot air in the oven and so reduce cooking time. The timings in this section have been worked out using a fan oven. If yours is a conventional oven, raise the heat given in the recipes by 10°C, and expect the recipes to take slightly longer.

Where you place a tray of biscuits or a cake in the oven will affect how they bake, especially if you have a conventional oven. Place them too close to one side of the oven and they will cook unevenly. Because of this, it is wise to turn cakes and biscuits when they begin to brown so that they colour and rise evenly.

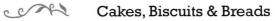

Steam

Bread benefits from being baked in a humid, steamy environment. Steam slows down the formation of the crust, allowing the bread to rise more, producing a lighter loaf. You can introduce steam to the oven by placing a small roasting tin on the bottom of the oven when you first turn the oven on to preheat. Then add hot water to the tin just after you put the bread in. Be careful not to scald yourself with the steam, as it will rise violently when you pour the water in.

Lining cake tins

Cake or loaf tins are generally greased and lined before baking, even if they are non-stick. As well as making it easier to remove the finished cake or loaf from the tin, lining with baking paper makes tins easier to clean. Use melted butter, brushed into all the corners and edges of the tin, and then cut non-stick baking paper to fit. This paper is coated to prevent sticking – and is especially good when used with meringues, which tend to stick to aluminium foil or greaseproof paper.

Testing whether cakes and breads are cooked

To test whether a cake is cooked, insert a skewer into the centre and remove it. If it comes away clean, the cake is cooked. This method will not work for cakes that are intentionally left slightly undercooked for a fudgy effect, such as the dark chocolate cake on page 290.

To test whether a bread is cooked, slip it from its tin and tap the bottom gently with your knuckles. If the bread gives a hollow sound, it is cooked.

Alternatively, a temperature probe can be inserted into cakes and breads once they have reached the end of their cooking time. If a temperature of 95°C has been reached at the centre, the cake or bread is cooked.

STORING BAKED GOODS

Always store cakes and biscuits in airtight containers to stop them becoming stale. Butter-based cakes and biscuits keep very well, but they do eventually grow stale if not eaten. In the event that you end up with some stale cake, you can use it up in a queen's pudding (see page 270).

Bread goes stale quickly. Even the act of freezing bread seems to hurry it past its best. To extend its keeping time, wrap it well in a cloth bag and store it in a cool place.

BARA BRITH

✳ **Serves 6–8** ✳ **Preparation time 25 minutes plus overnight soaking**
✳ **Cooking time 50–55 minutes**

'Plum breads', like this one, were, and are still, common and the recipes are almost impossible to distinguish from one another. Mrs Beeton gives many variants on this theme. Tea is used to moisten the fruit, and the resulting mixture requires no butter – a cake for hard times, you might think, but one that is delicious and healthy too. You can use any combination of tea and dried fruit, keeping the quantities the same.

400ml freshly made jasmine tea

350g dried dates

80g soft brown sugar

softened butter, for greasing

350g plain white flour

2 tsp baking powder

1 large egg, lightly beaten

25g flaked almonds

special equipment

a 1kg loaf tin

The day before you bake, make the jasmine tea. Place the dates in a large bowl and strain the tea over them. Stir in the sugar, cover and leave overnight.

When you are ready to bake, preheat the oven to 180°C/ gas mark 4. Grease the loaf tin with a little soft butter and line the base with a strip of non-stick baking paper.

Sift the flour and baking powder together into a bowl. Mix the beaten egg into the soaked dates then fold them into the flour mixture using a large metal spoon, working quickly but gently.

Transfer the batter to the loaf tin, smooth the surface and then scatter over the flaked almonds.

Set the loaf onto a baking tray and place in the centre of the oven for 50–55 minutes, turning the tin around after 30 minutes. The loaf is ready when a thin skewer pushed into the centre comes out cleanly, or a temperature probe registers 95°C. Remove from the oven and cool in the tin for 10 minutes. Transfer the cake to a wire rack to cool completely before storing in an airtight container. Serve in slices spread with butter and honey.

CARAWAY SEED CAKE

✳ **Serves 6–8** ✳ **Preparation time 20 minutes** ✳ **Cooking time 1 hour–1 hour 20 minutes**

Mrs Beeton adds a little brandy to her seed cake – a lovely addition, and quite the height of sophistication. Her recipe has been altered here only in that the proportion of flour has been reduced to show just how little you can get away with – the resulting crumb is moist and lighter than the citrus pound cake on page 288.

230g softened unsalted butter, plus extra for greasing

200g caster sugar

3 medium eggs at room temperature

75ml brandy

200g self-raising flour, sifted

1 tsp caraway seeds

pinch ground mace

few gratings of nutmeg

special equipment

a 1kg loaf tin

Preheat the oven to 160°C/gas mark 3. Grease the loaf tin with a little soft butter and line it with non-stick baking paper, leaving an overhang of 2cm on the long sides to help you lift the cake out of the tin when it is baked.

In a large bowl, beat the butter until it is very soft. Add the sugar and cream the two together until light and fluffy.

Lightly beat the eggs and brandy together then add this mixture, 2 tablespoons at a time, to the butter mixture, beating well after each addition. When two-thirds of the egg mixture has been incorporated, fold in 1 tbsp sifted flour using a large metal spoon. Then fold the remaining egg mixture into the batter.

Mix the caraway seeds and the spices with the remaining flour and sift over the batter. Fold it in carefully until there are no lumps. Pour the batter into the prepared loaf tin.

Place in the centre of the oven for 40–50 minutes, then reduce the heat to 150°C/gas mark 2, and bake for a further 25–30 minutes, or until the loaf is a deep golden brown. The loaf is ready when a thin skewer pushed into the centre comes out cleanly, or a temperature probe registers 95°C. If it is not cooked but is browning too much, turn the temperature down to 130°C/gas mark ½ and cover the top of the loaf with a piece of foil. Test again after 10 minutes. When it is done remove from the oven and cool in the tin for 10 minutes. Transfer the cake to a wire rack to cool completely before storing in an airtight container.

CITRUS POUND CAKE

✳ Serves 6–8 ✳ Preparation time 15 minutes ✳ Cooking time 1 hour

Mrs Beeton's pound cake uses a little almond and citrus to scent the crumb. It is a lovely mixture and quite fine on its own, without frosting or fillings. The simple combination is perfect with a cup of Earl Grey tea.

230g softened unsalted butter, plus extra for greasing

230g caster sugar

4 medium eggs at room temperature

½ tsp almond extract

280g self-raising flour, sifted, plus extra for dusting the tin

70g homemade candied peel (see page 359), cut into small chunks

25g ground almonds

special equipment

a deep cake tin, 20cm round or 17cm square

Preheat the oven to 160°C/gas mark 3. Grease the tin with a little soft butter, then line the base with non-stick baking paper.

In a large bowl, beat the butter until light and soft. Add the caster sugar and cream the two together until the mixture is light and fluffy and the sugar is well incorporated.

Beat the eggs lightly with the almond extract to break them up. Then add this mixture, 2 tbsp at a time, to the butter and sugar mixture, beating well after each addition. When two-thirds of the egg mixture has been incorporated, fold in 1 tbsp sifted flour using a large metal spoon. Fold in the remaining egg mixture and then sift in the remaining flour. Add the cut peel and almonds and fold everything together until all the ingredients are well distributed, but working gently to retain the lightness of the batter.

Pour the batter into the prepared tin and make a small depression in the centre. Place in the centre of the oven for 40 minutes, then reduce the heat to 150°C/gas mark 2 and bake for a further 20–25 minutes, or until the cake is firm to a light touch and a skewer inserted into the middle of the cake comes out cleanly. Or, insert a temperature probe into the centre of the cake. If it registers 95°C the cake is done.

Remove from the oven and cool the cake for 10 minutes in the tin before transferring to a wire cooling rack. When it is completely cool, store it in an airtight container. The lovely flavour of this cake develops further if it is left for 2–3 days before serving.

DARK CHOCOLATE CAKE

❊ **Serves 6–8** ❊ **Preparation time 15 minutes** ❊ **Cooking time 20 minutes**

A variation on Mrs Beeton's chocolate soufflé recipe, which appears in its original form on page 250, this cake uses whole rather than separated eggs, and includes butter. Those two elements combine to give a fudgy texture that is fantastic when served just warm, with whipped cream on the side.

150g slightly salted butter, plus extra for greasing

40g cocoa powder, plus extra for dusting

200g plain dark chocolate (65–70% cocoa solids)

5 medium eggs at room temperature

1 egg yolk at room temperature

70g soft brown sugar

150g caster sugar

3 tbsp brandy

90g plain flour

special equipment

a deep 23cm round spring-form cake tin and a large heatproof bowl

Preheat the oven to 160°C/gas mark 3. Grease the cake tin with a little soft butter, then pour some cocoa powder into the tin, rolling it around to coat the inside and tipping out any excess. Then line the base with non-stick baking paper.

Place the butter and chocolate in a large heatproof bowl and set it over a pan of barely simmering water on a low heat. Do not allow the bottom of the bowl to touch the water. Leave the chocolate to melt without stirring.

Place the eggs, egg yolk and sugars in the bowl of an electric mixer. Beat at high speed for 10–15 minutes, or until light and creamy, then add the brandy and beat until combined.

Sieve the cocoa and flour together. Working quickly but gently, fold the cocoa mixture into the egg mixture using a large metal spoon, ensuring that there are no lumps or bits of dry flour.

Pour the batter into the prepared tin and bake for 20 minutes. Once cooked, allow the cake to cool in the tin, then carefully remove the sides of the tin and slice with a sharp knife dipped in hot water.

The cake will remain deliciously moist and fudgy in the middle. Serve it at room temperature with some whipped cream and fresh raspberries on the side.

DARK GINGERBREAD

✳ Serves 6–8 ✳ Preparation time 20 minutes ✳ Cooking time 45 minutes

This is a classic gingerbread, dark and moist. I have reduced the quantity of flour from the original recipe to make a lighter cake and added some fresh root ginger to add spice and aroma. It can be iced or left plain and will keep for a week or more, after which it is best sliced and eaten spread with a little salted butter.

115g unsalted butter or lard, plus extra for greasing

225g black treacle

225g golden syrup

115g brown sugar, sieved if lumpy

50g finely grated fresh root ginger

375g plain flour

4tsp ground ginger

4tsp cinnamon

4tsp mixed spice

pinch salt

1 tsp bicarbonate of soda

¼ pint milk

3 medium eggs

for the icing

150g icing sugar

2 tbsp ginger wine or syrup

2 lobes of stem ginger in syrup, drained and finely chopped, to decorate

special equipment

a 23cm square baking tin

Preheat the oven to 180°C/gas mark 4. Grease the baking tin and line the base with non-stick baking paper.

Place the treacle, syrup, sugar and butter or lard in a medium-sized saucepan over a low heat and warm until the fat has just melted. Remove from the heat and stir in the grated root ginger.

Sift the flour, spices, salt and bicarbonate of soda together into a large bowl until well blended then add the melted ingredients stirring well to combine. Lightly beat the milk and eggs together and then pour them into treacle and flour mixture and stir to form a smooth, loose batter.

Pour the batter into the prepared tin and bake in the centre of the oven for 45 minutes, or until the gingerbread is evenly cooked and firm to the touch. Leave to cool in the tin on a wire rack for 15 minutes.

Make the icing by placing the icing sugar in a bowl and adding the ginger wine or syrup and mixing until you have a thick, pouring consistency. Turn the cooled gingerbread out of the tin, drizzle over the icing and sprinkle with the chopped ginger. Leave the icing to dry for 2–3 hours before serving. You can also transfer the gingerbread to an airtight container, but eat within 1 week of making.

LEMON SPONGE

✻ **Serves 10** ✻ **Preparation time 20 minutes** ✻ **Cooking time 40 minutes**

This versatile cake is especially nice served sliced with lemon curd (see page 360) and whipped cream. However, it can also be used, sliced and layered, in a trifle (see page 272 and note below) and the crumbs can be used in the queen's pudding on page 270.

25g unsalted butter, melted, plus a little extra for greasing

4 medium eggs

115g caster sugar

1 tbsp orange flower water

finely grated zest of ½ lemon

115g plain flour, sifted

special equipment

a deep 20cm round cake tin

Preheat the oven to 180°C/gas mark 4. Grease the cake tin with a little soft butter, then line the base with non-stick baking paper.

Using an electric mixer, whisk the eggs for a minute then add the sugar and orange flower water. Beat at high speed for 10–15 minutes until the mixture is light and mousse-like.

Working quickly but gently, fold in the lemon zest and flour, and then the melted butter. Make sure all of the ingredients are well incorporated and there are no lumps.

Pour the batter into the prepared tin and place in the centre of the oven. After 25 minutes turn the oven down to 160°C/gas mark 3 for a further 15 minutes. The cake is cooked when it is evenly browned all over or firm to a light touch and a skewer inserted into the middle of the cake comes out cleanly. Or, insert a temperature probe into the centre of the cake. If it registers 95°C the cake is done.

Note: If you are planning to bake this cake for use in the trifle recipe, use the method above but with the quantities given below, and bake in a 23cm square cake tin. The cake will take 25 minutes to bake at 180°C/gas mark 4.

3 medium eggs
85g caster sugar
½–1 tbsp orange flower water
85g plain flour
20g unsalted butter, melted, plus a little extra for greasing
zest of ⅓ lemon

HONEY MADELEINES

* **Makes about 20** * **Preparation time 20 minutes plus 40 minutes resting time**
* **Cooking time 10 minutes**

Mrs Beeton uses 'honey to taste' in her honey cake, which is unusually vague for her. Here, a more precise quantity is given, but honey can also be used in place of part of the sugar if you prefer. Based on Mrs Beeton's small sponge cakes, these madeleines have the added benefit of cooking quickly, overcoming the tendency of honey to brown too quickly in the oven.

120g unsalted butter, plus a little extra for greasing

50g English honey

3 medium eggs at room temperature

100g caster sugar

100g self-raising flour, plus extra for dusting the tins

25g ground almonds

special equipment

2 x 10-hole madeleine tins

Place the butter in a small pan to melt over a medium-high heat. Allow it to cook until it begins to brown lightly. As soon as it turns a light caramel colour, remove it from the heat and stir in the honey to halt the cooking process then set it aside to cool slightly.

Meanwhile place the eggs and sugar in a large bowl and whisk with an electric mixer until light and fluffy. This will take approximately 10–15 minutes.

Sift the flour and ground almonds together and fold into the mixture using a large metal spoon or a spatula. Then fold in the cooled butter and honey mixture until fully incorporated.

Cover and place in the fridge for 30 minutes.

Grease the madeleine tins with butter and dust them lightly with plain flour.

When the batter has chilled, divide it between the moulds. Let it rest for 10 minutes at room temperature while you preheat the oven to 160°C/gas mark 3.

Bake for 10 minutes, or until light golden and springy to the touch. Allow them to cool for 2–3 minutes in the tin (this will make them easier to remove) and then cool on a wire rack. Store in an airtight tin for up to 4 days.

PLAIN SCONES

* Makes 20 small scones   * Preparation time 10 minutes   * Cooking time 10–12 minutes

Scones and other little cakes raised with baking powder have always been popular and are quick to make. Mrs Beeton gives two recipes that are similar to our modern scone, breakfast cakes and soda buns, both of which have a neutral dough that is excellent when buttered or eaten with jam. She uses just a little sugar or none at all in some of her little cakes, substituting currants instead for sweetness. Should you want to try this, add 115g of currants in the place of the sugar. Split the scones when cool and fill with clotted cream and strawberry jam, or spread them with butter and heather honey.

450g self-raising flour, plus extra for dusting

115g cold unsalted butter, diced

pinch salt

60g caster sugar

175ml milk

1 tbsp lemon juice

special equipment

a 4–5cm round pastry cutter

Preheat the oven to 200°C/gas mark 6 and set 2 baking trays ready.

Place the flour, butter, salt and sugar into a food processor and blend until the mixture is very fine and lump-free. Pour the mixture onto a work surface and make a well in the centre. Stir the milk and lemon juice together in a bowl or jug, then pour into the well in the dry ingredients.

Using a large fork, work steadily out from the centre to mix the flour quickly and gently into the liquid until you have an even mixture with no wet or dry patches. Scrape up any dough sticking to the work surface using a spatula and incorporate this into the mix. Do not knead the mixture. Simply pinch it together with your fingertips until it forms a ball. If it seems a little dry, add a splash more milk.

Scatter some flour over your work surface, rolling pin and baking trays. Gently roll the dough out to a thickness of 3cm on the floured work surface. Dip your cutter into some flour and then stamp out a round in the dough sheet and place it on the baking tray. Dipping your cutter in flour between each cut will ensure the scones rise evenly.

When you have used all the dough, dust the scones lightly with flour. Bake in the centre of the oven for 10–12 minutes, or until well risen and a light golden-brown. The scones are ready when they sound hollow when tapped on the bottom. Transfer the scones to a wire rack until completely cool, then store in an airtight tin or freeze.

RICH FRUIT CAKE

✻ Serves 10–12 ✻ Preparation time 1 hour plus overnight soaking
✻ Cooking time 2 hours 30 minutes–3 hours

Mrs Beeton provided several recipes for fruit cakes, offering a different one for each occasion – among them a treacle-rich Christmas cake and a 'Bride or Christening' cake, both of which are quite different from the fruit cakes we are used to eating today. This rich fruit cake has been pared back to provide you with a basic recipe that can be spiced or altered to suit your own taste or the occasion. It is fruit-heavy and delicious. Like most rich fruit cakes, it benefits from being made a month or two before you intend to use it.

700g mixed dried fruit (raisins, sultanas and currants)

50g homemade candied peel, chopped (see page 359)

50g glacé cherries, halved

115g flaked almonds

60ml each brandy and sweet sherry

finely grated zest of 1 lemon

160g softened unsalted butter, plus extra for greasing

160g soft brown sugar

1 tbsp black treacle or molasses

3 medium eggs

3 tbsp milk

pinch salt

½ tsp ground mace

½ tsp freshly grated nutmeg

½ tsp mixed spice

200g sifted plain flour

special equipment

a deep 17cm round cake tin

Combine the dried fruit, peel, cherries, almonds, sherry and brandy in a large bowl. Stir, cover and leave overnight.

The next day, add the lemon zest to the fruit and stir well. Preheat the oven to 140°C/gas mark 1. Line a baking tray with a double layer of foil. Grease the tin and line the base and sides with non-stick baking paper. Secure a sheet of newspaper around the outside of the tin with a paperclip.

In a large bowl, cream together the butter and sugar until light and fluffy. Beat in the treacle or molasses. Beat the eggs and milk together and add to the butter mixture in 3–4 batches, beating well between each addition. Now sift together the salt, spices and flour and fold them into the mixture until just combined. Add the fruit and stir to distribute it evenly through the batter, then transfer the batter to the tin. Make a shallow depression in the middle.

Place the tin on the baking tray and cover with a sheet of foil, tucking it under the tin to keep it in place. Bake in the centre of the oven for 2½ hours, turning every 30 minutes, then check to see if the cake is cooked by inserting a skewer into the middle. If it comes out clean, the cake is done. If not, reduce the oven temperature to 130°C/gas mark ½ and retest after 30 minutes.

Cool the cake overnight in the tin, then carefully turn it out, leaving the baking paper in place, and store in an airtight container for a month or so before using. If you like, you can feed it every week for 3–4 weeks with 2–3 tbsp brandy. Simply drizzle the brandy onto the surface and let it soak in.

SCOTCH PANCAKES

✳ **Makes 20 pancakes** ✳ **Preparation time 5 minutes** ✳ **Cooking time 15–20 minutes**

Flat, griddle cakes of this type have been cooked for centuries on top of the stove or hearth, and they remain popular in Scotland – hence the name. This recipe is based on Mrs Beeton's nice breakfast cakes, but does not require the oven, and is therefore more economical. The syrup helps the pancakes brown evenly and keeps their crumb tender. They are excellent served with crisp bacon and marmalade.

225g self-raising flour

pinch salt

1½ tbsp golden syrup, warmed

1 tbsp sunflower oil, plus extra for oiling

2 medium eggs at room temperature

180ml whole or semi-skimmed milk

special equipment

a non-stick griddle

.Sift the flour and salt into a bowl and make a well in the centre. In another bowl or large jug, whisk the warmed syrup, oil, eggs and milk together. Pour the milk mixture into the flour mixture and whisk to combine. Be careful not to over-mix otherwise the cooked pancakes will not be tender. Do not worry if there are a few tiny lumps of flour.

The consistency by now should be that of very thick double cream. If the batter seems a little thick, add some extra milk.

Heat the griddle or a heavy-bottomed frying pan to medium-high and wipe with a little sunflower oil. Drop a dessertspoonful of the batter onto the griddle, spreading it slightly with the back of the spoon to make a round about 7.5cm in diameter. Repeat with another 4, so that you have 5 cooking at a time.

After about 1–2 minutes, or when a deep golden-brown skin has formed on the underside, flip the pancakes over using a spatula and cook for another 1–2 minutes until a skin forms underneath and the pancake feels springy to the touch.

Transfer to a warmed plate and cover with a clean tea towel. Wipe the griddle between batches to remove any debris and repeat with remaining batter until you have used it all up.

VICTORIA SANDWICH CAKE

✳ **Serves 8** ✳ **Preparation time 15 minutes** ✳ **Cooking time 25–30 minutes**

In 1861 the Victoria sandwich (which supposedly pays tribute to Queen Victoria's love of afternoon tea) had not yet been named. Instead Mrs Beeton included a recipe for Savoy cake. This similarly plain sponge was baked in a tall, elaborate mould – and in order to create the volume necessary for all that cake, Mrs Beeton used seven eggs, whisking the whites and yolks separately before folding them back together. In spite of all this grandeur, she recommended simply slicing the cake and spreading it with jam, 'which converts it into sandwiches'. Today, the cake is sandwiched together with jam before serving. As we use standard tins, fewer eggs are required and there is no need to separate them. Use a good quality, sharp raspberry jam, or make your own (see page 354). This cake can be eaten fresh or made a couple of days in advance to allow the jam to soak in.

eggs weighing 220–240g in total – approx 4 medium eggs

220–240g softened unsalted butter, plus extra for greasing

220–240g caster sugar, plus extra for dusting

220–240g self-raising flour

½ tsp vanilla extract

3–4 tbsp sharp raspberry jam

special equipment

2 x 20cm loose-bottomed cake tins

Preheat the oven to 160°C/gas mark 3. Grease the cake tins and line the bases with non-stick baking paper.

Crack the eggs into a bowl on a scale until you have 220–240g. Then measure out the butter, sugar and flour to the same weight as the eggs. In a large mixing bowl, beat the butter until it is light and fluffy. Add the caster sugar and cream the two together well. Lightly beat the vanilla into the eggs, then add the eggs 2 tbsp at a time to the butter mixture, beating well at each addition to prevent the mixture separating. When two-thirds of the egg has been incorporated, sift in 1 tbsp flour and stir. Add the remaining egg mixture, then sift in the remaining flour and fold it in using a large metal spoon until the mixture is free of lumps.

Split the batter between the tins, making a small indent in the middle of each. Bake in the centre of the oven for 25–30 minutes, or until risen, evenly browned and firm to the touch. Remove from the oven and run a knife round the inside edge of each tin. Cool the cakes for 10 minutes in the tins, then carefully turn them out onto a wire rack, peel away the baking paper and leave to cool completely.

Place one cake top-side down onto a serving plate. Spread the bottom evenly with the jam, then carefully set the other cake (top-side up) on top. Sprinkle with the caster sugar.

SHORTBREAD

✳ **Makes 30 fingers** ✳ **Preparation time 10 minutes plus 30 minutes chilling time**
✳ **Cooking time 50 minutes**

Mrs Beeton's original Scotch shortbread recipe contains caraway seeds, finely chopped blanched almonds and candied orange peel. Here, it has been pared back for simplicity, with semolina added for texture instead of the more highly flavoured nuts and seeds, but any or all of the original embellishments can be retained if you like. These are simply the finest biscuits to accompany the creamy puddings and fruit desserts found in this book, though it would be highly satisfying to enjoy one or two with nothing more than a cup of afternoon tea.

250g unsalted butter, diced

**120g caster sugar, plus
1 tbsp for dredging**

90g fine semolina

370g sifted plain flour

special equipment

a 20cm square baking tin

Beat the butter until it is soft, and then add the sugar, semolina and flour. Knead lightly to combine. Press the dough evenly into the tin then chill for 30 minutes.

Just before you are ready to bake preheat the oven to 150°C/gas mark 2. Place the shortbread in the centre of the oven for 50 minutes, or until it is an even pale golden-brown colour. Remove from the oven and dredge with the tablespoon of caster sugar. Leave to cool for 10 minutes in the tin, then cut into fingers. When it is completely cold, lift the biscuits out of the tin and place them in an airtight container. These will keep for up to 1 week.

ALMOND MACAROONS

✳ **Makes 50–60 shells** ✳ **Preparation time 15 minutes plus 20 minutes resting time**
✳ **Cooking time 15 minutes**

Although Mrs Beeton said of macaroons that it was 'almost or quite as economical to purchase such articles as these at a good confectioner's', that is certainly not the case today – which makes this recipe well worth a try. You will get a smoother, glossier result if your almonds are ground as finely as possible and you dry them in a warm place for a couple of hours before using them. These macaroons are especially good spread with fresh raspberry jam.

140g ground almonds

200g icing sugar

seeds scraped from 2 vanilla pods

4 medium egg whites

pinch cream of tartar

60g caster sugar

for the filling

raspberry jam (see page 354), to sandwich

special equipment

a piping bag fitted with a round nozzle

Before you begin, spread the ground almonds onto a baking sheet and leave them to dry in a warm place for 2 hours. Once they have dried, preheat oven to 140°C/gas mark 1. Line 2 baking sheets with non-stick baking paper.

Place the ground almonds, icing sugar and vanilla seeds into a food processor and blitz for 20 seconds to make the almonds as fine as possible and to combine them thoroughly with the sugar. Sift the mixture into a bowl.

Place the egg whites into the bowl of an electric mixer with the cream of tartar and beat on a medium speed until they become light and foamy. Increase the speed and add the caster sugar, a little at a time, until the sugar is fully incorporated and the mixture forms soft peaks.

Sift the almond mixture, one-third at a time, onto the egg whites, folding together after each addition. Continue to fold until the mixture becomes smooth and glossy, then spoon into a piping bag fitted with a round nozzle and pipe rounds 2–3cm in diameter onto the prepared baking sheets, leaving 3cm between the rounds. Leave to rest for 20 minutes to allow a skin to form on top of the macaroons, then bake for 15 minutes until set. Transfer the macaroons to a wire rack and leave to cool completely.

Use the raspberry jam to sandwich the macaroons together in pairs, and leave for 1 hour to allow the jam to soak in. The macaroons can be stored in an airtight container for up to 1 week, but they are best eaten after 24 hours.

SUNDERLAND GINGERNUTS

✳ **Makes 25 biscuits** ✳ **Preparation time 15 minutes** ✳ **Cooking time 15–20 minutes**

Mrs Beeton's spice mixture for these biscuits is lovely, with a little coriander being added for greater depth of flavour – an addition that is rarely seen today. The quantity of flour has been reduced to give a lighter, crisper result.

100g softened unsalted butter

75g caster sugar

20g black treacle or molasses

120g golden syrup

1½ tsp ground ginger

½ tsp ground allspice

½ tsp ground coriander

¾ tsp bicarbonate of soda

220g self-raising flour

100g demerara sugar

Preheat the oven to 180°C/gas mark 4. Line 2 baking sheets with non-stick baking paper.

Cream the butter and sugar in a large bowl until light and fluffy. Add the treacle or molasses and the syrup and beat the mixture until combined. In another bowl, sift all the ground spices, the bicarbonate of soda and the flour together then add to the butter mixture. Mix with your fingertips into an even dough that is free of lumps.

Pour the demerara sugar evenly on to a large flat dish. Now take a lump of dough about the size of a walnut, shape it into a ball and roll it in the demerara sugar, repeating with all the dough until the mixture is used up. Arrange the balls at least 4cm apart on the prepared baking sheets and flatten each one slightly using a fork. Bake for 5 minutes then turn the heat down to 160°C/gas mark 3 for a further 10–15 minutes.

The biscuits will rise and then fall. Once the surface of the biscuits cracks and they are firm and a dark golden brown all over remove them from the oven and leave them to cool for 10 minutes. Transfer the biscuits to a wire rack to cool completely and then store in an airtight container.

WELSH CAKES

✳ **Makes 15 cakes** ✳ **Preparation time 10 minutes** ✳ **Cooking time 30–35 minutes**

Mrs Beeton uses dripping or lard in many of her small cakes. The lard gives a 'short' dough that is best eaten warm with salted butter. Bilberry jam, common still in upland areas, makes the perfect accompaniment. Visit any Welsh market town and you will be able to buy these wonderful little cakes. They are often served with jam made from bilberries, which can be found growing on the upland heaths of Wales in the autumn.

150g self-raising flour, plus extra for dusting

pinch salt

50g caster sugar

½ tsp mixed spice

50g lard

30g currants

30g sultanas

1 egg

2 tbsp milk

special equipment

a non-stick griddle or frying pan and a 6.5cm round pastry cutter

Place flour, salt, sugar, mixed spice and lard in a food processor. Blend for 2 minutes or until evenly mixed.

Transfer to a bowl and stir in the currants and sultanas. In another bowl, beat the egg and milk together and pour them into the flour mixture. Using a large fork, quickly but gently fold everything together.

Scatter some flour on your work surface and dust your fingers with flour. Place the mixture on to the floured surface and bring it together into a ball using your hands. Scatter some flour on your rolling pin and roll the dough out to a thickness of 4mm. Stamp 15 rounds out of the dough using the cutter.

Preheat the griddle or frying pan on a medium–low heat then add the cakes a few at a time. Cook the cakes for 4–5 minutes, or until the undersides are golden brown. Turn the cakes over using a spatula and cook the other side. Transfer the finished cakes to a wire rack to cool while you cook the rest. Serve with unsalted butter and either jam or honey. These cakes can be stored in an airtight tin for up to 4 days or frozen for up to 1 month.

MILK LOAF

✳ **Makes 2 large loaves** ✳ **Preparation time 30 minutes plus 4 hours rising and resting time**
✳ **Cooking time 40–50 minutes**

This is an easy first loaf to make. The milk adds a light natural sweetness, whilst the plain flour makes for a tender crumb. Mrs Beeton gave a recipe from Eliza Acton using German yeast, which was relatively new and increasingly popular. Previously, cooks had obtained their yeast from ale houses, but this could be unpredictable for baking.

530ml milk

580g strong white flour, plus extra for dusting

190g plain white flour

10g dried yeast

15g salt

70g unsalted butter, melted, plus extra for greasing

special equipment

2 x 1kg loaf tins and a temperature probe

Warm the milk in a saucepan over a low heat to 30°C, then transfer it to a large bowl and add all the other ingredients except the butter. Mix with your hands until everything is evenly combined and sticky, then add the butter and squeeze it into the dough using your fingers. Cover with a tea towel and leave to rest in a warm place for 10–15 minutes, then scatter some flour over your work surface, place the dough on it and knead for 10–15 minutes, until it is fully developed, smooth and satiny. Place the dough back in the bowl, cover with a clean, damp tea towel and leave in a warm place for 1½–2 hours, or until it doubles in volume.

Grease the 2 loaf tins. Set the dough back onto the floured work surface and divide it in half. As gently as possible, shape each half into a round, then cover with a clean, dry tea towel and leave to rest for 5 minutes. Finally, flatten each round, roll into a cylinder and place in a prepared tin. Place the tins on a baking sheet and cover with a clean tea towel. Allow them to rise again in a warm place for 45 minutes, or until the loaves have almost doubled in volume and the bread is rising proud of the tin. Towards the end of the rising time preheat the oven to 220°C/gas mark 7.

Uncover the loaves and use a small, very sharp knife to slash the tops 3–4 times diagonally. Then place them into the oven. After 10 minutes, turn the oven down to 180°C/gas mark 4 and bake for a further 30–40 minutes, or until the loaves are dark golden brown. Once they are cooked (see page 285 for how to check), remove the loaves from the tins and place them on a wire rack to cool, then store in an airtight tin for up to 2 days.

ENGLISH MUFFINS

❋ Makes 10 muffins ❋ Preparation time 10 minutes mixing plus 2 hours rising time
❋ Cooking time 20–30 minutes

Mrs Beeton toasted her muffins, not too dark, and piled them high well buttered to melt together, just as she did with her toast. They are straightforward to make and delicious.

230ml milk

5g dried yeast

400g strong white bread flour, plus extra for dusting

100g plain white flour

10g salt

15g caster sugar

20g melted butter, plus a little extra for greasing

fine semolina, for dusting

special equipment

10 x 10cm muffin or poaching rings, a pastry cutter of the same size, a non-stick griddle or heavy-bottomed frying pan and a temperature probe

Pour the milk and 150ml water into a small pan and warm to 40°C over a low heat, then pour into a large bowl. Whisk in the yeast, and then sift in 200g strong white bread flour, stirring until you have a smooth consistency. Cover the bowl with a clean, damp tea towel and leave in a warm place for 1 hour, or until doubled in volume.

Sift all the remaining ingredients, except the butter and the semolina, into the bowl. Mix thoroughly with your hands, making sure no bits of dry flour are left. Add the melted butter and mix well. Continue to knead and squeeze in the bowl for 5 minutes, until the dough feels smooth and elastic but not hard, then cover the bowl again and leave in a warm place for 30 minutes, or until almost doubled in volume. Meanwhile, dust 2 baking sheets with semolina. Use a little melted butter to grease 10 muffin or poaching rings and arrange them on the baking sheets.

Flour your work surface, set the dough onto it and gently press it out to a thickness of 2cm, using your hands. Use the pastry cutter to stamp out rounds, placing each one in a muffin ring as you go and re-rolling the dough if necessary. Cover the baking sheets with a clean, dry tea towel and leave the muffins to rise in a warm place until the dough reaches the top of the rings and is beginning to dome.

Heat the griddle or frying pan over a medium-high heat. Using a palette knife or spatula, carefully lift each muffin, still in the ring, and place it into the pan. Depending on the size of the pan, you may be able to cook 4–5 muffins at once. Cook for 4 minutes on each side, or until they sound hollow when tapped. Place the muffins on a wire rack, remove the rings and leave to cool while you cook the next batch. They can be stored in an airtight tin for up to 2 days.

MALTED SODA BREAD

✳ **Makes 2 large loaves** ✳ **Preparation time 20 minutes** ✳ **Cooking time 50 minutes**

Mrs Beeton gives a recipe for soda bread that uses just 'flour' – and you can of course use whatever type you like. This updated recipe uses malted flour, which adds a delicious flavour. It is wonderful with smoked salmon or cheese and lovely toasted with bacon and marmalade the next day. Leavened with bicarbonate of soda, rather than yeast, it can be made from scratch in just over an hour.

375g plain flour

375g malted flour

150g porridge oats, plus extra for sprinkling

2 tsp bicarbonate of soda

1½ tsp salt

25g caster sugar

350ml milk

475g plain yoghurt

50g black treacle or molasses, warmed gently in a small pan

75g butter, melted, plus extra for greasing

special equipment

2 x 1kg loaf tins

Preheat the oven to 200°C/gas mark 6. Grease the loaf tins and line each with a piece of non-stick baking paper, leaving a slight overhang along the long sides of each tin. This will help the bread rise evenly.

Sift all the dry ingredients into a large bowl, mix them together and make a well in the centre. In another bowl, combine the milk, yoghurt, treacle or molasses and the melted butter, mixing well so there are no lumps. Working quickly, add this to the dry ingredients and combine with a large fork to form a soft, stretchy dough.

Divide the dough equally between the two tins, pressing the batter gently into the corners of the tins. Wet your fingers and gently smooth the surface of the mixture.

Sprinkle the top of the loaves with a few oats and bake in the centre of the oven for 20 minutes. Then turn the oven down to 180°C/gas mark 4 and bake for a further 30 minutes, or until the loaves have browned well and have risen evenly. Test the bread to see if it is ready by tipping it from the tin and knocking the bottom of the loaf. If it sounds hollow, the bread should be ready. Or, insert a temperature probe into the centre of each loaf. If it registers 95°C the loaf is done.

Remove the loaves from the tins and transfer to a wire rack to cool for 20 minutes before cutting. Serve still slightly warm or store in an airtight container and eat within 3 days.

WHOLEMEAL BREAD

✳ **Makes 2 large loaves** ✳ **Preparation time 40 minutes plus 4 hours rising and resting time**
✳ **Cooking time 40–50 minutes**

The flours that are available to us today vary enormously from those Mrs Beeton used. The change is partly due to improvements in milling technology, which have made flour whiter and whiter, and partly thanks to the fact that we now appreciate the benefits of wholemeal flour when for centuries it was considered coarse and fit only for the poor.

550ml water

620g strong wholemeal flour

150g strong white flour, plus extra for dusting

7g dried yeast

15g salt

70g unsalted butter, melted

special equipment

2 x 1kg loaf tins and a temperature probe

Warm the water to 30°C in a saucepan over a low heat, then pour it into a large bowl and add all the other ingredients except the butter. Mix with your hands until everything is evenly combined, then add the butter and squeeze it into the dough using your fingers. The dough will feel sticky.

Leave the dough to rest in a warm place for 20 minutes covered with a damp tea towel. When you are ready to knead, scatter some flour over your work surface and place the dough on it. Knead the dough for 2–3 minutes then cover it and leave it to rest for 5 minutes. Repeat, kneading for 2–3 minutes and resting for 5 until the dough is elastic and soft but not sticky. Place the kneaded dough in a bowl, cover with a clean, damp tea towel and leave in a warm place for 1–1½ hours, or until it has doubled in volume. Towards the end of the rising time grease the 2 loaf tins.

On a floured work surface, divide the dough in 2. Gently shape each half into a round, cover with a clean, dry tea towel and leave to rest for 5 minutes, then flatten each round, roll into a cylinder and place in a prepared tin. Put the tins on a baking sheet, cover with a clean tea towel and leave in a warm place for 45 minutes, or until the loaves are rising proud of the tins. Towards the end of the rising time preheat the oven to 220°C/gas mark 7.

Using a sharp knife, slash the tops of the loaves 3–4 times diagonally, then place them into the oven. After 10 minutes turn the oven down to 180°C/gas mark 4. Bake for 30–40 minutes more, or until the loaves are dark golden brown. Once they are cooked, remove the loaves from the tins and cool on a wire rack. Store in an airtight tin for up to 2 days.

ENRICHED DOUGH FOR SWEET BUNS

✳ **Preparation time 20 minutes plus 1–1 ¼ hours rising and resting time**

The following four recipes give only a small indication of the range of English yeasted cakes and buns. Historically, yeasted sweet cakes were far more common than they are now – we tend to use eggs to leaven cakes today, as they are widely available year round (which they weren't historically) and relatively inexpensive. These recipes often have a very regional basis, but they can all be made from the same basic dough, with only minor adjustments. The basic dough recipe is given here.

80ml water

75ml whole milk

5g dried yeast

220g strong white flour

2 egg yolks

55g plain white flour, plus extra for dusting

¾ tsp salt

30g caster sugar

30g butter, melted

special equipment

a temperature probe

First, heat the water and milk in a small saucepan over a low heat until the mixture is tepid, not more than 30°C.

In a large bowl, whisk this mixture with the yeast and 130g of the strong flour until the ingredients combine into a smooth batter. Cover and leave in warm place for 45 minutes to an hour, or until doubled in size.

Beat the egg yolks into the batter then combine the remaining flour, salt and sugar together and add to the batter. Use your hands to bring all the ingredients together and knead for 2 minutes. Next add the melted butter a little at a time and continue to mix until all the butter is incorporated. Rest the dough, covered with a damp tea towel, in a warm place for 15 minutes then proceed as advised for each recipe.

HOT CROSS BUNS

❋ Makes 8 large buns ❋ Preparation time 3 hours including rising and resting time
❋ Cooking time 15–20 minutes

1 quantity enriched dough
(see page 315) but made
with 7g dried yeast and an
extra 25g butter

30g raisins

50g chopped mixed peel

25g sultanas

1 tsp mixed spice

1 tsp ground cinnamon

for the cross paste

100g plain flour

20g caster sugar

for the glaze

50g apricot jam (see page 352)

1 tbsp caster sugar

special equipment

a piping bag fitted with a
small round nozzle

Make the dough as directed, with a little extra yeast, then add an additional 25g melted butter at the end.

After 15 minutes resting, uncover the dough and add the raisins, chopped mixed peel, sultanas, mixed spice and ground cinnamon. Blend them in by breaking up the dough and kneading in the ingredients. When fully combined, turn the dough out onto a lightly floured work surface and knead for 10 minutes, or until it feels soft and smooth and the added ingredients are evenly distributed. The dough should feel slightly tacky but not sticky. Add a little flour as you knead if it is too sticky. Shape the dough into a round and place it in a lightly oiled bowl. Cover with a clean, dry tea towel and leave to rise in a warm place for 1–1½ hours, or until almost doubled in size.

Line a baking tray with non-stick baking paper. Flour your work surface and place the dough onto it. Divide the dough evenly into 8 pieces, shape each one into a round ball and arrange them on the baking tray, spaced about 2cm apart and covered loosely with cling film. Leave in a warm place for 30 minutes, or until almost doubled in size.

Meanwhile, preheat the oven to 180°C/gas mark 4 and make the cross paste. Sift the flour and sugar into a bowl, add 75ml water and mix to a thick, smooth paste. Place this into a piping bag fitted with a small round nozzle and pipe a cross onto each bun. Bake for 15–20 minutes, or until the buns are golden brown. While the buns are baking make the glaze. Place a small pan over a medium heat. Add the apricot jam, caster sugar and 50ml water. Heat until simmering, then cook until the sugar and jam have dissolved and the mixture has reduced by one-third.

Using a pastry brush, paint the glaze onto the buns as they come out of the oven. Serve immediately, split open and spread with salted butter, or store in an airtight tin for up to 3 days. The buns can also be frozen for up to 1 month.

CHELSEA BUNS

✳ Makes 7 ✳ Preparation time 3 hours including rising time ✳ Cooking time 20 minutes

1 quantity enriched dough
(see page 315)

100g softened unsalted butter,
plus a little extra for greasing

50g soft brown sugar

½ tsp freshly grated nutmeg

180g currants

4 tsp caster sugar, for dusting

special equipment

a 25cm round spring-form
cake tin

Make the enriched bread dough and leave it to rest, covered, in a warm place. After 15 minutes, dust your work surface with flour and place the dough on top. Knead for about 10 minutes, or until the dough feels smooth and satiny, then place it into a lightly oiled bowl, cover with a clean, dry tea towel and leave to rise for 1–1½ hours, or until almost doubled in size.

Meanwhile, make the filling by creaming together the butter, brown sugar and grated nutmeg until pale and fluffy. Add the currants and stir in well.

Grease the spring-form cake tin, line it with non-stick baking paper and set it aside. When the dough is ready, place it on the lightly floured work surface and press out to a flat sheet. Using a rolling pin, roll to a rectangle about 30 x 35 cm, allowing the dough to rest for a couple of minutes if it shrinks back from the desired size, then re-roll until you have the dimensions specified.

With the longest edge facing you, spread the filling mixture evenly over the entire surface of the dough then roll the dough up into a tight cylinder. Trim the edges to neaten the roll then, at 5cm intervals, cut through the dough to make 7 equal rounds. Arrange 6 of the rounds, flat-side down and evenly spaced apart, around the inside edge of the prepared tin and place the remaining round in the centre. Cover with cling film and leave to rise in a warm place for 30 minutes, or until the rounds have increased in size by about half and are beginning to push up against each other. Towards the end of the rising time preheat the oven to 160°C/gas mark 3.

Remove the cling film from the buns, dust them with 2 tsp caster sugar and bake for 20 minutes, or until the buns are golden brown. Once cooked, dust again with the remaining caster sugar, remove from the tin all in one piece, and cool before serving. The buns can be stored for 2–3 days in an airtight tin or frozen for up to 1 month.

CORNISH SAFFRON BUNS

✳ **Makes 8 buns** ✳ **Preparation time 3 hours including rising time**
✳ **Cooking time 15 minutes**

10 saffron strands

1 quantity enriched dough (see page 315)

80g finely chopped homemade candied orange or grapefruit peel (see page 359)

for the glaze

1 egg yolk

1 tbsp milk

Place the saffron strands in a small bowl and add 1 tbsp boiling water and leave to cool.

Make the enriched bread dough as directed in the recipe, adding the saffron water to the sponge once it has developed. Add the candied peel with the remaining flour and mix to incorporate.

Place the dough on the work surface and knead for about 10 minutes, or until it feels soft, smooth and slightly tacky but not sticky. If it is too sticky, add a little flour as necessary while you knead. Shape the dough into a round and place it in a lightly oiled bowl. Cover with a clean, dry tea towel and leave to rise for 1–1½ hours, or until almost doubled in size.

Line a baking sheet with non-stick baking paper and set it aside. Place the dough onto the floured work surface and divide it evenly into 8 pieces weighing about 70g each. Shape each piece into a round ball and arrange, spaced about 4cm away from one another, on the prepared baking sheet. Cover loosely with cling film and leave in a warm place for approximately 30 minutes, or until almost doubled in size.

Towards the end of the rising time, preheat the oven to 180°C/gas mark 4. In a small bowl beat the egg yolk and milk together. Brush the top of the buns with the glaze and bake in the centre of the oven for 15 minutes, or until the buns are a deep golden brown and a probe inserted into the centre of a bun reads 95°C. Serve them warm with unsalted butter and lemon curd or honey. Store, when cold, in an airtight tin for up to 3 days, or freeze for up to 1 month.

LEMON SALLY LUNN

✳ Serves 6 ✳ Preparation time about 3 hours including rising time
✳ Cooking time 15–20 minutes

**1 quantity enriched dough
(see page 315)**

**finely grated zest of
1 lemon**

for the glaze

2 tbsp caster sugar

zest and juice of 1 lemon

special equipment

**a 20cm round spring-form
cake tin and a temperature
probe**

Make the enriched bread dough. Mix in the lemon zest and leave the dough to rest, covered, in a warm place.

After 15 minutes, dust your work surface with flour, uncover the dough and place it on the work surface. Knead the dough for about 10 minutes, or until it feels smooth and satiny, then place it into a lightly oiled bowl, cover with a clean, dry tea towel and leave to rise for 1–1½ hours, or until almost doubled in size.

Grease the cake tin, line it with non-stick baking paper and set it aside. Place the risen dough onto the floured work surface and gently press it down to de-gas it then shape it into a tight round ball. Place the ball into the prepared tin and let it rest for 5 minutes. Press the dough down so it only comes up as far as the edge of the tin then cover loosely with cling film. Leave it to rise for 30 minutes to 1 hour, or until the bun has doubled in size. Towards the end of the rising time preheat the oven to 160°C/gas mark 3.

Bake for 15–20 minutes. Meanwhile make the glaze by placing the sugar, lemon juice and zest and 2 tbsp water into a small pan over medium heat. Let simmer until it has reduced by one-third and is the consistency of light syrup.

When the surface of the bun is a deep golden brown or a temperature probe inserted in the centre reads 95°C the bun is finished. Remove it from the oven and, using a pastry brush, glaze the bun using up all of the syrup. Any excess will run into the tin and be absorbed by the bun. Cool the bun in the tin. To serve, cut into slices and sandwich with either whipped cream or butter and jam. Store in an airtight tin for 2–3 days, or freeze for up to 1 month.

SAUCES

The purpose of a sauce is to complement food. Always be careful to match the right sauce to the right food so that the sauce never dominates. When seasoning a sauce aim for an assertive, but not salty, finish.

INGREDIENTS

Stocks

A good-quality homemade stock forms the foundation of a successful sauce. Stocks can be made in quantity and then stored in the freezer in small amounts so that you have them to hand when cooking. You can find recipes for the most useful stocks in the Soups & Stocks chapter.

Commercial or dried, concentrated stocks lack the body and flavour of a good homemade stock, and so are not ideal for using in sauces. They have little natural gelatine, which means they cannot be reduced down to a sticky glaze the way a homemade stock can be.

Commercial stock can also be high in salt, while good-quality homemade stocks rarely require extra salting thanks to the concentration of natural minerals and salts in the ingredients you use to make them.

Wine and spirits

Wine and certain other stronger forms of alcohol can be delicious used in sauces but unless their alcohol content is burnt off during cooking, they can dominate a sauce. Boiling is sufficient to evaporate away the alcohol in wine. Stronger spirits, such as brandy or rum, must be handled differently. Once these have been added to the pan, ignite the fumes with a lit match to burn the alcohol off. Take care when flaming sauces, however. If you are wearing long sleeves make sure they are tucked back and cannot be set alight, and ensure that you are not standing too near to any overhanging curtains.

A light red or white wine is best for cooking. Avoid using very fine wines (you are better off drinking these), strongly alcoholic wines or those with a very distinctive flavour. Anything too dark or tannic will stain the food, as the pigments do not break down quickly. Do not use old wine or dregs for cooking because any taint will be transferred straight to the sauce.

Butter

Butter (along with milk and cream) often forms the base of a sauce. Unsalted butter is generally used to enrich cream sauces, as well as hollandaise and beurre blanc, because it allows you to decide how much or how little salt to add. Butter can also be added in small quantities at the end of the cooking process to enrich and add gloss to a sauce, or to sweeten a sharp sauce.

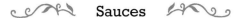

Eggs

Eggs are used in many sauces, for example, to thicken custards, or to stabilise emulsified sauces such as mayonnaise or hollandaise. Buy the best eggs you can afford for this purpose. Not only will their flavour be carried through to the finished sauce, the quality of their fat and protein will make a difference to the result.

Thickeners

Various forms of flour can be used to thicken a sauce.

Plain, soft, wheat flour: This is used to make a roux-based sauce, where the flour and butter are cooked together before stock, milk or cream are added. Cooking the flour and butter together for longer before adding the liquid produces a toasted, or brown, roux, with a rich, nutty flavour. Brown roux is traditionally used for meat-based sauces.

Beurre manié: Kneading together equal quantities of soft wheat flour and butter, uncooked, coats the flour particles in butter and creates a beurre manié. When this is whisked into hot simmering stocks, the butter melts and thickens the sauce without causing lumps. If you are planning to use this mixture to thicken a gravy, use 10g each of butter and plain flour for a lightly thickened result.

Arrowroot: This is the finest starch that can be used to thicken sauces. Meat sauces in particular benefit from the clear, unclouded result arrowroot produces. Arrowroot should be mixed with a little cold water or stock before being whisked into a sauce, and then simmered for a few minutes to cook it completely.

Cornflour: This thickener gives a lighter result than can be achieved using wheat flour. To use cornstarch, mix it with a little cold water to a loose, creamy consistency before whisking it briskly into the hot sauce base. Allow this to simmer for a few minutes to cook the starch thoroughly. Potato starch can be used in place of cornflour and gives similar results.

A NOTE ON GRAVY

Gravy is the sauce made from the caramelised juices of roasted meat left behind in the roasting tin. Adding wine and/or stock to this makes the gravy base, but if you are using wine, allow it to boil for a minute to burn off the alcohol first. Then thicken the liquid with beurre manié, or cornflour or arrowroot mixed with a little water, as described above. Simmer, stirring, to loosen any caramelised bits still adhering to the roasting tin, and to allow the thickener to finish cooking. When the gravy has cooked, allow it to sit for a minute then spoon off any fat that floats to the surface, or use a separating jug.

TECHNIQUES

Roux-based sauces

A roux is simply a cooked mixture of fat, usually butter, and flour that is used to thicken milk- or stock-based sauces. To make a roux, use a medium-sized saucepan with a heavy base. This will distribute the heat evenly, making the sauce less likely to burn. Melt the butter over a low to medium heat. Sift in the flour, stirring all the while. Cook the two together so they bubble and foam and you begin to smell a light, nutty aroma.

Now stir in the liquid a little at a time, stirring constantly and allowing the mixture to simmer between each addition. It is better to use hot liquid. If you stir a cool liquid into the roux, the sauce will cook much more slowly and may become lumpy if not stirred thoroughly. Once all of the liquid has been added simmer the sauce gently, stirring constantly, until the starch in the flour is fully cooked and the sauce is glossy. The sauce can be served immediately or stored, chilled and covered, for several days.

Emulsions

Sauces that are made by blending various ingredients together, either hot or cold, are called emulsions. The key to the success of an emulsion is the rate at which the ingredients are blended. For example, when adding oil or melted butter to egg yolks, add it at a rate of no more than one-third of the volume of the egg yolk mixture at any one time. Only when the mixture is smooth and evenly combined should more oil or melted butter be added in. If the sauce thickens too quickly, adding a tablespoon of warm water will liquify it a little, and then the remaining oil or fat can be added.

Emulsified sauces can be kept warm over a bowl or pan of warm, but not boiling, water. They cannot be reheated once cold. Cold emulsified sauces, such as mayonnaise or vinaigrettes, can be stored, tightly wrapped, in the fridge for a few days. Do not keep sauces containing raw eggs for more than three days.

Egg and cream liaisons

The stock from a fricassee or civet can be thickened by adding it to a liaison (mixture) of egg yolk and cream. A measure of the hot sauce base is blended into the liaison and the resulting mixture is poured back into the remainder of the hot stock and placed over a low heat. As the egg yolk and cream cook gently, they thicken the stock. The sauce is then strained through a very fine sieve to serve.

BECHAMEL SAUCE

✳ Makes 500ml ✳ Preparation time 5 minutes
✳ Cooking time 45 minutes including 30 minutes infusing

Béchamel sauce, historically, arose as an amalgam of a stock-based sauce with milk or cream, which is exactly what Mrs Beeton gives in her original recipe. Today, as we are often catering for non-meat eaters, it tends to be made with milk in place of the stock. You can, of course, use half chicken stock and half milk or single cream if you like. Make sure you allow the vegetables and aromatics plenty of time to infuse. For a truly faithful rendition of the original recipe, add a couple of cloves with the bay leaf.

500ml whole milk

½ medium-sized onion, peeled and diced

½ small carrot, peeled and diced

1 tsp black peppercorns

1 bay leaf

35g butter

35g plain flour

salt (optional)

grated nutmeg (optional)

Put the milk, onion, carrot, peppercorns and bay leaf in a saucepan over a medium heat. Bring the mixture to a simmer then remove from the heat. Cover with a lid and leave for 30 minutes to infuse.

When the milk has finished infusing, make a roux. Melt the butter in a small pan over a medium heat. Add the flour and cook for 5 minutes, stirring, until the mixture starts to foam and gives off a delicate toasting aroma. If the flour begins to turn brown or burn at the edges, immediately remove the pan from the heat and dip the base in cold water.

Now bring the milk back to a simmer and strain it through a fine sieve into a large jug, discarding the vegetables. Place the roux back onto a gentle heat and whisk a little of the hot milk into it, blending it in completely before adding a little more. Repeat until all the milk has been added, then continue to simmer the sauce gently for 3–4 minutes until it is glossy, silky and free of lumps. If the sauce tastes floury continue cooking for 1–2 minutes, then season with a little salt and a few gratings of nutmeg, if desired. This sauce can be stored in the fridge, covered closely with cling film, for up to 4 days.

Note: For a simple and tasty cheese sauce, add 80–100g grated Isle of Mull Cheddar and ½ tsp English mustard powder to the hot béchamel sauce, blend well and serve.

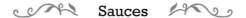

APPLE SAUCE

✳ **Serves 4** ✳ **Preparation time 10 minutes** ✳ **Cooking time 15 minutes**

Mrs Beeton would have used an old variety of apple for her sauce. Our now ubiquitous Bramley had only just been discovered and the first trees did not appear for sale until after her book was published. The butter adds natural sweetness, while the new additions of bay leaf and shallot lend a savoury note that makes this sauce more appealing to the modern palate. Serve with cooked game, pork or poultry.

20g unsalted butter

1 shallot, peeled and finely chopped

1 bay leaf

2 large cooking apples, peeled, cored and chopped into small pieces

pinch salt

sugar, to taste

Place the butter in a small saucepan over a medium heat. Add the shallot and bay leaf. Cook for 2–3 minutes, stirring. Add the finely chopped apple and cook until the apple begins to break down. Add a splash of water as the apple cooks to keep it just moist enough to prevent it catching or burning. Add the salt and a little sugar to taste. Continue to cook, stirring occasionally, until the apple is soft. Cool, remove the bay leaf and serve at room temperature.

HORSERADISH SAUCE

✳ **Serves 8** ✳ **Preparation time 10 minutes**

Mrs Beeton recommends horseradish sauce a lot – and it almost sums up the British taste for piquant in one recipe. It is the perfect complement to a cold piece of beef or smoked fish – adding a little lemon zest gives a welcome freshness.

200ml double cream

½ tsp caster sugar

1 tsp white wine vinegar

½ tsp English mustard powder, or to taste

50g piece fresh horseradish root

lemon juice, to taste

½ tsp finely grated lemon zest (optional)

salt and freshly ground black pepper

Place the cream, a pinch of salt and the sugar, white wine vinegar and mustard powder in a large bowl and beat until the mixture begins to form soft peaks.

Peel the horseradish root and rub with a little lemon juice to prevent it going brown. Finely grate the root into the cream, stirring it in and tasting as you go. Stop when it is strong enough for your taste. Stir in the lemon zest, if using, and season to taste. Chill until ready to serve but use on the day of making.

BREAD SAUCE

✳ Serves 4 ✳ Preparation time 10 minutes
✳ Cooking time 1 hour including 30 minutes infusing time

Either milk or stock can be used for this sauce, though milk gives a creamier result. This sauce has the classic milk seasonings of pepper, mace and bay to add piquancy. As Mrs Beeton says, it should be used alongside game or poultry.

500ml whole milk

1 small onion, peeled
and quartered

1 bay leaf

½ tsp black peppercorns

3 cloves

2 blades mace

100g stale white breadcrumbs

15g butter

20ml double cream

grated nutmeg, to taste

salt and freshly ground
black pepper

Place the milk, onion, bay leaf, peppercorns, cloves, and mace and a few gratings of nutmeg in a saucepan over a medium heat. Bring the mixture to simmering then remove from the heat. Cover with a lid and leave for 30 minutes to infuse.

Strain the milk through a fine sieve into a clean pan set on a low heat, discarding the vegetables and whole spices. Add the breadcrumbs and cook gently, stirring occasionally for 10–15 minutes, or until the sauce is very thick but still soft and smooth. Beat in the butter and cream, and season the sauce with about ¼ tsp each salt and black pepper. Transfer to a warmed gravy boat or serving jug, cover and rest for 15–20 minutes in a warm place. Grate a little nutmeg over, beat it in and serve.

FISH CREAM SAUCE

✳ Serves 4 ✳ Preparation time 15 minutes ✳ Cooking time 45 minutes

Mrs Beeton's cream sauce for fish is a simple mixture of cream with salt, cayenne, and a little mace or lemon juice, thickened with butter and flour. She also suggests adding shallots for flavour. This updated version shows how this kind of sauce has developed over the intervening period, using fish stock, wine and vermouth to add layers of flavour. The result is a more rounded sauce that will appeal to the modern palate. Fennel and garlic, which were available but not well used in Victorian Britain, have also been added to the shallots as they pair well with fish.

150g fish bones, preferably flatfish

150g white fish trimmings

1 small carrot, peeled

1 small stick celery, trimmed

1 small piece fennel, trimmed

½ small onion, peeled and halved

2 tsp sunflower oil

100g shallot, peeled and finely sliced

½ bulb fennel, finely sliced

1 small garlic clove, peeled and finely sliced

1 bay leaf

50ml white wine

50ml dry white Vermouth (Noilly Prat), plus extra to serve

300ml double cream

lemon juice, to taste

2 tbsp finely chopped fresh chervil, parsley or tarragon, to serve

salt

First make the stock by placing the fish bones and trimmings and the pieces of carrot, celery, fennel and onion, along with 750ml cold water, into a pan over a medium heat. Bring the stock almost to simmering then turn the heat to low and cook for 20 minutes. Remove from the heat and pour through a fine sieve into a bowl, discard the bones and vegetables.

Pour the sunflower oil into a medium saucepan over a medium heat. Add the finely sliced shallot, fennel and garlic along with the bay leaf and cook gently until the vegetables are soft, but not coloured.

Add the white wine and Vermouth and cook until the liquid has almost all evaporated, then add the stock and simmer until reduced by three-quarters. Finally, add the double cream and cook until the liquid has reduced by half.

Season with lemon juice and salt to taste, then pass the mixture through a fine sieve into a sauceboat or serving jug. Just before serving, add ½ tbsp dry Vermouth and sprinkle over the finely chopped herbs.

BEURRE BLANC

✳ Serves 4 ✳ Preparation time 5 minutes ✳ Cooking time 15 minutes

This sauce, a French classic, is similar to Mrs Beeton's many butter sauces, but avoids the use of flour, so it is a really versatile and easy sauce to make. Use the best unsalted butter and you will find that it amalgamates more easily with the vinegary shallots.

1 large or 2 small shallots, peeled and finely sliced

100ml dry white wine

1 tbsp white wine vinegar

1 tbsp single cream

200g chilled unsalted butter, cut into 20 cubes

lemon juice, to taste

white pepper, to taste

Place the sliced shallot, wine and vinegar in a small stainless steel pan over a medium heat. Bring to a simmer and cook, stirring occasionally, until all of the liquid has evaporated. Whisk in the cream and turn the heat down very low, resting the pan on just half the ring to avoid overheating the sauce. Add the butter in chunks, beating rapidly to amalgamate until it is all incorporated and the sauce is smooth. Do not allow the butter to melt or turn to oil. If it does, throw in a small splash of cold water or an ice cube and beat well to emulsify. Strain the sauce through a fine sieve into a small pan, add a squeeze of lemon juice and a pinch of white pepper to taste, and serve immediately with poached or grilled fish. This sauce does not keep for more than 30 minutes.

PARSLEY & GARLIC BUTTER

✳ Makes 100g ✳ Preparation time 5 minutes

Mrs Beeton's parsley butter was suggested as an accompaniment to boiled fowls – which we rarely cook today. However, the addition of a little garlic turns the original recipe into a versatile butter for the modern kitchen. It is whipped to ensure that it does not run when heated.

100g softened unsalted butter

large bunch of parsley, leaves only, finely chopped

2 garlic cloves, finely chopped

½ tsp Maldon or other flaky salt

Place the butter in a medium-sized bowl and whip until creamy, pale and fluffy. Add the parsley, garlic and salt and whip until combined.

Cover and chill until required. It will keep for 2 days in the fridge.

HOLLANDAISE SAUCE

✽ Serves 4 ✽ Preparation time 15 minutes ✽ Cooking time 10 to 15 minutes

Mrs Beeton's Dutch sauce for fish contains a lot less butter than this modern recipe, and a lot more acid (in the original both vinegar and lemon juice are used). Today, we prefer a less sharp sauce, and we commonly serve it not only with fish but also with vegetables such as asparagus, or poured over eggs.

250g unsalted butter

2 large egg yolks

½ tsp lemon juice

salt to taste

special equipment

a heatproof glass or ceramic bowl

Place the butter in a small pan over a medium heat. When it has melted, turn the heat off and keep the pan warm to one side.

Place a heatproof glass or ceramic bowl over a pan of barely simmering water over a low to medium heat. Make sure that the base of the bowl does not touch the water.

Add the egg yolks and lemon juice to the bowl along with ½ tsp water, whisking continuously until they become pale and fluffy. Whisk the hot butter into the egg mixture a little at a time until it is fully incorporated. Continue to whisk until the sauce is thickened and hot. Remove the pan and bowl from the heat to stop it cooking any further and season to taste with a little salt. The sauce can be kept warm over the water for 30 minutes but then must be used, as it will not keep.

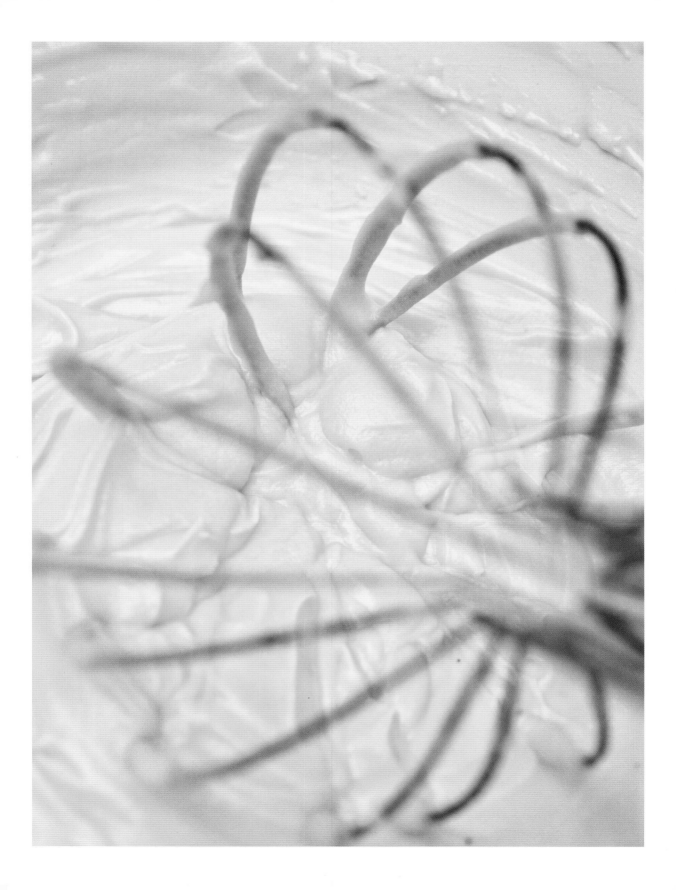

MAYONNAISE

✳ Serves 4 ✳ Preparation time 10 minutes

Mrs Beeton noted that patience is needed to make this sauce well, and she is right. The liaison works only if each addition of oil is fully incorporated before more is added. You can experiment with the mix of oils – but using a majority of mild oil will keep the sauce light so that it does not overpower the rest of the meal.

1 very fresh whole egg plus 1 yolk

½ tbsp Dijon mustard

1 tbsp white wine vinegar

1 scant tsp Maldon or other sea salt, or ½ tsp fine salt

2 garlic cloves, peeled and crushed (optional)

250ml light olive oil

3 tbsp water

50ml strong extra virgin olive oil

lemon juice to taste

Place the whole egg and the extra yolk, mustard, vinegar, salt and the crushed garlic, if you are making garlic mayonnaise, into the jug of a blender and whiz for 10 seconds until creamy. With the motor still running, slowly add the light olive oil in a thin stream, pausing every few seconds to allow the sauce to emulsify before you add more oil.

Continue until the oil is fully incorporated. You should notice that the sauce thickens as you go, and the mixture turns paler. Leave the machine running, add 3 tbsp water and mix for 2 minutes, then slowly add the extra virgin olive oil as before.

Add ½ tsp lemon juice and adjust to taste with a little more lemon juice and salt, if you like. To gain a finer texture, pass the mayonnaise through a sieve before serving.

For a firmer mayonnaise, add 50–100ml more extra virgin olive oil, then add a very little cold water to thin it to the consistency you desire. Store in the fridge in a sealed jar or covered closely with cling film, and eat within 2 days.

Note: Mayonnaise can split if too much oil is added at once. If this happens, the mixture will turn quickly from a thickening sauce to a liquid, oily mass. To rectify this, start with a clean bowl and add another egg yolk mixed with 1 tbsp tepid water. Beat the two together lightly and then, carefully, add the split mayonnaise a little at a time, beating well with each addition. You should end up with only slightly more mayonnaise than you initially intended, but it saves throwing away your first batch.

SALAD CREAM

✳ Serves 4 ✳ Preparation time 5 minutes ✳ Cooking time 15 minutes

Mrs Beeton gave two cream dressings for salad – delicious sauces that cling to crisp, fresh leaves. They are similar in fact to the mustardy remoulade sauce used in the French kitchen, but more refined and delicate: perfect when used to dress cos lettuce and radishes. The recipe below is based on one of the originals, with the quantities adjusted slightly to balance the flavours. This quantity will coat approximately 200g of salad leaves.

1 egg

1 tsp mustard

1 large pinch salt

1 large pinch sugar

1 pinch white pepper

1 pinch cayenne pepper

1 tbsp cider or white wine vinegar

6 tbsp single cream

Place the egg in a small pan of cold water and place it on a high heat. Bring to a boil, then reduce the heat to low and cook for 8 minutes. Remove the pan from the heat and lift out the egg with a slotted spoon. Place the egg in a bowl of cold water for five minutes to cool, then peel it and remove the yolk from the white. The white can be reserved for another recipe, or for sprinkling on the salad when ready to eat.

Place the yolk in a medium bowl and mash it with the mustard, salt, sugar, peppers and vinegar until there are no lumps. Slowly stir in the cream, mixing the dressing well to amalgamate. Chill until ready to use. This salad cream will keep for up to 2 days in the fridge.

To use, simply place 200g salad leaves in a large bowl, drizzle over the dressing and toss well to amalgamate. If using, chop the egg white finely and scatter over the salad. Serve immediately.

EVERYDAY CUSTARD

✳ Serves 6 ✳ Preparation time 5 minutes
✳ Cooking time 30 minutes including 15 minutes infusing time

This quick recipe uses cornflour to thicken the sauce. It is an economical way of making custard and is perfect for a trifle (see page 272).

1 tbsp cornflour

450ml whole or Jersey milk

80g caster sugar

1 vanilla pod, split lengthways

4 large egg yolks

special equipment

a heatproof glass bowl
and a temperature probe

In a medium-sized bowl, mix the cornflour and just enough milk to make a thin paste. Set this aside and place the remaining milk, half the sugar and the vanilla pod in a pan. Slowly bring to a boil, whisking often to prevent sticking. Once it has boiled, remove the pan from the heat, cover with a lid and leave for 15 minutes to infuse.

Meanwhile, place the eggs yolks and the remaining sugar in a heatproof glass bowl and whisk until pale and fluffy.

Now remove the vanilla pod from the milk and scrape the seeds from the pod back into the pan. Place the pan over a medium heat. When the mixture is simmering, pour it onto the cornflour mixture in the bowl, stir, and then pour it back into the pan. Simmer for 2–3 minutes, still stirring, to cook the sauce. If the sauce still tastes floury at this point, continue cooking on a low heat for another 1–2 minutes.

Beat the egg yolk mixture once more and then pour the simmering sauce onto it, whisking constantly to combine thoroughly.

Rinse out the milk pan and half fill it with hot water. Place it over a medium heat and set the bowl of custard mixture on top, making sure that base of the bowl does not touch the water. Cook, stirring continuously, until the custard thickens. If you like, test with a temperature probe as you stir. The sauce needs to cook to 80–83°C to thicken. If you notice that the sauce is curdling at the bottom of the bowl, remove it from the heat immediately.

Strain the cooked custard through a sieve into a serving jug or a cold, clean bowl to stop it cooking any further. Either serve immediately or, if using for a trifle, cool the custard, cover it closely with cling film and store in the fridge for up to 3 days.

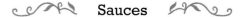
SPECIAL CUSTARD

✳ Serves 4 ✳ Preparation time 5 minutes
✳ Cooking time 30 minutes including 20 minutes infusing time

This recipe takes Mrs Beeton's suggestion of using cream instead of milk and gives a luxurious custard that is perfect for a treat. You may find that when you add the hot cream to the eggs it thickens perfectly without requiring further cooking – if not, simply cook out over simmering water as the recipe suggests.

350ml double cream

50g caster sugar

1 vanilla pod, split lengthways

5 egg yolks

special equipment

a medium-sized heatproof glass bowl

Place the cream, half the sugar and the vanilla pod in a small saucepan over a medium heat. When it reaches simmering point, remove the pan from the heat, cover with a lid and leave for 20 minutes to infuse.

While the cream is infusing, whisk the egg yolks and the remaining sugar together in a medium-sized heatproof glass bowl until light and fluffy. Then half-fill another saucepan with hot water and set it over a medium heat.

Once the cream has infused, remove the vanilla pod and, using a small knife, scrape the seeds into the cream. Then return the cream to the heat and bring to a boil. Just as the cream begins to rise up the sides of the pan, give the eggs a whisk and pour the cream over them, beating to blend the mixture well. Then place the bowl over the pan of water, making sure that the base of the bowl does not touch the water. Stir until the custard thickens. If the sauce begins to curdle, remove it from the heat immediately. Pour the custard through a sieve into a cold, clean bowl or jug and serve.

Note: Sauces that are thickened with egg yolks need to be heated to allow the yolks to coagulate, but overheating causes the mixture to curdle. To avoid this, custards are usually finished in a bowl over a pan of gently simmering water, which can take time. To speed up the process, it is possible to use a microwave. Once the hot cream or milk has been added to the yolks, place the mixture in a microwave and cook it in 30-second blasts, stirring well after each to check the thickness of the liquid.

JAMS, JELLIES & PICKLES

Preserving food that would otherwise be wasted, by making jams and pickles, is an old technique that is still highly valued in the British kitchen. Fruit and vegetables can be preserved in many ways, using sugar, salt, vinegar and heat, often in combination, to inhibit the growth of microbes that would otherwise cause the food to spoil.

THE DIFFERENT TYPES OF PRESERVE

Jam: The essence of a good jam – made using pieces of fruit and sugar – is its flavour. This is enhanced by using top-notch ingredients and limiting the cooking time to just enough to cook the jam and achieve a 'set'. A natural gelling compound, pectin, is present in most fruits, but not always in sufficient quantities to set the jam, even if it is boiled for hours. Commercially prepared pectin, either in liquid form or added to sugar to make 'jam sugar', encourages jam to set even with a limited boiling time.

Jams are best eaten within a month or two of being made, in which case they can be made with three parts sugar to four parts fruit, which will give the best balance of fruit and sugar. For a jam that will keep for longer, use equal quantities of sugar and fruit. The higher sugar content helps prevent fermentation or the growth of moulds. Jams made with jam sugar, or those with added liquid pectin, should begin to set at 105°C. For notes on setting jam, see page 351.

Note that preserving sugar and jam sugar are not the same thing. Jam sugar has added pectin, whereas preserving sugar is simply a clear form of white sugar, which will give good results when used for making preserves.

Jelly: Jellies, in this context, are made from the juices of cooked fruits and are particularly useful for fruits that have tiny seeds, such as currants and blackberries. The fruit is first cooked with a little water, then placed in muslin over a bowl or pot. The muslin retains any debris or pips while the juice drips through the fabric. The juice is then cooked with sugar to 105°C, usually with added pectin, to obtain a set.

Fruit cheeses and butters: These preserves are based on the sieved pulp of cooked fruits. Fruit butter get its name from its texture. Fruit cheese is traditionally kept in straight-sided jars or pots for ease of removal, which makes them resemble a small cheese, hence the name. Fruit cheeses and butters are an excellent way of preserving strongly flavoured fruits, such as damson and quince, and they are delicious served with cheese. Fruit butters are generally made with three parts sugar to four parts fruit, while fruit cheeses are made with equal quantities of each.

Curds: These short-lived preserves are made with eggs, butter, sugar and, usually, citrus fruit juices, cooked on a low heat over a pan of simmering water. Other sharp fruits like currants can be made into curds, too. Curds should be kept in the fridge and eaten within a month of being made.

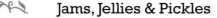

Marmalades: Either a single or a mixed variety of citrus fruits can be made into marmalade. In England the most common, and best, marmalades are made from Seville oranges. These are available in the middle of winter and into early spring, but you can freeze the oranges for use at other times of the year. Because citrus fruits contain a high percentage of pectin, marmalades are usually made with a high proportion of water, unlike jams.

Candied peel and fruit: Fruit is candied by soaking it in increasing concentrations of sugar syrup over a number of days. The resulting product is very sweet and can be stored when wet or after it has been dried. Although it is possible to candy whole fruits, such as clementines and oranges, the easiest method, and one of the nicest, is to candy your own citrus peel. Thick-skinned oranges and grapefruit, in particular, make excellent candied peel that's far better than any kind of peel you can buy. It is best to make a large quantity at once for drying, storing or freezing. Candied peel that has been sliced and dipped in chocolate makes an excellent gift.

Bottled fruits and vegetables: The technique for bottling fruit and vegetables to preserve them involves sterilising filled jars either in a hot water bath or a low oven. The resulting preserves will keep for an indefinite period of time. Although this technique is common on the continent, it is sadly no longer much practised in the UK. This is a shame, as it is a very handy way of storing fruit, especially in a glut when you might not have the space to freeze it. Because it is the heat that preserves the fruit, bottling retains more of the character of the fruit than freezing, and it can be done with or without sugar. Sauces made from fruit and vegetables, and condiments that do not have a high sugar or salt content, and which would otherwise spoil, can also be preserved successfully by bottling.

Always be careful to use the right equipment if you choose this method of preserving, otherwise you may end up with jars that shatter during heating. Very deep pans and preserving (Kilner) jars specifically designed for the purpose are available from good kitchen shops.

Pickles: Pickling is the preservation of pieces of fruit or vegetables in a mixture of vinegar, sugar and spices, and many fruits and vegetables can be made into pickles. They can be cooked, as in the case of beetroot, or raw, as in the case of onions. Firm vegetables are often soaked in a mild brine solution overnight to soften and flavour them prior to pickling. Pickles should usually be left for a minimum of one month before eating to allow them to mature, though three months is best. Thereafter they will keep for up to one year before losing their freshness.

Chutneys: A blend of fruit and/or vegetables is cooked with spices into a soft, reduced mass to make chutney. Sugar and vinegar are added for their preservative qualities. Chutneys should be left for a minimum of one month, or up to three months, before eating to allow them to mature. Chutneys can keep for up to one year before losing their freshness.

SOURCING INGREDIENTS

When preserving, always use fruit and vegetables that are in the peak of their season. They will then be at their most flavourful and should be at their lowest price, and you may be able to buy them by the crate or box from pick-your-own farms, farmers' markets or greengrocers at a keen price. (It is always worth haggling when stocks are high.) Look for fruit and vegetables that are plump, fresh, unbruised and dry and avoid buying fruit that is over-ripe – even if it is labelled 'good for jamming'. Also avoid fruit that is under-ripe because its flavour will not have developed fully.

PRESERVING EQUIPMENT

Pans: A large, heavy, stainless steel jam-making (or maslin) pan is essential for home jam-making. Most of the pans on the market are of 9-litre capacity, with graded metric and imperial measurements on the inside. Buy one with two handles for ease of pouring. Aluminium pans are not suitable for making most preserves because the metal is easily dissolved by the fruit acids and vinegars you will be using.

Jam funnels: A wide-necked jam funnel is very useful when transferring hot preserves into jars. These can be metal or silicone. Before using, sterilise them in boiling water for two or three minutes.

Jars: Any modern glass jars should be suitable for preserves, but they will need to withstand temperatures of up to 120°C, because they must be sterilised in a low oven before use. Jar lids with rubberised seals must be boiled for 2–3 minutes to sterilise them. Kilner jars with rubber seals and clasps are excellent for this purpose.

Whatever you use, it is important to get a good seal to prevent drying out or spoilage. Metal lids are not appropriate for most preserves because fruit acids and vinegars will dissolve the metal. Plastic lids can be used, as can waxed-paper discs and cellophane, so long as they are secured well with string or an elastic band.

Ladles and spoons: Ladles and spoons for making jam must be scrupulously clean and non-absorbent to avoid any cross-contamination of flavours from other food. It is a good idea to keep your jam-making equipment separate and only use it for that purpose. A heatproof, silicone spatula is very useful for scraping out the pan.

QUANTITIES

When first making preserves, only attempt to make a small quantity. Jams and jellies in particular are best made in quantities of no more than one kilogram at a time so that they come to a boil quickly, preserving more of the fruit flavour and colour. If you find yourself faced with a large glut of fruit, work with two pans at once. One pan can be used to warm the fruit and dissolve the sugar, while the jam in the other pan is finishing. This way, you can easily make a series of small batches.

SETTING JAMS AND JELLIES

The individual recipes included in this chapter include many of the techniques commonly used when making preserves. The method for checking whether the setting point has been reached is the same for all jam and jelly recipes. Before beginning your jam or jelly, put one or two saucers in the fridge to cool, then follow the method described below:

Mixtures of fruit or fruit juices and sugar will come to a boil at a temperature over 100°C. As the water is driven off by boiling, the temperature will increase and the sugar concentration will rise. To test for temperature, make sure that your thermometer or probe is held in the main body of the jam. If it is held too near the bottom or top the reading will be inaccurate. As the mixture of fruit and sugar approaches 105°C, it will noticeably thicken, because at this point the pectin will begin to gel together to form a mesh. How long this takes depends on many factors, such as sugar content and acidity. You can see how far the pectin has meshed (in other words, if the jam or jelly has reached a setting point), by using the cold-saucer test.

To test for a set, spoon a small amount of the mixture onto one of the cold saucers you have placed in the fridge. Let it sit for a minute, then push the edge with your finger. You should notice that the surface wrinkles. If it does not, continue to cook the jam for a couple of minutes and then test it on a cold saucer again.

If the jam reaches a temperature above 107°C and has not yet reached a setting point, remove it from the heat. You can ladle it into the jars at this point but you will find that your jam does not set perfectly. If you prefer, you can add additional lemon juice, which is high in pectin, in the ratio of 1 lemon for each 500g of fruit in the initial mixture, then reboil. After adding the lemon juice, you should find that the jam sets. If you use jam sugar, which also contains added pectin, you should find that the jam sets every time without the addition of extra lemon juice.

APRICOT JAM

※ **Makes 1.5 kg – 3 or 4 jars** ※ **Preparation time 15 minutes** ※ **Cooking time 25 minutes**

There is more than a hint of high summer in this wonderful jam. Mrs Beeton scented it with the kernels of the apricots, which impart a delicious bitter-almond flavour. It is well worth spending the minute or two it takes to extract the kernels from the stones. Pay particular attention to this jam as it cooks – the skins of the apricots have a habit of sticking to the bottom of the pan.

1kg fresh apricots

750g jam sugar

juice of 1 lemon

special equipment

a stainless steel preserving pan, a small hammer and a sugar thermometer or temperature probe

Heat the oven to 120°C/gas mark ½ and place your clean jars on a baking sheet in the oven. Put a couple of saucers in the fridge for testing the set.

Halve the apricots, reserving the stones. Place the fruit in a large stainless steel pan with the jam sugar, lemon juice and 200ml water. Stir gently to amalgamate and leave to sit for 5 minutes.

Meanwhile, using a small hammer, break 10 of the stones and release the kernels. Place these in a small pan of water and bring to the boil. Cook for 2 minutes, then drain and cool in a bowl of cold water. Skin the kernels, chop finely and add to the pan of fruit.

Now place the large pan over a medium heat. Stir to dissolve the sugar into the fruit, then turn the heat up and bring to a rapid boil, stirring to prevent the apricot skins sticking to the bottom.

Boil the mixture rapidly for 3–4 minutes. When the jam has reached 105°C and begins to thicken, start testing for setting point using the cold-saucer method on page 351.

When the jam is ready, remove it from the heat and allow it to form a skin. Remove and discard any scum that has formed, then pot the jam into the warm, sterilised jars. Cover the surface of the jam with a waxed-paper disc and seal the jar with cellophane.

BLACKCURRANT JAM

❋ **Makes approx 1.5kg – 3 or 4 jars** ❋ **Preparation time 30 minutes**
❋ **Cooking time 20 minutes**

When they are in their peak season, in the middle of July, you will find blackcurrants in farm shops and markets. Carefully pick the berries from their stems and remove any greenish berries before weighing the fruit and proceeding with the jam. This jam has an intense flavour and is a good keeper.

1kg blackcurrants

750g jam sugar

special equipment

a stainless steel preserving pan and a sugar thermometer or temperature probe

Heat the oven to 120°C/gas mark ½ and place your clean jars on a baking sheet in the oven. Put a couple of saucers in the fridge for testing the set.

Place the blackcurrants in a stainless steel pan with 200ml water and bring to a gentle simmer over a low heat for approximately 5 minutes, until the fruit breaks down. Add the sugar and stir until it has dissolved.

Turn up the heat and bring the fruit to a rolling boil, stirring constantly to prevent it catching.

Boil rapidly for 3–4 minutes, and when the temperature of the fruit has reached 105°C and the mixture begins to thicken, start testing for setting point using the cold-saucer method on page 351.

When the jam is ready, remove it from the heat and allow the jam to form a skin. Remove and discard any scum that has formed, then pot the jam into the warm, sterilised jars. Cover the surface of the jam with a waxed-paper disc and seal the jar with cellophane.

BERRY JAM

* Makes approx 1.5kg – 3 or 4 jars * Preparation time 10 minutes
* Cooking time 15 minutes

This recipe works well with strawberries, raspberries or brambles. For the best flavour it should only be made with dry, ripe fruit in peak season. Make only as much as you will eat in a month or two, as lightly set jams like this one do not keep forever. Mrs Beeton added redcurrant juice to her berry jams for its pectin and acidity, but a little lemon juice and jam sugar, used in combination, make a delicious jam that should set quickly.

900g fruit, stalks removed

750g jam sugar

2 tbsp lemon juice

special equipment

a stainless steel preserving pan and a sugar thermometer or temperature probe

Heat the oven to 120°C/gas mark ½ and place your clean jars on a baking sheet in the oven. Place a couple of saucers in the fridge for testing the set.

Chop the berries in half if they are large, then mix the fruit, sugar and lemon juice in a large stainless steel pan. Place the pan over a medium heat and stir gently as the fruit begins to release its juice. After 2 or 3 minutes turn the heat to high and scrape any sugar back from the sides of the pan into the mix. Boil rapidly for 3–4 minutes, stirring continuously to prevent the jam burning on the bottom of the pan.

When the temperature of the fruit has reached 105°C and the mixture begins to thicken, start testing for setting point using the cold-saucer method on page 351.

When it is ready, remove from the heat and allow the jam to form a skin. Remove and discard any scum that has formed, then pot the jam into the warm, sterilised jars. Cover the surface of the jam with a waxed-paper disc and seal the jar with cellophane.

SEVILLE ORANGE MARMALADE

✻ **Makes approx 3kg marmalade – 6 to 8 jars** ✻ **Preparation time hour 30 minutes**
✻ **Cooking time 2 hours to soften peel plus 1 hour to finish**

The bitter Seville orange, with its sharp juice and aromatic zest, has been valued in the kitchen since long before its sweet cousin arrived in England around 400 years ago. Mrs Beeton was clearly keen on both, using them widely in her preserves. The intensity of the Seville is unmatched, though, and this makes it superb for making marmalade.

1.4kg Seville oranges

2.8kg preserving sugar

1 lemon, sliced

special equipment

a stainless steel preserving pan, a muslin square and a sugar thermometer or temperature probe

Place the oranges in a large stainless steel pan with 3 litres of water and bring to a boil, then simmer the fruit gently for 2½ hours or until its skin is tender and the water has reduced to about 2.5 litres.

Remove the oranges to a colander set over a large bowl to catch the drips, and reserve the liquid in the pan. Still over the colander, cut the oranges in half and scoop the pith, pulp and seeds out into a bowl, then slice and reserve the peel. You should end up with roughly 1.9 litres of juice, 700g of sliced peel and 625g of pulp and seeds. If your volume of juice is less than this, add some of the reserved cooking water to make up the difference.

Place 2 saucers in the fridge to chill for testing the set, and put your clean jars in a cool oven, 120°C/gas mark ½. Return the liquid and peel to the pan. Wrap the pith, pulp, seeds and sliced lemon in a muslin square, tie securely and drop that into the pan too. Over a high heat, simmer for 10 minutes until the peel is tender. Add the sugar, stirring well until fully dissolved, and then bring to a rapid boil over a high heat. Continue stirring frequently until the mixutre reaches 105° or starts to thicken, then test for the setting point using the cold-saucer method on page 351.

Remove the pan from the heat and allow the marmalade to stand for 10 minutes to form a skin, so that the peel will not rise when it is put into jars. Remove and discard any scum that has formed , then pot the marmalade into the warm jars, cover the surface with a disc of waxed paper and seal with cellophane. Store in a cool, dark place and use within 1 year of making.

CANDIED PEEL

* Makes about 2kg * Preparation time 20 minutes
* Cooking time approx 6 hours over 3 days plus 2 days air-drying

Although Mrs Beeton did not give a recipe for candied peel, it was listed as an ingredient in many of her cakes and puddings. If you are a regular orange or grapefruit eater, this is an excellent way of using up the peel which you would otherwise throw away. Candied peel makes a wonderful addition to many of the cake recipes in this book.

12 pink or red grapefruit or large oranges

3–4 kg granulated sugar

special equipment

a large stainless steel preserving pan

Make 2 cuts around each grapefruit at right angles allowing you to peel off the skin in 4 segments, leaving the fruit intact. The fruit can then be eaten or juiced.

Place the peel in a large stainless steel pan. Cover with cold water, bring to the boil, and then discard the liquid. Repeat this process twice more, draining the peel after the third blanching. You will end up with about 1.5kg of blanched peel, depending on the size of the fruit.

Make the syrup by dissolving 2kg sugar in 2 litres of water. Add the peel, return to the heat and simmer very gently for approximately 2 hours, or until the peel is translucent and very tender. Remove from the heat and cool overnight.

The next day, transfer the peel to a bowl, measure the volume of the syrup and add sugar at the rate of 1kg per litre. Place over a medium heat and stir to dissolve the sugar, then increase the heat and bring to a rolling boil. Pour back over the peel and leave to cool overnight.

The next day, remove the peel and boil the syrup again, then pour back over the peel and once again leave overnight to cool.

Once cooled, strain and arrange the peel on a wire cooling rack over a tray to catch drips. Allow it to dry at a warm room temperature for two days, until the peel begins to feel dry to the touch.

Once it is absolutely dry, pack in sealed jars, filling up the space in between the slices with granulated sugar. If you prefer moist peel, it can be frozen instead.

LEMON CURD

* Makes approx 1.2kg – 3 or 4 jars * Preparation time 20 minutes
* Cooking time 30 minutes

Although Mrs Beeton did not give a recipe for lemon curd as such, the filling for her lemon cheesecakes is effectively the same thing. To complete her recipe, simply spoon the curd into puff pastry cases in much the same way you would make jam tarts. This short-keeping preserve can also be used to fill a lemon sponge (see page 293) – simply mix with an equal quantity of lightly whipped double cream.

6–8 large, juicy lemons

225g unsalted butter

550g caster sugar

5 medium eggs and
2 egg yolks

special equipment

a large ceramic or heatproof
glass bowl

Place 3–4 clean jars on a baking sheet and into an oven heated to 120°C/gas mark ½.

Finely grate the zest of the lemons, then cut them in half and squeeze, straining the juice through a sieve into a bowl. Measure the juice: you need 250ml. If you have any excess, keep it in the fridge and use within 2 days.

Cut the butter into small pieces and place in a large ceramic or heatproof glass bowl over a pan of gently simmering water. Add the sugar and the lemon zest and juice, and stir with a wooden spoon until the sugar has completely dissolved.

Lightly beat the eggs and yolks and strain through a sieve into the mixture, stirring over a gentle heat to cook.

Continue to stir until the mixture thickens, which it will do at about 85°C, then remove it from the heat and pour into the warm jars. Cover the surface of the curd with a waxed-paper disc and seal the jar with cellophane.

Once cool, store in the fridge and use within 1 month.

BOTTLED PLUMS

* Makes 3 x 1-litre Kilner jars * Preparation time 30 minutes
* Cooking time approx 1 hour

This is a simple way of preserving plums or other soft fruit for winter use, especially if you do not have a freezer large enough to hold a glut of produce. The temperatures and times given are specific to achieve a product that will not perish, so you will need a sugar thermometer or temperature probe to make this recipe.

2kg purple plums

1kg granulated or caster sugar (you will require 300–400ml syrup for each 1-litre jar, see method)

special equipment

a sugar thermometer or temperature probe and 3 x 1-litre Kilner jars (standard jars not made for preserving are at risk of exploding)

Halve the plums, and remove and discard the stones. Place a large, deep pan of water over a medium heat. The pan must be deep enough to cover the jars when filled.

Make the syrup by heating 2 litres of water in another saucepan and adding the sugar. Bring to the boil, stirring occasionally, and simmer for 2 minutes, then cool to 65°C.

Ensure that the pan of water is at about 40°C, then pack the halved plums into the jars, pushing them in firmly. Pour the hot syrup over the plums, ensuring that there are no air bubbles and filling the jars right up to the brim. Place the seals on top and screw on the lids, tightening them right up and then slackening by a quarter turn.

Place a sheet of newspaper in the bottom of the pan, and then stand the jars into the water, ensuring that they are covered to a depth of at least 50mm.

Turn the heat up and quickly bring the water to a simmer (about 90°C). Adjust the heat as necessary to maintain this temperature for 20 minutes. When you have finished, carefully lift the jars from the hot-water bath and tighten the screw-on lids. Cool, then store in a cool, dark place and use within 1 year.

BLACKCURRANT CHEESE

✳ **Makes 750g – about 3 or 4 jars** ✳ **Preparation time 10 minutes** ✳ **Cooking time 30 minutes**

In the style of Mrs Beeton, although not strictly one of her recipes, this preserve is included to use up the remains of the blackcurrant cordial recipe on page 384. It gives a richly flavoured fruit cheese that can be served with terrines or cheeses, or simply cut into chunks, dipped in caster sugar and enjoyed as a sweet.

800g blackcurrants – or you can use the pulp discarded after making blackcurrant cordial (see page 384). In this case, use only 400g sugar.

600g jam sugar

special equipment

a large stainless steel preserving pan

Place your jars on a clean baking sheet in a low oven at 120°C/gas mark ½.

Purée the fruit thoroughly in a food processor, then pass through a fine sieve into a large stainless steel pan. Add the sugar, and cook over a medium heat, stirring constantly, until a rapid boil is achieved, then reduce the heat to low and cook until the mixture thickens and a spoon drawn across the bottom of the pan leaves a clean trail. This will take approximately 15–20 minutes.

Pot the cheese into your sterilised jars, cover the surface of the cheese with a waxed-paper disc and seal the jar with cellophane. Store in a cool, dark place and use within 1 year of making.

DAMSON CHEESE

✳ **Makes 1.8kg – 4 or 5 jars** ✳ **Preparation time 30 minutes**
✳ **Cooking time 1 hour 30 minutes**

Mrs Beeton gave several recipes for fruit cheeses, which are really only cooked fruit pastes. This is a long-keeping preserve that is ideal served as a condiment with cheese.

1.5kg damsons

200ml water

approx 1–1½ kg preserving or granulated sugar

2 tbsp lemon juice

special equipment

a large stainless steel preserving pan and a small hammer

Pick over the fruit, removing any debris and leaves and discarding any bruised or damaged fruit, then place in a large stainless steel pan. Bring to a simmer over a low to medium heat. Turn the heat down low and simmer uncovered until the stones easily come away from the fruit and the damsons break down completely. Stir occasionally to prevent the fruit sticking to the bottom of the pan and catching. This will take approximately 30 minutes depending on the ripeness of the fruit.

Put the cooked fruit through a fine sieve, reserving the stones. Pick out 30 stones and crack each with a small hammer. You will see a small brown kernel inside. Peel and remove the white flesh inside, chop the kernels finely and add to the pulp. You should end up with about 1.2kg.

When you are ready to finish the cheese, place your clean jars on a baking sheet in a cool oven, 120°C/gas mark ½.

Weigh the sieved pulp and add the same weight of sugar. Place both these ingredients in the pan, stirring over a low heat to dissolve the sugar. It is faster to finish the pulp in two batches, so remove half to a large bowl and continue to cook the portion that remains in the pan. Turn the heat up to medium and cook, stirring constantly with a heatproof spatula or flat wooden spoon, until a rapid boil is achieved. Reduce the heat to low and cook until the mixture thickens and a spoon drawn across the bottom of the pan leaves a clean trail. This will take approximately 15–20 minutes.

Pot the first batch of cheese into the sterilised jars, and then finish the second batch. Cover the surface of the cheese with a waxed-paper disc and seal the jar with cellophane. Store in a cool, dark place and use within 1 year.

QUINCE CHEESE

* **Makes 2.1kg – 4 or 5 jars** * **Preparation time 30 minutes** * **Cooking time 4 hours**

Quince trees, with their delicate pink flowers, have long been popular in British gardens, but in the last 150 years their fruit has declined in popularity. However, thanks to renewed interest in traditional English produce, it is once again becoming more widely available. If you would like to use English quinces a good supplier is listed at the back of the book.

1½ kg pear or Japonica quinces

approx 2kg granulated sugar

If you are using pear quinces, rub off any fur. Wash and chop the fruit into small pieces, including the peel and cores. Discard any black or brown pieces.

Place the quinces in a large stainless steel pan. Cover with water and bring to the boil over a high heat, then turn down to the lowest setting and cook until all the quince pieces are tender. Do not cover, but stir occasionally to prevent sticking and to ensure that the fruit is evenly cooked. This will take approximately 3 hours.

When the quinces are tender and breaking down, puree the fruit along with any liquid in a jug blender and pass through a fine sieve. Place 4–5 clean jars on a baking sheet and put them into a cool oven, 120°C/gas mark ½.

Weigh the pulp. This recipe should yield approximately 1.9kg. Weigh out the same amount of sugar, return both ingredients to the pan and stir over a low heat to dissolve the sugar. It is faster to finish the pulp in two batches, so remove half to a large bowl and continue to cook the portion that remains in the pan. Turn the heat up to medium and cook, stirring constantly with a heatproof spatula or flat wooden spoon, until a rapid boil is achieved. Then reduce the heat to low and continue to stir until the mixture thickens and a spoon drawn across the bottom of the pan leaves a clean trail. This will take approximately 15–20 minutes.

Pot the first batch of cheese into the sterilised jars and then finish the second batch. Cover the surface of the quince cheese with a waxed-paper disc and seal the jar with cellophane. Store the cheese in a cool, dark place and use within 1 year of making.

QUINCE JELLY

* **Makes about 1.6kg – 3 or 4 jars** * **Preparation time 30 minutes**
* **Cooking time 4 hours spread over 2 days**

This delicate, amber-coloured preserve can be served with terrines (see page 102) or game pies, but it is also very nice when used as a glaze to fruit tarts, or in apple pies. Japonica quices are small, very hard but commonly grown fruits from decorative trees and can be used in combination with, or as opposed to, the pear quinces.

1½ kg pear or Japonica quinces

approx 750g jam sugar

special equipment

a stainless steel preserving pan, a jelly bag or muslin and a sugar thermometer or temperature probe

If you are using pear quinces, rub off any fur. Wash and chop the fruit into small pieces, including the peel and cores. Discard any black or brown pieces.

Place the quinces in a stainless steel pan, cover with water and bring to the boil, then turn the heat to low and simmer until the fruit is completely soft, topping up the water as necessary to ensure the fruit is always just covered. This will take 2–3 hours. Stir occasionally to ensure that the fruit is not catching on the bottom of the pan. Once cooked, strain the hot liquid carefully through a jelly bag or muslin-lined sieve. Do not squeeze or press the pulp through, or the jelly will turn cloudy. It can be left to drip overnight.

When you are ready to finish the jelly, heat the oven to 120°C/gas mark ½ and place your clean jars in the oven on a baking sheet. At the same time, place a couple of saucers in the fridge. Discard the pulp and measure the liquid (you should have around 1 litre). Return this to the cleaned pan over a medium heat. For every litre of liquid, add 750g jam sugar to the pan and stir to dissolve.

Bring the mixture to a rapid boil, stirring regularly to prevent sticking. Keep at a rolling boil until setting point is reached. Once the jelly mixture reaches about 105°C and begins to thicken, start testing for setting point using the cold-saucer method on page 351. Once setting point has been reached, remove the pan from the heat and allow the jelly to sit for a minute to form a skin. Remove and discard any scum that has formed and pot the jelly into the sterilised jars. Cover the surface of the jelly with a waxed-paper disc and seal each jar with cellophane.

APPLE JELLY

* Makes approx 2.4kg – 5 or 6 jars * Preparation time 20 minutes
* Cooking time 1 hour 30 minutes spread over 2 days

A very handy jelly to have in the larder, this can be used to glaze tarts and pies, is lovely on toast and can be served with game. Bramleys have good acidity and make an excellent jelly. If you use a different variety of cooking apple, adjust the sugar to taste.

2½ kg Bramley apples, freshly picked or slightly under-ripe

approx 1.6kg jam sugar

juice of 3 lemons

special equipment

a sugar thermometer or temperature probe

Peel the apples and chop them into small pieces. Place in a stainless steel pan and add enough cold water to just cover – you will need about 2 litres. Bring to the boil over a high heat, then simmer gently, topping up as necessary to ensure the apples remain just covered, until the fruit is completely broken down and soft. Strain the hot cooked apples through a jelly bag or a muslin-lined sieve over a large bowl, and leave to drip overnight if possible. From these quantities, you should expect a yield of approximately 1.8kg of pulp (this can be used in place of the quince pulp in the recipe for quince cheese – see page 364) and 2 litres of juice.

When you are ready to finish the jelly, place your clean jars on a baking sheet in a cool oven at 120°C/gas mark ½, and place a couple of saucers in the fridge for testing the set of the jelly when finished. Measure the juice. For every 500ml juice, weigh out 400g jam sugar. Place the juice and sugar in a large pan over a high heat, stirring continuously until the sugar has dissolved. Add the lemon juice, mix well and then divide the mixture into two roughly equal parts (this will enable to you to finish the jelly quickly, preserving the flavour).

Bring one half to a rapid rolling boil and cook until it reaches 105°C, stirring frequently to prevent sticking. Begin to test for setting point when it starts to thicken, using the cold-saucer method on page 351. Once a setting point has been reached, remove the jelly from the heat and allow it to form a skin.

Remove and discard any scum that has formed and pot the jelly into the sterilised jars. Cover the surface of the jelly with a waxed-paper disc and seal the jar with cellophane. Repeat the process with the other half of the mixture.

PLUM JELLY

* Makes approx 1.8kg – 4 or 5 jars * Preparation time 1 hour 30 minutes over 2 days
* Cooking time 15 minutes

Mrs Beeton used either damsons or greengages for most of her plum preserves.
Each plum has a distinct flavour, so choose the ones you like the most. You can gather
cherry plums from old hedgerows in late July and early August. Whichever plum you
use, the result is a clear, brilliant, tart jelly that is lovely eaten with a fresh cream cheese
or served with game dishes in the winter as an alternative to redcurrant jelly.

**1.5kg cherry plums or
other small plums, stalks
removed**

approx 900g jam sugar

special equipment

**a stainless steel preserving
pan, a jelly bag or muslin
and a sugar thermometer or
temperature probe**

Place the washed plums in a stainless steel pan with 600ml
water. Cook over a medium heat until the juices run and
the fruit breaks down completely. Strain the hot, cooked
plums through a jelly bag or muslin-lined sieve over a
large bowl, and leave to drip overnight.

When you are ready to finish the jelly, place your clean
jars on a baking sheet in a cool oven, 120°C/gas mark ½.
Place a couple of saucers in the fridge for testing the set.
Measure the juice: allow 750g jam sugar for each litre of
liquid. This recipe should yield about 1.2 litres juice, which
would require 900g of jam sugar. Place the juice and sugar
in a clean stainless steel pan. Dissolve the sugar first over
a low heat, stirring frequently to prevent sticking, then
bring the jelly to a rolling boil and cook until it reaches a
temperature of 105°C.

When the mixture begins to thicken, start testing for
setting point using the cold-saucer method on page 351.
When it is ready, remove from the heat and allow the jam
to form a skin.

Remove and discard any scum that has formed, then pot
the jam into the warm, sterilised jars. Cover the surface
of the jelly with a waxed-paper disc and seal the jar with
cellophane.

LEMON MINCEMEAT

❋ **Makes approx 2.8kg – about 6 jars** ❋ **Preparation time 15 minutes**
❋ **Cooking time 3 hours**

Mrs Beeton's light, fresh lemon mincemeat is unusual in that it contains only currants –
no raisins, sultanas or other vine fruits such as you would find in most modern recipes.
Along with the lemon, this gives it a pleasant bitterness in contrast to the richness of the
suet and spice.

**zest and juice of
2 large lemons**

**2kg Bramley cooking
apples, peeled, cored
and coarsely grated**

225g suet

450g currants

225g caster sugar

80g candied peel

2 tsp mixed spice

Preheat the oven to 120°C/gas mark ½.

Mix all the ingredients together in a large ovenproof dish
until well combined. Transfer to a steel bowl or roasting
tray, place in the preheated oven and cook, stirring
occasionally, for 3 hours. Wash 6 jam jars and place them
on a baking sheet in the oven with the mincemeat for the
last half hour to sterilise them.

When the mixture has cooked, pot into the jars, covering
the surface with a waxed-paper disc and sealing the jars
with cellophane.

Keep in a cool, dark place for at least 2–3 months and then
use within 1 year of making.

APPLE CHUTNEY

✳ **Makes approx 3.7kg – 8 to 10 jars** ✳ **Preparation time 25 minutes** ✳ **Cooking time 1 hour**

Chutneys, along with many other spiced ketchups and sauces, were often brought home to the British kitchen by military gentlemen who had developed a taste for the exotic while overseas. We are now able to buy fresh spices imported monthly into Europe. This must be taken into consideration when looking at the quantities used in historic kitchens, where spices would have invariably taken many months to arrive from abroad, resulting in considerable loss of flavour. This chutney offers a superb way to use up a glut of apples. Its warm, autumnal spice mix, based largely on coriander seeds, works exceptionally well with apple.

2kg Bramley or other cooking apples, peeled and cored weight

1kg shallots, peeled and finely sliced

500g sultanas

300g soft brown sugar

300g granulated sugar

1 litre cider vinegar

2 tbsp whole coriander seeds

1 tsp ground ginger

1 tsp ground cinnamon

special equipment

a stainless steel preserving pan

Place the washed jars on a baking sheet in a cool oven, 120°C/gas mark ½.

Chop the apples into 1cm dice and add to a large stainless steel pan with all the other ingredients. Place the pan on a high heat and bring to a boil, stirring to dissolve the sugar. Simmer on a medium-high heat, stirring regularly, until the chutney is thick. This will take approximately 1 hour depending on the size of the pan and the surface area from which the liquid is evaporating. Take great care not to let the chutney burn – you will have to stir constantly as it begins to thicken, scraping the bottom of the pan carefully with a heatproof spatula or wooden spoon.

When the chutney is ready, place it into the sterilised jars. Seal and store in a cool, dark place for at least 1 month and then use within a year of making.

PICKLED BEETROOT

✳ Makes approx 1.6kg – 4 or 5 jars ✳ Preparation time 15 minutes
✳ Cooking time 1–2 hours

A deep, brilliant pickle to serve with cold pork pies or cheeses. Make this pickle in the late summer when the beetroot are mature and taste their best. Rather than boil the beetroot, I roast them to concentrate their flavour, and I use a mildly spiced vinegar to cure them, which gives the pickled beetroot an aromatic edge.

1kg unpeeled young beetroots

20 juniper berries

salt, to taste

for the spiced pickling vinegar

300ml cider vinegar

200ml white wine vinegar

70ml water

½ tsp coriander seeds

1 tsp allspice berries

2 tsp juniper berries

½ tsp blade mace

2 bay leaves

200g granulated sugar

special equipment

a roasting tin

Preheat the oven to 200°C/gas mark 6.

Top and tail beetroot, wash them well, and place them in a roasting tin lined with foil. Add the juniper berries and a generous pinch or two of salt, cover with another sheet of foil and seal very tightly on all sides. Put the roasting tin in the oven and cook for 1–2 hours, depending on size, until the beetroot are cooked through and tender.

While the beetroot are cooking, place all the ingredients for the pickling vinegar into a pan, bring to a boil and simmer for 5 minutes. Leave to cool.

Once the beetroot are cooked, remove them from the oven and leave to cool. Reduce the oven temperature to 120°C/gas mark ½ and place 4–5 jars into the oven to sterilise for half an hour. When the beetroot are cool, peel them, cut each into 8 even pieces and put into the jars. Cover with spiced pickling vinegar, seal the jars and store in a cool, dark place for at least 1 month and use within 1 year.

PICKLED SHALLOTS

* Makes approx 2kg * Preparation time 1 hour plus overnight brining
* Cooking time 20 minutes

These classic pickled shallots are excellent with Mrs Beeton's pork pie – make them when shallots are at their peak in the late summer because they don't store well – or use baby onions. If you like a spicier pickle, add a couple of chillies to the spiced vinegar. Mrs Beeton cooked her pickled onions to remove their strength, but today we prefer them pickled raw and full of bite.

20g salt

2kg shallots

for the spiced pickling vinegar

800ml cider vinegar

200ml white wine vinegar

200ml water

5g blade mace

5g coriander seeds

5g allspice berries

2 bay leaves

2 cinnamon sticks

10g mustard seeds

200g granulated sugar

special equipment

a large stainless steel preserving pan

Add the salt to 2 litres of water in a large pan, place over a medium heat and stir to dissolve. Remove from the heat and leave to cool.

Soak the shallots in their skins in a large bowl of warm water, and begin to peel them, trimming the tips and removing the roots carefully, so that you leave the root plates intact. This will help to stop the shallots falling apart.

Place the peeled shallots in the cooled brine, cover and leave to soak overnight.

Put all of the ingredients for the spiced vinegar in a large stainless steel pan. Bring to a simmer over a high heat, stirring to dissolve the sugar, then leave to cool overnight.

The next day, remove the shallots from the brine and rinse. Pack the shallots into clean and dry preserving jars (there is no need to sterilise if you are using non-reactive lids). Pour in the spiced vinegar, ensuring that the liquid covers all the shallots and that there are no air bubbles. Seal and store in a cool, dark place for at least 1 month and then use within 1 year of making.

TOMATO CHUTNEY

✳ **Makes approx 3kg – 7 jars** ✳ **Preparation time 25 minutes** ✳ **Cooking time 1 hour**

Mrs Beeton provided many recipes for using up quantities of the many fruits that we are often faced with gluts of at the end of summer. She gave a recipe for a chutney that blended apple and tomato together, but as each of these fruits benefits from different spice treatments they are better preserved separately. This tomato chutney, with its bird's-eye chilli kick, is one of the best ever for eating with sausages for a weekend breakfast, or for enjoying in the autumn at a bonfire party.

2kg tomatoes, chopped into small pieces

1kg onions, peeled and chopped into small pieces

500g raisins

70g fresh root ginger, peeled and finely grated

6 garlic cloves, peeled and finely chopped

300g granulated sugar

300g soft brown sugar

1 tsp allspice berries

1 stick cinnamon

1 bird's-eye chilli, or other hot chilli, cut in half lengthwise

1 litre cider vinegar

special equipment

a large stainless steel preserving pan

Place several clean jars on a baking sheet in an oven preheated to 120°C/gas mark ½.

Place all the ingredients into a large stainless steel pan and bring to the boil, stirring to dissolve sugar. Turn down the heat and simmer, stirring constantly, until the chutney has thickened. This will take approximately 1 hour depending on the size of your pan and the surface area from which the liquid is evaporating. Take great care not to let the chutney burn. As it begins to thicken, scrape the bottom of the pan carefully with a heatproof spatula or wooden spoon to prevent it catching.

When the chutney is ready, pot it into the sterilized jars. Seal and store in a cool, dark place for at least 1 month and then use within 1 year.

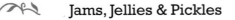

RASPBERRY VINEGAR

❋ **Makes approx 2 litres** ❋ **Preparation time 10 minutes over 3 days**

This recipe uses up the pulp left over from making the raspberry jelly on page 261. Mrs Beeton used raspberry vinegar diluted with water as a tonic. In fact, because it is so intensely fruity, it also makes a super addition to dressings or to game dishes. Try using a splash when cooking liver – it is a delicious combination.

1.5kg raspberries (or raspberry pulp, see page 261)

1kg caster sugar

1 litre white wine vinegar or cider vinegar

special equipment

a large stainless steel or ceramic bowl and a jelly bag or muslin

Place the raspberries or raspberry pulp in a large stainless steel or ceramic bowl and crush lightly. Add the sugar and the vinegar and cover. Steep together for 3 days and then strain the vinegar through a colander lined with muslin suspended over a large bowl. Alternatively, use a jelly bag and stand. Transfer the vinegar into vinegar bottles that have non-reactive seals. Store in a cool, dark place for at least 1 month, and then use within 1 year.

DRINKS

Y ou can make your own fruit cordials, fruit cups and party drinks very economically indeed. This chapter contains some suggestions for both soft drinks and drinks with alcohol, along with guidelines on how to brew the perfect cup of tea or coffee, and a very indulgent way to make hot chocolate.

COLD DRINKS

Fruit cordials

Cordials are drinks based on pressed or dripped juice. Blackcurrants, with their strong flavour, make a very popular cordial. For superlative flavour, make cordials with freshly harvested, ripe fruit in season. Frozen fruit is a good substitute if fresh is not available. Once made, cordials keep for only a few days.

Fruit cups and party cocktails

While it is customary to serve alcoholic drinks at parties, it is not always responsible to serve concentrated alcoholic drinks if you are not serving food at the same time. The rosé and Champagne cups in this chapter are both delicious while being light on alcohol content – just the thing for parties and picnics.

Ginger beer and other sparkling drinks

Homemade ginger beer, and bottle-fermented wines such as Champagne, contain live yeasts, which ferment sugars and produce carbon dioxide. The result is a potentially volatile mix that creates pressure inside the bottle and can shatter glass and cause plastic bottles to explode. If you plan to make yeast-based sparkling drinks at home, only use proper beer bottles, which can be bought from kitchen or home-brew supply shops.

TEA

W hat we know as tea derives from an evergreen plant related to the camellia. The new shoots of the tea bush are highly prized and generally make the finest tea. Once picked, the leaves are either dried immediately to produce green tea, or fermented until dark to make black tea. The flavour and character of each tea variety and region of origin varies enormously, so try as many as you can until you find one (or several) you really like. The best-quality tea is sold in leaf form from specialist shops. It does not keep forever so only buy 100–200g at a time. To keep it fresh, store the tea sealed in an airtight container in a cool, dark place.

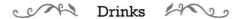

To make tea, using either leaves or bags, boil plenty of fresh water in a kettle. Pour a little of the freshly boiled water into the teapot and swirl it around to warm the pot, while the rest of the boiling water cools down in the kettle for a minute or so. Pour away the water from the teapot and add the tea, using one level teaspoon of loose-leaf tea per cup, plus one teaspoon 'for the pot'. If you are using bags, use one per person. Pour the water – about 200ml per cup – over the tea, put the lid on the pot and leave to steep. For a light-coloured tea, leave the pot to steep for one and a half minutes. If you prefer your tea stronger steep it for a maximum of five minutes. Do not steep strong teas for too long, or you will stew them, making them taste bitter.

COFFEE

The two major varieties of coffee that are grown today are *Coffea arabica* and *Coffea canephora* (also known as Robusta). The coffee bean is covered with a fleshy coat, inside which is a pale green bean. It is possible to buy raw coffee beans and roast them at home, but most of us buy beans ready-roasted to varying degrees – the darker the roast, the more intense the flavour. For example, high-roast blends of single varieties, which are among the darkest, are used for making espresso. Many of the flavour compounds in coffee are volatile, so it is important to buy your coffee often and in small quantities from a dealer who roasts their beans regularly. Alternatively, you can purchase it in vacuum packs and, once opened, store it in the fridge or freezer in an airtight container to keep the coffee fresher for longer.

Whatever method you prefer to use to make coffee, use one dessertspoon (7g) per cup plus one for the pot. Leave the kettle to stand for a few minutes after boiling, so that the water drops a few degrees in temperature (the ideal temperature for brewing coffee is 94°C), and then pour the water over the coffee – use about 200ml per cup for a medium-strength brew. Stir, then leave to brew for two or three minutes before serving.

GINGER BEER

✳ **Makes 2–2.5 litres** ✳ **Preparation time 10 minutes, plus 3 days brewing time**

This drink is great fun to make but be warned that it must be left to brew for three days before serving. The addition of yeast makes the beer fizzy so it must be stored in bottles able to withstand high pressure. These are widely available from home-brew shops. To serve, you can add a little extra sugar to Mrs Beeton's original recipe if you have a sweet tooth, or drink it straight up, just as she intended, for a dry, refreshing draught.

80g fresh root ginger, sliced

200g caster sugar, plus extra to serve

¼ tsp cream of tartar

2 lemons, sliced

¼ tbsp fresh yeast

special equipment

home-brewing bottles (3–4 x 750ml or 8–10 x 250ml bottles) and a temperature probe

Place the ginger, sugar, cream of tartar and 200ml cold water in the jug of a liquidizer. Blend until smooth, then pour into a large bowl. Add 2.3 litres boiling water, and the lemon, then cool until it is just warm to the touch, or a temperature probe registers 38°C.

Now place the yeast in a small bowl, stir in a tablespoonful of the liquid and mix to blend. Add this mixture to the remainder of the cooled liquid and leave overnight.

Sterilise the bottles: remove any rubber seals, then place the washed bottles on a baking sheet lined with newspaper and put them in a low oven heated to 120°C/ gas mark ½ for half an hour. Place the rubber seals in a small pan of boiling water and simmer for 5 minutes, then allow them to air dry on a tray covered with a clean cloth.

Leave the bottles in the oven to cool, then replace the seals and seal until you are ready to fill them.

Strain the mixture through a fine sieve into a large jug for ease of pouring and decant into the bottles. Wrap each bottle in a few layers of newspaper and stand them in a bucket covered with a towel in case of an explosion. Store them at room temperature.

After 3 days place the bucket in a sink, lift off the towel and unwrap and open as many bottles as you need. To serve, place ½ tsp caster sugar in the bottom of each glass, add a few ice cubes and top up with the beer. The beer can be kept for up to 1 month in a cool, dark place.

LEMONADE

✳ **Makes approx 1 litre** ✳ **Preparation time 10 minutes plus 2 days steeping**

Mrs Beeton recommended a beaten egg white or some sherry to improve this lemonade, but it is just perfect as it is. Use the best lemons you can find, preferably unwaxed ones. If you cannot get unwaxed ones, scrub your lemons well in warm water before grating the zest off them.

finely grated zest of 2 lemons

juice of 3 lemons

150g caster sugar or 120g mild English honey

Place all the ingredients in a large jug and top up with 1 litre of water. Cover with cling film and leave to steep in a cool place or in the fridge for 2 days, stirring occasionally.

After 2 days, strain the lemonade into a clean jug and store, covered with cling film, in the fridge.

Use within 7 days of making.

BLACKCURRANT CORDIAL

✳ **Makes approx 400ml** ✳ **Preparation time 10 minutes plus 24 hours dripping**

No other fruit has a flavour as intense as the blackcurrant, making it ideal for a wonderfully refreshing cordial. Freeze any glut of berries you acquire in the summer and you can make this throughout the winter – it is better to use previously frozen fruit as it releases its juice more readily than fresh. If you have fresh fruit, put it in the freezer overnight before using. Mrs Beeton's recipe used whitecurrants, which are not so easily available today, and had whiskey blended into it. However, keeping the cordial alcohol-free means it can be made up with spring water for children – and it is also delicious mixed with English sparkling wine for a more grown-up drink. The blackcurrant pulp left over when you drip the juice can be used to make the blackcurrant cheese on page 362.

800g very ripe blackcurrants, frozen and thawed and picked over to remove leaves and stalks

300g caster sugar, plus up to 100g extra to taste

special equipment

a jelly bag or a sieve lined with muslin

Place the blackcurrants and the sugar in the jug of a blender and purée. Transfer to a jelly bag, or a sieve lined with muslin, suspended over a deep large bowl to catch the drips. Cover everything with a sheet or cloth and leave to drip overnight.

The next day, pour the dripped juice in a jug. Either discard the blackcurrant pulp or use it to make blackcurrant cheese. You should end up with approximately 400ml juice. Add a little more caster sugar to taste. If you prefer a more syrupy cordial, add up to 100g of sugar.

Store the cordial in the fridge for up to 7 days or pour it into a resealable container and freeze for up to 1 month. To serve, dilute in the ratio of 1 part cordial to 2 parts water.

ROSE WINE CUP

✳ **Makes 1.8 litres or 12 servings** ✳ **Preparation time 5 minutes plus 1 hour steeping**

This delicate aperitif stretches a nice bottle of rosé wine into a lighter, longer drink to enjoy on a warm day. Mrs Beeton used this method with Claret, but rosé gives a more refreshing result. Maraschino is a delicate liqueur based on a rare cherry and can be bought from good vintners.

70ml Maraschino or Curaçao

a few borage leaves or 6 pieces cucumber peel or salad burnet

750ml light rosé wine

250g crushed ice

750ml chilled soda water

freshly grated nutmeg, to taste

Place the borage, cucumber peel or salad burnet in a small jar. Pour over the Maraschino or Curaçao. Seal and leave to steep.

After 1 hour strain the mixture into a large glass jug or punch bowl. Pour in the wine and stir. Add the crushed ice and soda water.

To serve, grate a little nutmeg onto the top of each drink.

CHAMPAGNE CUP

✳ **Makes 1.65 litres or 12 servings** ✳ **Preparation time 5 minutes plus 2 hour steeping**

This light cocktail will help launch a party elegantly, and is low enough in alcohol to be enjoyed without reproach. Mrs Beeton used borage leaves to scent the cocktail base, but you can substitute cucumber skin or salad burnet, which have a similar flavour.

4 borage leaves or the peel from a 4cm piece of cucumber or 4 salad burnet sprigs

150ml Curacao, Triple sec or Cointreau

750ml Champagne, chilled

750ml soda water, chilled

Bruise the borage leaves, salad burnet or cucumber by rubbing them between your fingers for a few seconds, then place in the jar. Pour in the Curaçao, and cover.

After a minimum of 2 hours strain the infused Curaçao through muslin into a jug.

To serve, pour a dessertspoonful into the bottom of each glass, half fill each glass with Champagne, and top up with soda water.

BRAMBLE LIQUEUR

✴ **Makes approx 1.2 litres** ✴ **Preparation time 5 minutes plus 2 months steeping**

This marvellous liqueur takes its inspiration from Mrs Beeton's whiskey cordial and exemplifies her pleasure in taking simple ingredients and creating something special with them. Replacing the whiskey with a more neutral vodka or gin allows the flavour of the fruit to dominate. This fruit combination captures the glossy, purple-black allure of fresh wild blackberries, but the recipe also works with other fruits, such as sloes or wild damsons: just prick them all over before immersing them in the alcohol. Storing the finished liqueur in tinted bottles helps to stop the colour fading.

800g ripe brambles, picked over to remove any debris

200g caster sugar

600ml vodka or gin

special equipment

a 1.2-litre Kilner or preserving jar, a sieve lined with muslin and 2–3 tinted bottles with screw caps

Pack the brambles into the jar and add the sugar, shaking so that it sifts down and fills the gaps between the fruit. Pour in the vodka or gin and seal.

Keep in a cool, dark place for 2 months. For the first 7 days give the jar a shake once a day.

After 2 months strain the liqueur through a sieve lined with muslin into a jug for ease of pouring. Pour the liqueur into bottles and seal. Use within 1 year of making.

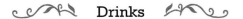
ORANGE BRANDY

✳ **Makes approx 1.5 litres**   ✳ **Preparation time 5 minutes plus 7 days steeping**

The Seville orange is largely produced for the British market because we never lost our desire for making Seville orange marmalade (see page 356). However, during the short period of time Seville oranges are available here in January and February, you can also use them for making Mrs Beeton's delectable orange brandy, which can be served on its own or poured over ice.

zest of 3 Seville oranges

200ml Seville orange juice (approximately 6–7 oranges)

1 litre brandy

400g caster sugar

special equipment

a 1.5-litre Kilner or preserving jar, a sieve lined with muslin and a tinted bottle with a screw cap

Using a potato peeler, remove the peel from the oranges and place it in the bottom of the jar. Add the juice, brandy and sugar, then stir well and seal the jar. Stir daily over the next 7 days then strain through a sieve lined with muslin into a jug for ease of pouring. Pour the orange brandy into a bottle and seal. Store the bottle in a cool, dark place for 1 month before using.

To serve, add a dessertspoonful of the brandy to a glass of English sparkling wine for a delightful aperitif, or pour it over ripe strawberries for a fruity treat.

DRINKING CHOCOLATE

❋ Makes 300ml or 1 serving ❋ Preparation time 1 minute
❋ Cooking time 5 minutes

Mrs Beeton used half water and half milk for her hot chocolate, but this recipe uses all milk for a richer result and gives the option of adding honey for an even more indulgent drink. The freshly grated chocolate gives a luxurious, silky texture, but you can use cocoa powder for a lighter result if you prefer.

260ml semi-skimmed milk

1 tsp English honey or ½ tsp caster sugar, to taste

60g dark chocolate, (65–75% cocoa solids), grated, or 2 tsp cocoa powder

Place the milk in a saucepan over a medium heat. Add the honey or sugar and bring to a simmer.

Whisk the grated chocolate or the cocoa powder into the hot milk until the chocolate has melted and the mixture is smooth. Simmer for 1 minute, add more honey or sugar to taste and serve.

PRODUCERS & SUPPLIERS

Spices

Green Saffron Spices

Unit 16, Knockgriffin, Midleton, Cork, Ireland

Tel 00 353 21 463 7960

www.greensaffron.com

Arun and Olive Kapil's family business imports and grinds premium spices from family farms across India.

Fish

Ben's Fish

Rewsalls Old Barn, Rewsalls Lane, East Mersea, Colchester, Essex CO5 8SX

Tel 01206 386833

www.bensfishmersea.co.uk

This supplier of fresh, seasonal fish and game is run by Ben Woodcraft, who was an inshore fisherman for 20 years and now liases directly with local fishermen, farmers and growers from around the east coast. Ben's Fish is also a good supplier of English quinces.

Wingham's Fresh Fish

108 Queen Street, Withernsea, East Yorkshire HU19 2HB

Tel 01964 614239.

Shaun Wingham is one of a small number of license holders permitted to catch Wild Salmon, Sea Trout and MSC certified wild Sea Bass from the Holderness Coast fishery – one of the most sustainably managed in the UK. His wife Penny manages the shop, which is well worth a visit.

Meat

Anna's Happy Trotters

Burland, Holme Farm, Howden, East Yorkshire DN14 7LY

Tel 01430 433030

www.annashappytrotters.com

Delicious and well butchered Yorkshire free-range pork from one of our finest pig farmers, Anna Longthorp.

The Blackface Meat Company

Weatherall Foods Limited, Crochmore House, Irongray, Dumfries DG2 9SF

Tel 01387 730 326

www.blackface.co.uk

This small family business rears Blackface sheep and Galloway cattle in the south west of Scotland. Their superb mutton, lamb, game, beef and pork is produced with care and attention.

Borrowdale Herdwick

Yew Tree Farm, Rosthwaite, Borrowdale, Cumbria CA12 5XB

Tel: 01768 777675

www.borrowdaleherdwick.co.uk

A small farm rearing the area's traditional Herdwick sheep, where the animals enjoy a full life, slowly growing on the beautiful fells of Borrowdale. The animals are available as hogget or mutton. Their rich, nutty flavour is exceptional.

Fletchers Reediehill Deer Farm

Auchtermuchty, Fife KY14 7HS

Tel 01337 828369

www.seriouslygoodvenison.co.uk

Nicola and John Fletcher are experts in producing farmed Red deer. Their meat is reared to exceptionally high standards and tastes delicious.

Graig Farm

Dolau, Llandrindod Wells,
Powys LD1 5TL

Tel 01686 627979

www.graigfarm.co.uk

This farm supplies a wide range of organic products, including meat and poultry, from its online shop. All of their produce is cared for to high standards.

Langley Chase Organic Farm

Kington Langley,
Wiltshire SN15 5PW

Tel 01249 750095

www.langleychase.co.uk

A small organic farm producing award-winning Manx Loaghtan lamb and mutton which is truly delicious and unique.

Offley Hoo Farm

Hoo Lane, Great Offley, Hitchin,
Hertfordshire SG5 3ED

Tel 01462 769302

www.offleyhoofarm.co.uk

Jonathan Birchall, BBC Farming Today farmer of the year 2011, and his wife Sarah, produce exceptional rare breed Longhorn beef, Wiltshire Horn lamb and rare breed pigs.

Peele's Norfolk Black Turkeys

Rookery Farm, Thuxton, Norwich,
Norfolk NR9 4QJ

Tel 01362 850237

www.peelesblackturkeys.co.uk

A producer of Norfolk Black turkeys for four generations. The birds are reared outside and allowed to mature slowly on a diet of home-grown wheat, barley, oats and beans. Their flavour is unlike any other bird and tastes like turkey should.

Rhug Estate

Corwen, Denbighshire LL21 0EH

Tel 01490 413000

www.rhug.co.uk

An organic farm and butchery supplying a variety of meat including Aberdeen Angus beef, Salt Marsh lamb, Chicken, Game and traditional Duroc pork. All the meat (with the exception of the game, which is sourced as locally as possible) is organic and comes from their own farms.

St Brides Farm

High Kype Road, Sandford,
Strathaven ML10 6PRT

Tel 01357 529989

www.stbridespoultry.co.uk

Free range chickens and ducks are produced on this small poultry farm just outside of Strathaven, favouring slower growing, flavourful breeds which naturally thrive in the free-range setting.

SausageMaking.org

0845 643 6915

www.sausagemaking.org

An online site that sells all you need to make your own bacon, sausages, salami and hams.

Cheese and dairy

George Mews Cheese

106 Byres Road,
Glasgow G12 8TB

Tel 0141 334 5900

www.georgemewescheese.co.uk

Specialising in unusual cheeses, George has a carefully balanced selection of world-class British and European artisan cheeses.

Moorlands Cheesemakers

Lorien House, South Street, Castle Cary,
Somerset BA7 7ES

Tel 01963 350634

www.cheesemaking.co.uk

Katrin Loxton sells everything you need to make
your own cheeses at home, from various forms of
rennet and cultures to complete cheesemaking
kits.

Neal's Yard Dairy

108 Druid Street,
London SE1 2HH

Tel 020 7500 7520

www.nealsyarddairy.co.uk

Neal's Yard buy and mature cheese from about
seventy cheesemakers on farms around Britain
and Ireland. They sell the cheese to shops and
restaurants all over the world, and to the public
from their two shops in London.

Paxton and Whitfield

93 Jermyn Street,
London SW1Y 6JE

Tel 020 7930 0259

www.paxtonandwhitfield.co.uk

One of the most respected cheesemongers
in the country, with a long established history
in fine cheese retailing.

PGT Hook & Son

Longleys Farm, Harebeating Lane, Hailsham,
East Sussex BN27 1ER

Tel: 01323 449494

www.hookandson.co.uk

Father and son Phil and Steve Hook farm Longleys
Farm organically and supply extremely natural,
pure, unpasteurized milk, cream and butter from
their sustainably managed cows. They offer a mail
order service from their website.

Tea and coffee

Ceylon 1

1-5 Vyner Street, London E2 9DG

Tel 07540723460

www.ceylon1.com

Ceylon 1 imports and sells tea from the organic
and fair trade estates in Sri Lanka – which produce
some of the best tea in the world – and sells it both
online and from a stall at London's
Borough Market.

Monmouth Coffee Company

36 Maltby Street, Bermondsey,
London SE1 3PA

Tel 020 7232 3010

www.monmouthcoffee.co.uk

Monmouth roast coffee from small farms, estates
and cooperatives across the world at their roasting
site in Bermondsey, and are continually on the
lookout for new varieties and growers to add to
their list. Their shops sell freshly roasted beans as
well as the finished article.

Equipment

Lakeland

Alexandra Buildings, Windermere,
Cumbria LA23 1BQ

Tel 015394 88100

www.lakeland.co.uk

Lakeland provides an array of innovative
cookware, appliances and utensils. The
company places enormous value on customer
satisfaction, and uses customer feedback to
develop its vast range.

Nisbets Catering Equipment

Fourth Way, Avonmouth,
Bristol BS11 8TB

Tel 0845 140 5555

www.nisbets.co.uk

This is one of the UK's largest suppliers of catering
equipment, and a great source of larger scale
cooking equipment such as stock pots.

Useful organisations

The British Association for Shooting and Conservation

Marford Mill, Rossett,
Wrexham, LL12 0HL

Tel 01244 573 000

www.basc.org.uk

BASC promote and protect sporting shooting of all types throughout the UK, and produce Codes of Practice detailing the law surrounding shooting game.

The Dexter Cattle Society

www.dextercattle.co.uk

The Dexter Cattle Society helps farmers find markets and buyers for their cattle and keeps a directory of suppliers and locations where this fantastic beef can be purchased.

FARMA

Lower Ground Floor, 12 Southgate Street,
Winchester, Hampshire SO23 9EF

Tel 0845 45 88 420

www.farmersmarkets.net

The National Farmers' Retail & Markets Association represents the sale of local food and fresh farm products direct to the public through farmers' markets and farm shops. Visit their website for a list of certified markets and suppliers in your area.

Freedom Food Limited

Wilberforce Way, Southwater, Horsham,
West Sussex RH139RS

Tel 0300 123 0014

www.rspca.org.uk/freedomfood

Freedom Food is the RSPCA's farm assurance and food labelling scheme. It is the only UK farm assurance scheme to focus solely on improving the welfare of farm animals reared for food.

Marine Stewardship Council

Marine House, 1 Snow Hill,
London EC1A 2DH

Tel 020 7246 8900

www.msc.org

The Marine Stewardship Council fishery certification program and seafood ecolabel recognise and reward sustainable fishing. This global organization works with fisheries, seafood companies, scientists, conservation groups and the public to promote the best environmental choices in seafood.

Rare Breeds Survival Trust

Stoneleigh Park, Nr Kenilworth,
Warwickshire CV8 2LG

Tel 024 7669 6551

www.rbst.org.uk

The Rare Breeds Survival Trust is a charity that concerned with conserving Britain's native farm livestock. Contact them for lists of rare breed suppliers and producers in your area.

Slow Food UK

Slow Food UK, 6 Neal's Yard, Covent Garden,
London WC2H 9DP

Tel 020 7099 1132

www.slowfood.org.uk

Slow Food UK is part of the global Slow Food movement. It has thousands of members and connections with local groups around the UK that link the pleasure of artisan food to community and the environment.

Soil Association

South Plaza, Marlborough Street,
Bristol BS1 3NX

Tel 0117 314 5000

www.soilassociation.org

The Soil Association is a charity campaigning for planet-friendly food and farming. It offers guidance to consumers looking for local suppliers of organic food as well as advice for organic growers and businesses.

SEASONAL BUYING

Even in Mrs Beeton's time gardeners were in the habit of forcing fruits into early cropping inside heated greenhouses, or holding back grapes in storage, their cut stems held in charcoal water. Indoor growing is big business today and has extended the seasons of many of our most popular fruits and vegetables significantly – yet the availability of fresh, locally grown fruits and vegetables can still change rapidly. Some, such as strawberries or asparagus, have a very limited season and it is worth knowing when to expect them. These pages contain a rough guide to seasonal UK produce and major European crops, but since exact timings the crops can vary with latitude, altitude and local microclimates it is always worth talking to your local producers and suppliers and asking them which fruits and vegetables will be the next to appear. Tropical crops have not been included as they tend to be available year-round.

FRUITS AND VEGETABLES

January

Vegetables: beetroot, Brussels sprouts, cabbage, carrots, celeriac, celery, chicory, garlic, horseradish, Jerusalem artichokes, kale, leeks, mushrooms (cultivated), nettles, onions, parsnips, potatoes (maincrop), purple sprouting broccoli, radicchio, radishes, salsify, shallots, swede, turnips **Fruits:** apples, blood oranges, clementines, pears, rhubarb (forced), satsumas, Seville oranges, tangerines

February

Vegetables: beetroot, Brussels sprouts, cabbage, carrots, cauliflower, celeriac, chicory, garlic, Jerusalem Artichokes, kale, leeks, mushrooms (cultivated), nettles, onions, parsnips, potatoes (maincrop), purple sprouting broccoli, radicchio, salsify, shallots, swede, turnips **Fruits:** apples, blood oranges, pears, rhubarb (forced)

March

Vegetables: beetroot, Brussels sprouts, cabbage, carrots, cauliflower, chicory, garlic, jersey royal new potatoes, Jersualem artichokes, kale, leeks, mushrooms (cultivated), nettles, onions, parsnips, potatoes (maincrop), purple sprouting broccoli, radicchio, shallots, salsify, swede, wild garlic **Fruits:** apples, blood oranges, pears, rhubarb (outdoor)

April

Vegetables: broccoli, cabbage, carrots, cauliflower, chard, chicory, cucumber, garlic, jersey royal new potatoes, kale, leeks, lettuces & salad leaves, St George mushrooms, mushrooms (cultivated), nettles, onions, potatoes (maincrop), purple sprouting broccoli, radicchio, samphire, salsify, spinach, watercress, wild garlic **Fruits:** rhubarb (outdoor)

May **Vegetables:** asparagus, broad beans, broccoli, cabbage, carrots, cauliflower, chard, cucumber, garlic (fresh), Jersey royal new potatoes, lettuces & salad leaves, Morel mushrooms, mushrooms (cultivated), nettles, new potatoes, onions, potatoes (maincrop), radishes, rocket, St George mushrooms, samphire, spinach, watercress, wild garlic **Fruits:** (outdoor), elderflower

June **Vegetables:** artichokes (globe), asparagus, broad beans, broccoli, cabbage, cardoons, carrots, cauliflower, chard, courgettes, cucumber, garlic (fresh), Jersey royal new potatoes, kohlrabi, lettuces & salad leaves, Morel mushrooms, mushrooms (cultivated), nettles, new potatoes, onions, peas, potatoes (maincrop), radishes, rocket, samphire, spinach, spring onions, tomatoes (greenhouse) turnips, watercress, wild garlic **Fruits:** blackcurrants, blueberries, cherries, elderflower, gooseberries, strawberries, wild raspberries, wild strawberries

July **Vegetables:** artichokes (globe), asparagus, aubergine, beetroot, broad beans, cabbage, cardoons, carrots, cauliflower, courgettes, cucumber, fennel, French beans, garlic (fresh), kohlrabi, lettuces & salad leaves, mushrooms (cultivated), nettles, new potatoes, onions, peas, peppers, potatoes (maincrop), radishes, rocket, spring onions, summer black truffle, romanesco, runner beans, samphire, spinach, spring onions, sweetcorn, tomatoes (greenhouse), turnips, watercress **Fruits:** blackcurrants, black mulberries, bilberries, blueberries, brambles, cherries, cherry plums, gooseberries, loganberries, peaches, raspberries, redcurrants, strawberries, tayberries, whitecurrants, wild raspberries, wild strawberries

August **Vegetables:** artichokes (globe), aubergine, beetroot, broad beans, cabbage, cardoons, carrots, cauliflower, celery, cobnuts, courgettes, cucumber, fennel, French beans, garlic, kohlrabi, leeks, lettuces & salad leaves, marrow, mushrooms (cultivated), nettles, onions, peas, peppers, potatoes (maincrop), radishes, rocket, romanesco, runner beans, spinach, spring onions, tomatoes (outdoor), turnips, watercress, wild mushrooms **Fruits:** apricots, black mulberries, bilberries, blueberries, brambles, cherries, cherry plums, discovery apples, gooseberries, greengages, loganberries, peaches, raspberries, redcurrants, strawberries, tayberries, whitecurrants, wild raspberries, wild strawberries

September **Vegetables:** artichokes (globe), aubergine, beetroot, broad beans, broccoli, butternut squash, cabbage, cardoons, carrots, celery, chicory, cobnuts, courgettes, cucumber, fennel, French beans, garlic, horseradish, kale, kohlrabi, leeks, lettuces & salad leaves, marrow, mushrooms (cultivated), nettles, onions, parsnips, peas, peppers, potatoes (maincrop), purple sprouting broccoli, radicchio, radishes, rocket, romanesco, runner beans, shallots, spinach, spring onions, swede, sweetcorn, tomatoes, turnips, walnuts, watercress, wild mushrooms **Fruits:** bilberries, blueberries, brambles, cherries, cherry plums, damsons, discovery apples, elderberries, gooseberries, greengages, Marjories seedling plums, peaches, raspberries (late season), redcurrants, strawberries, Victoria plums, whitecurrants, wild raspberries, wild strawberries

October

Vegetables: beetroot, broccoli, Brussels sprouts, butternut squash, cabbage, cardoons, carrots, cauliflower, celeriac, chestnuts, chicory, cobnuts, cucumber, fennel, garlic, horseradish, Jerusalem artichokes, kale, kohlrabi, leeks, marrow, mushrooms (cultivated), onions, parsnips, peppers, potatoes (maincrop), pumpkin, purple sprouting broccoli, radicchio, radishes, rocket, romanesco, runner beans, salsify, shallots, spinach, spring onions, swede, sweetcorn, truffles (black), truffles (white), turnips, watercress, wild mushrooms
Fruits: apples, damsons, pears, quince, raspberries (late season), sloe berries

November

Vegetables: beetroot, broccoli, brussels sprouts, cabbage, carrots, cauliflower, cardoons, celeriac, celery (blanched), chestnuts, chicory, garlic, horseradish, Jerusalem artichokes, kale, kohlrabi, leeks, mushrooms (cultivated), onions, parsnips, potatoes (maincrop), pumpkin, purple sprouting broccoli, radicchio, radishes, rocket, salsify, shallots, swede, sweetcorn, truffles (black), truffles (white), turnips, watercress, wild mushrooms
Fruits: apples, pears, quince, raspberries (late season), sloe berries

December

Vegetables: beetroot, broccoli, Brussels sprouts, cabbage, carrots, cauliflower, celeriac, celery (blanched), chestnuts, chicory, garlic, horseradish, Jerusalem artichoke, kale, leeks, mushrooms (cultivated), onions, parsnips, potatoes (maincrop), purple sprouting broccoli, radicchio, radishes, salsify, shallots, swede, truffles (black), truffles (white), turnips, watercress, wild mushrooms **Fruits:** apples, clementines, pears, quince, satsumas, tangerines

HERBS

Herbs enable us to vary the flavour of familiar meats and fish, their oils contributing wonderfully to the scent of the kitchen. Buy plants and keep them at home on a windowsill or in a window box, or plant them out in the garden.

Spring: borage, chervil, chives, coriander, dill, mint, parsley, rosemary, sorrel, thyme

Summer: basil, borage, chervil, chives, coriander, dill, hyssop, mint, oregano, parsley, rosemary, sage, savoury, sorrel, tarragon, thyme

Autumn: basil, chives, coriander, oregano, mint, parsley, rosemary, sage, sorrel, tarragon, thyme

Winter: chives, mint, parsley, rosemary, sage, thyme

GAME

The charts below give the seasons for game birds and animals. The laws concerning the shooting and sale of ground game in particular change regularly. See the BASC website (www.basc.org.uk) for the most up-to-date information.

Gamebirds & Waterfowl

Pheasant
1 October – 1 February in England, Wales and Scotland
1 October – 31 January in Northern Ireland

Grey partridge
1 September – 1 February in England, Wales and Scotland
1 September – 31 January in Northern Ireland

Red-legged partridge
1 September – 1 February in England, Wales and Scotland
1 September – 31 January in Northern Ireland

Red grouse
12 August – 10 December in England, Wales and Scotland
12 August – 30 November in Northern Ireland

Duck and goose
1 September – 31 January in England, Wales and Scotland
1 September – 31 January in Northern Ireland

Common snipe
12 August – 31 January in England, Wales and Scotland
1 September – 31 January in Northern Ireland

Woodcock
1 October – 31 January in England, Northern Ireland and Wales
1 September – 31 January in Scotland

Wood pigeon
No close season in England, Wales, Scotland and Northern Ireland subject to complying with the terms and conditions of the relevant game licence

Ground Game

Brown mountain hare
1 January – 31 December in England, Wales and Scotland on moorland and unenclosed land

12 August – 31 January in Northern Ireland

Rabbit
1 January – 31 December in England, Wales and Scotland on moorland and unenclosed land

No close season in Northern Ireland

Deer

Red deer	Stag	1 August – 30 April in England and Wales 1 July – 20 October in Scotland 1 August – 30 April in Northern Ireland
	Hind	1 November – 31 March in England and Wales 21 October – 15 February in Scotland 1 November – 28/29 February in Northern Ireland
Fallow deer	Buck	1 August – 30 April in England and Wales 1 August – 30 April in Scotland 1 August – 30 April in Northern Ireland
	Doe	1 November – 31 March in England and Wales 21 October – 15 February in Scotland 1 November – 28/29 February in Northern Ireland
Sika deer	Stag	1 August – 30 April in England and Wales 1 July – 20 October in Scotland 1 August – 30 April in Northern Ireland
	Hind	1 November – 31 March in England and Wales 21 October – 15 February in Scotland 1 November – 28/29 February in Northern Ireland
Roe deer	Buck	1 April – 31 October in England and Wales 1 April – 20 October in Scotland
	Doe	1 November – 31 March in England and Wales 21 October – 31 March in Scotland

GLOSSARY OF COOKING TERMS

Many languages have influenced the British kitchen, but none so much as French – hardly surprising since French food has often been held up as the benchmark for excellence, in Mrs Beeton's time as well as in our own. Long before the Michelin guide began to report on British restaurants, French chefs were working for British royalty and could be found in the kitchens of many large country houses. Perhaps the most famous of these was Antonin Careme, chef to the Prince Regent (later George IV), who set the standard for future chefs to emulate. Mrs Beeton knew of him by name and reputation. The list below is intended to help explain the more commonly used terms – many, but not all, of which come from the French.

agar-agar   a vegetable setting agent made from seaweed

al dente   a term used to describe foods such as pasta, rice and vegetables that are cooked but still have a firmness to the bite

arrowroot   a powdered starch made from the roots of a tropical plant. It is used to thicken sauces, giving a lovely transparent result

au gratin   describes a cooked dish topped with a browned crust, usually made by finishing with grated cheese or breadcrumbs and browning under the grill

bain marie   a large pan or tin used as a waterbath to cook or warm food that is too delicate to withstand direct heat

baking powder   a raising agent made from bicarbonate of soda and cream of tartar

baste   to moisten meat or poultry during the roasting process by pouring over fat or liquid

beat   to mix food energetically to introduce air, using a wooden spoon, whisk or electric mixer to make a mixture light and fluffy

béchamel   a classic flavoured white sauce (see page 329)

beef   the meat from cattle

beurre manie   a paste made from butter and flour that is used to thicken hot sauces

beurre noisette   butter heated until it has coloured to a rich brown, then mixed with vinegar or lemon juice and, often, capers

bisque   a shellfish stock or soup, often with added cream

blanch   to boil briefly, often in order to loosen the skin from nuts and kernels, to part-cook green vegetables or to remove strong or bitter flavours

blender   a machine used for blending or puréeing, particularly in the preparation of soups and sauces. It can be in the form of a jug into which liquids are poured, or hand held (known as a wand or stick blender) for use in a bowl or saucepan

blend   to combine ingredients to give a smooth mixture

boil   to heat a liquid to the point at which it bubbles vigorously and begins to vapourise – 100°C in the case of water

bone   to remove the bones from fish, meat or poultry

braise   to cook slowly in a covered pan or dish, with liquid

bran   the outer husk of a grain of wheat or oats

brine   a saltwater solution used for preserving and pickling

brown   to colour the surface of a food by cooking it in hot fat, caramelising the sugars and developing flavour

butter muslin   a fine cotton cloth used for straining jellies, stocks and dairy products. It should be scalded before use.

caper   the pickled flower bud of the plant *Capparis spinosa*

caramel   a confection made by melting sugar. A simple caramel can be made by gently warming a mixture of sugar and water to 170–180°C, until the sugar melts and turns golden brown

casserole   a deep, lidded cooking pot made from an ovenproof material

cheesecloth   see butter muslin

chill   to cool food without freezing, usually in a refrigerator

chine to separate the backbone from the ribs in a joint of meat, to make carving easier

chinois a conical sieve with a very fine mesh used for straining soups, sauces and purées to give a very smooth result

clafoutis a baked batter pudding made with fruit, often cherries (see page 268)

clarify (of stock) to remove sediment or filter using egg white (see page 20)

clarified butter pure butterfat, made by heating butter and lifting the fat from the liquid milk that forms underneath. Clarified butter does not burn as easily as butter and has a longer shelf life

cocotte a small dish in which eggs, mousses and souffles are baked

coeur a la creme a heart-shaped mould of cream or curd cheese

compote a dish of stewed fruit in sugar syrup, served cold

colander a metal or plastic basket used for draining food such as cooked vegetables

conserve a sweet preserve usually made with whole fruits

consistency texture, used to describe cakes and doughs

coral (of lobster) the ovaries and preformed eggs of a hen lobster, found in the tail; (of scallops) the orange roe, which is often detached before cooking

cornflour the ground kernels of corn/maize, used for thickening liquids and sauces

court bouillon a stock flavoured with herbs and vegetables, to be used for poaching fish

couverture chocolate made especially for cooking, which contains a high proportion of cocoa butter. It has a glossier apprearance and is easier to handle than standard chocolate

crimp to press pastry together decoratively, to seal

curd the solids left after milk is soured, following the removal of the whey

curdling the process whereby fresh milk or sauce separates into solids and liquid. This can be intentional, as when making cheese, or unfortunate – for example when creamed butter and sugar split with the addition of eggs

cure to preserve fish or meat by salting, smoking or drying

deep fat fry to cook food by immersing it in oil

de-glaze to add liquid to a pan after roasting or sautéeing in order to dissolve any juices or sediment left in the base of the pan, picking up their flavour

devil to cook with spicy seasoning

dice to cut food into small cubes

dough a mixture of flour, liquid and sometimes fat for baking into bread or cakes

dredge to sprinkle food with flour or sugar

dress to prepare poultry, game or shellfish

dripping the fat which drips from meat, poultry or game during cooking

dumpling a small ball of dough or stuffing that is steamed or poached, and often served with soup or stews

dust to sprinkle lightly, for example with flour, sugar or spices

emulsion a suspension of tiny droplets of one liquid in another liquid

flake to separate the flesh of fish into small pieces following the natural structure

flambé or **flame** to remove the alcohol from hot food by lighting the fumes

flameproof describes cookware or utensils which can be used with direct heat or in a hot oven

fold in to combine ingredients carefully with a whisk, metal spoon or spatula in order to retain any air that has been incorporated into the mixutre

fool a dessert of whipped cream or custard folded with fruit purée

forcemeat a seasoned mixture of breadcrumbs or meat and vegetables, often used to stuff birds before cooking. Now more commonly known in this context as stuffing

freeze to preserve food by chilling and storing well below 0°C

fricassee a stew, usually of chicken or veal

fromage blanc a light, soft curd cheese

game wild or wild-reared birds or mammals, shot within a restricted season (see page 77)

gelatine a setting agent derived from the bones of animals, used for setting jellies

giblets the neck, gizzard, liver and heart of poultry or game

glaze a glossy finish given to food, usually by brushing with beaten egg or milk before cooking, or with sugar syrup after cooking

gluten the main protein component of some flours, notably wheat flours

gravy a sauce made from the juices exuded from meat, poultry or game during cooking, combined with stock or water and starch

green bacon unsmoked bacon, may be either from the loin or belly

griddle a flat iron plate used for cooking ingredients such as bread or scones, particularly on top of the hob but also in the oven

griskin backbone, spine or chine of pork

hang to suspend meat or game in a cool, dry place until matured and tenderised

haricot when mature, a type of white bean, the young, unripe pod of which is also eaten as a green vegetable

herbs plants used for their aromatic properties

hogget a sheep aged between one and two years of age

honey a sweet, sugar-rich product derived from nectar made chiefly by honeybees

hull to remove the green calyx from fruits such as strawberries or raspberries

infuse to combine aromatic herbs and/or vegetables with a liquid such as stock or milk (or, in the case of tea making, water) and leave them for a period of time to impart their flavour

jelly a liquid set with gelatine or another gelling agent

joint to cut an animal or piece of meat into smaller pieces by cutting through the joints to separate the bones. Also a piece of meat for roasting

jugged (of game) cooked in a covered pot, usually with blood added for gravy; (of kippers) cooked in a jug

lard natural or refined pork fat

larding threading strips of fat through lean meat before cooking, to add flavour and prevent the flesh from drying out

legumes podded vegetables such as peas, beans and lentils

leveret a hare aged up to 1 year old

lexia a large raisin, usually stoned

liaison a thickening or binding agent, for example a roux, arrowroot mixture, egg yolk or cream

Macedoine a mixture of various kinds of vegetables or fruits cut into small dice

macerate to soften food, often fruit, by adding sugar

maslin pan jam pan

maître d'hôtel cooked and/or served with parsley

marbled (of meat) containing intramuscular, as opposed to surface, fat

marinade a mixture of oil, wine or vinegar used to tenderise or flavour meat

medallions round pieces of meat, usually of steak or loin, usually fried

meringue a light mixture of beaten egg whites and sugar

Mirepoix a mixture of finely chopped vegetables, usually onion, carrot and celery

molasses the liquid that remains once sugar has been crystallised

muslin see butter muslin

mutton the name given to sheep that are over two years old at slaughter

nibbed (of nuts, usually almonds) chopped

ovenproof describes cookware or crockery that can be used in the oven

par-boil to part cook in water

parfait a chilled or frozen dessert

pasty an oval-shaped pastry case with savoury or sweet filling

pâté   a cooked meat or vegetable puree

PDO   Product of designated origin, a European designation for protected foods

pectin   a gum-like substance which acts as a setting agent in jams and jellies. It is found naturally in some fruits and vegetables, notably lemons

pickle   to preserve meat or vegetables in brine or vinegar

pith   the bitter white tissue that is found inside the rind of citrus fruits

poach   to cook food in simmering liquid

pork   the meat from pigs, which can be cured to make bacon or ham

preserve   to keep food in good condition by treating it with salt, vinegar or sugar

pulp   the soft, fleshy tissue of fruit or vegetables, or the result of cooking or mashing fruit

purée   food that has been blended or passed through a sieve to give a smooth texture

ramekin   a small ceramic, ovenproof dish, often used for soufflés or creams

reduce   to concentrate a liquid, for example a sauce or stock, by boiling it until a portion has evaporated

render   to slowly cook meat and trimmings so that they release their fat

rennet   a substance extracted from the stomach lining of calves. It is used to coagulate milk for junket, and for making cheese

roast   to cook in the oven or on a spit over an open flame

roux   a mixture made from equal quantities of fat and flour cooked together and used as a thickening agent for sauces

sabayon   a light, beaten mixture of egg yolks or whole eggs and sugar

sauté   to fry food in hot shallow fat, turning it frquently, until it is evenly browned

scald   to heat cream or milk to just below boiling point. Originally, the main purpose of this was to eliminate harmful bacteria and enzymes (which are no longer present in pasteurised milk), but other purposes include encouraging the growth of yeast when making bread, or helping other ingredients to infuse

score   to cut shallow gashes into the surface of food before cooking

sear   to brown meat rapidly using a fierce heat to seal in the juices

seasoned flour   flour mixed with salt and pepper, and sometimes other spices, often used to coat meat or fish before cooking

season   to add salt, pepper, spices, herbs or other ingredients to food to add flavour or (at the end of the cooking time) to correct the balance of flavours

sediment   a solid residue left in the bottom of a tin after roasting meat or poultry

setting point   the stage of cooking a jam or jelly at which it will set when cooled

sift   to pass flour or sugar through a sieve to remove any lumps and/or incorporate air

simmer   to cook in liquid that is kept just below boiling point

skewer   a metal or wooden stick used to hold food in place during cooking

skillet   a heavy cast iron frying pan

skim   to remove residue from the surface of a liquid, for example fat from stock or scum from jam

soufflé   a baked dish consisting of a sauce or purée, usually thickened with egg yolks and lightened with beaten egg whites, which rises during cooking

soused   pickled in brine or vinegar

spring-form   describes a cake tin with hinged sides and a loose bottom

steam   to cook food in the steam that rises from a pan of boiling water

steep   to soak in liquid, in order to hydrate

sterilise   to destroy germs by heat or chemical means

stew   to simmer food slowly in a casserole or covered pan

stir   to mix with a circular motion, using a spoon or fork

stockpot   a large, deep pan for making stock

strain to separate liquids from solids by passing through a sieve or muslin

stuffing see forcemeat

suet a hard fat from around the kidneys of animals, usually cattle

sweat to gently soften chopped vegetables in hot oil or butter

sweetbreads a collective name for the pancreas and thyroid glands of animals, usually lambs or calves

syrup a sugar dissolved in water or another liquid

terrine an earthenware pot used to make and serve pâté. Also its contents

truss to tie a bird or piece of meat into a neat shape using string

turnover a savoury or sweet pastry made by folding a round or square of pastry in half over a filling, usually of fruit, forming a semicircle or triangle (see page 223)

vanilla sugar sugar with a vanilla flavour, usually made by storing caster sugar with used vanilla pods in order to extract the oils

venison the meat from deer

vinaigrette a dressing for salad or vegetables, made with base of oil and vinegar

whey the liquid part of milk that is left after the curds have been removed in the process of cheese making

whip to beat eggs or cream until they are thick and increased in volume

whisk a looped wire utensil that is used to introduce air into ingredients such as eggs or cream

yeast a fungus used to leaven bread

yoghurt milk that has been cultured with bacteria, most commonly *Lactobacillus*

zest the coloured outer skin of citrus fruits in which the highly flavoured oils are contained

INDEX

RECIPE INDEX

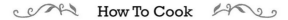

ACKNOWLEDGEMENTS

Mum, Sandra, has helped without question in the kitchen and office both in the process of testing the recipes and in organising manuscripts and printing endless reams of paper – you are a blessing.

Dad, Louise, Oscar, Fanny, and the girls, all helped me along the way, nibbling and advising. Woof!

A hearty and welcome addition to this book was made by Adam Sellar, a great chef, and the best baker, who helped me at every stage along the way both in testing the recipes, and as an opponent on the squash court to work off the calories.

The wonderful Amanda Harris let me realise the vision of bringing Isabella's book back to life, allowing me to go right back to the beginning. Thank you for lighting the blue touch paper and standing back.

The brilliant Debbie Woska sat alongside me through the edit, sculpting text and clarifying meaning – you could not have worked harder or made more of an effort. Also to the copy editor, Constance Novis, proofreader Diona Murray-Evans and indexer Cherry Ekins, many thanks.

To all the design team – Julyan Bayes, Lucie Stericker, Sammy-Jo Squire, Nicky Morgan, Leila and crew, and the photographer Andrew Hayes-Watkins and team for making the book look as lovely as it does.

Thanks also to all the team at Orion – Nicki, Elizabeth and Lisa, and the rest. Also to Michael Dover who answered my call.

Suppliers and helpers were many:

Thanks to Shaun and Penny Wingham, who supplied the freshest fish, and Alan Turner who provided the most delicious Dexter beef.

Also to Mike and Steve Wilson and Graham Clubley, who not only supplied many cuts of fabulous meat but also sang and gave encouragement with great patience in helping me map the animals.

To Ben and Amanda Woodcraft on Mersea Island for lovely fish, game and quinces, and to Andy Bing and all the team at Loch Duart for the best salmon.

To Hazel and Jo Relph who provided brilliant Herdwick sheep, and Jonathan and Sarah Birchall for their delicious Wiltshire Horn lamb and Longhorn beef.

George and crew at Fresh and Fruity in Hedon for always having a smile and a laugh, and for providing great fruit and veg.

Tom and Andy thank you for being there.

Matthew Canwell, Veronica Davidson and team at Lakeland Ltd., who continually innovate and improve, and helped enormously in providing tins and equipment for me to use when testing the recipes – thank you.

Also to the staff at the Brotherton Library in Leeds who provided intelligent support when I first looked for Isabella.

Thanks to Kathryn Hughes who has done most of all to unravel the Beeton myth and get us closer to the woman

Finally, to Isabella herself: thank you.

Gerard Baker